Laboratory for Liberty

Journal of the Commons House of Assembly from the

the subject of Complaint: And in the course of their Inquiry, they have added such observations and remarks, as they judged might serve to illustrate and explain the several Matters which have been laid before them, and which the House have been pleased to refer to their Consideration.

Your Comee think it necessary in the first place to take notice, That his Maty King Charles the 2d by his Royal Charter bearing Date the 13 June in the 17 year of his Reign granted to eight Lords Proprietors in the said Charter named "All that "Province, Territory or Tract of Land Situate lying & being "within his Dominions in America extending North & Eastward "as far as the North End of Carohtacke River or Gullet, upon "a strait westerly Line to Wyonoke Creek which lies within "or about the Degrees of thirty six and thirty Minutes of "Northern Latitude and so West in a direct Line as far as "the South Seas.

That in pursuance of an Act of Parliament passed in the second year of his present Majestys Reign, Seven of the late Lords Proprietors of Carolina have surrendered to his Maty seven eighth parts of Carolina, and that since the said Surrender, his Maty hath been pleased to grant a Charter for establishing the Colony of Georgia, in which Charter (amongst others) are Words to the effect following (to wit) His Maty "doth give & grant of seven undivided parts the whole into "eight equal parts to be Divided of all those Lands, Countrys "and Territorys Situate lying & being in that part of South "Carolina in America which lies from the most Northern "Stream of a River there commonly called the Savannah "all along the Sea Coast to the Southward unto the most "Southern Stream of a certain other great Water or River "called the Alatamaha and Westward from the heads of "the said Rivers respectively in direct Lines to the SouthSeas "and all that Space Circuit & precinct of Land lying within "the said Boundarys with the Islands in the Sea lying "opposite to the Eastern Coast of the said Lands within twenty "Leagues of the same which are not already Inhabited or "Settled by any Authority derived from the Crown of Great "Britain.

Your Comee from the above recited Charters & Acts of Parliament are furnished with the following very obvious Remarks.

First It appears that by the Charter to the late Lords Proprietors all the Lands from the Latitudes of 36 Deg. and 30 Min. to the Lat. of 29 Deg. Northern Lat. were granted to the said late Lords Proprietors.

Secondly. That on the surrender made to the Crown

GEORGE EDWARD FRAKES

Laboratory for Liberty

The South Carolina Legislative Committee System 1719-1776

THE UNIVERSITY PRESS OF KENTUCKY

Lexington   1970

FRONTISPIECE: *Page 213 of the Journal of the Commons House of Assembly of South Carolina for December 15, 1737.* From The Journal of the Commons House of Assembly, *edited by James Harrold Easterby. Courtesy of the South Carolina Department of Archives and History*

The University Press of Kentucky is a statewide cooperative scholarly publishing agency serving Berea College, Centre College of Kentucky, Eastern Kentucky University, Kentucky State College, Morehead State University, Murray State University, University of Kentucky, University of Louisville, and Western Kentucky University.

Editorial and Sales Offices: Lexington, Kentucky 40506

TO CATHERINE DAVIES FRAKES

Contents

Foreword

This study of the South Carolina legislative committee system is an attempt to illuminate the role of committees in the growth of colonial self-government. Partly because of frontier developments, the legislative committee became an institution which helped to solve many governmental problems of a New-World community. In a sense, the committees provided workshops for ideas that were to bring about legislative supremacy and, finally, independence.

Origins of the committee system can be traced, in part, to the parliamentary committees of medieval England. In 1670 Englishmen brought the committee system to South Carolina. Thereafter provincial legislative committees played a vital role in solving the problems of frontier economy and defense as well as in the emergence of self-government from 1719 to 1776.

One of the first steps toward greater home rule, the South Carolina revolution of 1719 against proprietary control, was largely a product of legislative and extralegal committee activity. In the decades of royal rule that followed, important developments occurred within the committee system. Among them was the elimination of royally appointed councilors from certain types of joint legislative committees. The dominance of joint committees by the Commons House of Assembly demonstrated that the colonists gradually increased control over their own affairs. Events on the frontier associated with Indian affairs and land development help explain this transition.

Expansion of the legislative committee system resulted in Commons

House control of important governmental functions related to expenditure of money. Often these expenditures were made during periods of inter-colonial and frontier warfare. Other types of committees—commissions, vestries, grand juries, and other boards—were used throughout South Carolina and had an important voice in local government. Most of the leading provincial South Carolinians became acquainted with problems of self-government in this frontier colony through experience on legislative or local government committees.

After 1761, when royal officials began to tighten their control over the colony, Commons House committees steadfastly opposed attempts to reduce their legislative power. The result of this struggle was a political deadlock which almost paralyzed constitutional government after 1769.

Powerful extralegal organizations controlled by executive committees appeared in the 1760s, both in Charles Town and on the frontier. These extralegal bodies rallied South Carolinians to their cause. Political leaders formed "general committees" that gave direction to the independence move-ment, and Commons members used their experience in leading home-rule forces. By 1775, a province-wide network of local extralegal committees augmented the General Committee's power. The new Provincial Congress which was formed in 1775 relied upon a committee, the Council of Safety, as its executive body. South Carolina colonists had modified an Old-World parliamentary institution in a frontier environment to make it a vital part of their legislative program. Committees of the Provincial Congress helped bring about the colony's declaration of independence and first state con-stitution.

This study of South Carolina's legislative committee system thus illus-trates the development of an institution which was vitally important in the growth of representative government in America.

A number of primary materials are of particular value in studying the politics and institutions of colonial South Carolina. The journals of the Commons House and those of the Upper House and the Council are ex-cellent sources of information. The student of South Carolina history is fortunate to have the fine collection of the South Carolina Archives as well as the materials of the South Caroliniana Library of the University of South Carolina, the Charleston Library Society collections, and the resources of the South Carolina Historical Society in Charleston to assist him.

Although the number of additional public and private papers that have been published is not great, numerous materials from British archives have been copied and are now available at the South Carolina Archives Department in Columbia, and at the Library of Congress. A number of these sources are now duplicated on microfilm. In addition, selected volumes of the journals of both houses of the South Carolina General Assembly have been published, edited by Charles Lee, James H. Easterby, Alexander S. Salley, and others.

Some of the information drawn from these primary materials should be clarified. A major source of misunderstanding in colonial history is the existence of the Julian or "Old Style" calendar and the modern calendar. I have converted all Old Style dates into the modern dating system throughout the text. However, when authorities I cite use Old Style dates in primary sources, I have retained the Old Style dates in my notes.

A recently published study of South Carolina political history by the late M. Eugene Sirmans was particularly helpful to me in clarifying the political aspects of my subject. His book differs from mine in that his is a chronological investigation of politics before 1763. My study is basically an institutional treatment of the internal operations of the assembly and influential extralegal bodies with particular emphasis on the period following the French and Indian War.

This study grew out of research for my doctoral dissertation. I am indebted to my teachers at the University of California, Santa Barbara, for their help in the preparation of this work, especially the members of my doctoral committee, Professors Henry M. Adams, A. Russell Buchanan, Rollin W. Quimby, and Robert Norris. In particular, I am grateful for the assistance of my adviser, Dr. Wilbur R. Jacobs, whose criticism and guidance have been invaluable.

Many other persons, too numerous to mention, have assisted me in my work. Of these, I would like to thank my classmates Professor David Kamens, Dr. Yasuhidi Kawashima, Professor Allan Rogers, Mr. Frank Bunker, Dr. Thomas Reeves, and Dr. Marvin Zahniser, who have given me excellent suggestions on this subject. I am also indebted to colleagues at Santa Barbara City College and the University of California, Santa Barbara, especially Mrs. Ruth Little, Mr. Donald Sawyer, Dr. Curtis Solberg, Mr. Raymond Loynd, Mr. Robert Easton, Miss Donna Page, Mrs. Donna Ellison, Mrs. Jeannette Dawson, and Mrs. Dorothy Annable. In addition I want to express my appreciation to Dr. Ruth Bourne for reading my manuscript.

The following have been of great assistance in my research for this work: the staffs of the University of California, Santa Barbara, Library; the Southern Historical Collection of the University of North Carolina; the University of Virginia Alderman Library; the Henry Huntington Library; and the University of California libraries at Berkeley and Los Angeles. I would particularly like to thank the University of California, Berkeley, Library for the use of its Legislative Collection, and the Santa Barbara Campus Library for the use of the Louis K. Koontz Collection of British and French manuscripts. Individual librarians who were exceptionally helpful were: Mrs. Granville Prior of the South Carolina Historical Society; Drs. William R. Tansill and David Mearns and their staff of the Library of Congress; Dr. Charles Lee, director of the South Carolina State Archives Department; and Mr. E. I. Inabinett and Mrs. Clara Mae Jacobs of the South Caroliniana Library of the University of South Carolina. I would also like to thank Mr. Kenneth Timings of the Public Record Office in London for making South Carolina materials in Class Five available through Professor Wilbur R. Jacobs, who was in London in the summer of 1965.

I also want to thank my three children, Jimmy, Laura, and Bobby, for their cooperation and patience. Most of all, I am indebted to my wife, Catherine Davies Frakes, for her support, assistance, and confidence.

CHAPTER I

The Background of the Legislative Committee System

The widespread use of committees in virtually every phase of society is such an accepted part of modern American life that the importance of the committee's role in shaping our institutions is often overlooked. A number of factors explain the general use of committees in America today. In government, the committee system is one of the best known alternatives to authoritarian rule. And in a nation where self-government has become a way of life, the committee approach reflects some of our national beliefs. Moreover, committees are an excellent training ground for inexperienced legislators.[1]

Our tradition of committee activity can be traced to the days of the colonial frontier. It is part of our democratic legacy. The foundations laid down in the colonial period have been built on in the years since.

Committees were among the institutions brought by Englishmen to the New World.[2] South Carolina was one of the frontier colonies that made extensive use of legislative committees,[3] modifying principles originated and developed in the British Parliament. Throughout the colony's formative, pioneer years, legislative committees were partly responsible for nurturing a spirit of self-government and for shaping the direction of South Carolina's political development in the eighteenth century.

Committees were used in Great Britain as early as the fourteenth century, some 300 years before the first colony in Virginia. By the time of the Stuart era in the seventeenth century the use of parliamentary committees was well established. These committees had their antecedents in the *curia regis,* the royal council of Norman, Angevin, and Plantagenet kings. Seeds of the legislative committee system can be traced back to the reign of Edward I (1273–1307), when parliamentary groups were originally established. One of the earliest official legislative committees is mentioned in the records of the House of Commons in 1340.[4]

In the first printed journals of the House of Commons, issued in 1547, we find additional records of special committees. During the reign of Queen Mary, committees examined the qualifications of members of Parliament. Conference committees with the House of Lords and committees on taxation were operating in 1563.[5] Fourteen years later Sir Thomas Smith in his treatise, *Commonwealth of England,* wrote about the use of committees in framing bills as a regular part of parliamentary procedure:

The committies are such as either Lords in the higher House, or Burgesses in the Lower House, doe choose to frame the Lawes upon such Bills as are agreed upon, and after ward to bee ratified by the same Houses.

Smith also wrote that:

It chanceth sometime that some part of the Bill is allowed some other part hath much controversie and doubt made of it; and it is thought if it were amended it would go forward. Then they choose certaine Committees of them who have spoken with the bill and against it, to amend it, and bring it againe so amended as they amongst them shal think meet.[6]

In the reign of Elizabeth I, the first "steering" and standing committees were formed. A significant development was open discussion in committees.

---

[1] George Galloway, *History of the House of Representatives,* pp. 70, 80, 94–96. Also see James David Barber, *Power in Committees.*

[2] William Augustus Mancuse, "The Origin and Operation of the State Legislative Committee System" (Masters thesis, University of Virginia, 1924), pt. 1:1–10; Ralph Volney Harlow, *A History of Legislative Methods in the Period before 1825,* pp. 9, 116–17.

[3] South Carolina was ruled as a proprietary colony from 1663 to 1719. From 1719 to 1721, the colonists governed themselves while awaiting news of their petition for royal status. Between 1721 and 1776, South Carolina was a royal colony. See M. Eugene Sirmans, *Colonial South Carolina: A Political History, 1663–1763,* pp. 55, 67–71, for an understanding of this early period of legislative activity.

[4] John Franklin Jameson, "The Origin of the Standing-Committee System in American Legislative Bodies," *Political Science Quarterly* 9 (1894): 246–47.

[5] Ibid., p. 247.

[6] Sir Thomas Smith, *De republica Anglorum, A Discourse on the Commonwealth of England,* pp. 79, 93.

A further precedent was set with the founding of parliamentary standing committees on privileges and elections, on religion, and on grievances.[7]

Still other parliamentary committee functions developed before 1600. An example was the committee to consider statutes that were about to expire. Such a committee was later formed in South Carolina's colonial legislature.[8] Of all these early British parliamentary committees, the development of the standing committee on privileges and elections appears to have been the most important step in the growth of committee operation.

By the eve of the Stuart period, the parliamentary committee system functioned with three general types of legislative committees.[9] All were later found in colonial legislatures. These included ad hoc committees (temporary committees assigned special tasks), committees that framed legislation, and standing sessionary committees operating for the length of a session of the House of Commons. A third type, committees of the whole house, sometimes called general or grand committees of the Commons, permitted members to discuss issues freely without the rules of parliamentary procedure. When such a practice was followed, the Speaker left the chair and joined the discussion.[10]

As England's government changed during the rule of the Stuarts, so did the parliamentary committee system. By the time of the English Civil War, committees on trade and courts of justice were active along with earlier committees on religion, grievances, and privileges and elections. These five bodies often functioned as committees of the whole in the House of Commons. Later, similar committees in a different setting would play an important part in the operation of the South Carolina provincial legislature as well as in other colonial assemblies.[11]

Under Charles II additional changes occurred in the committee system. The first recorded mention of an extrasessionary committee—one meeting out of the regular session—was made in 1621. After 1625 committees could

---

[7] Jameson, "Standing-Committee System," p. 249; Robert Luce, *Legislative Procedures and the Course of Business in the Framing of Statutes,* pp. 87–88.

[8] See *Colonial Records of South Carolina: The Journals of the Commons House of Assembly,* 1736–1750, ed. James Harrold Easterby, Ruth Green, and Charles Lee, vols. 1–9, passim [hereafter cited as *JCHA* (Easterby)]; *The Journals of the Commons House of Assembly of South Carolina,* ed. Alexander Samuel Salley [hereafter cited as *JCHA* (Salley)]. Also see Jameson, "Standing-Committee System," pp. 259–61.

[9] Jameson, "Standing-Committee System," pp. 251–52.

[10] Harlow, *Legislative Methods,* p. 92.

[11] Mancuse, "Legislative Committee System," pt. 1:10–20; and Jameson, "Standing-Committee System," p. 255.

hear counsel and witnesses as well as subpoena individuals and records for examination. Formation of subcommittees was also initiated in the early Stuart period.[12]

During the Long Parliament and Commonwealth period the importance of committees increased.[13] Committees were given both rooms and protection so they could work without disturbance. During the actual fighting of the English Civil War, committees in both houses of Parliament began to acquire executive tasks.

In the days of the later Stuarts, the committee system was carried to the South Carolina frontier. A split in the direction of committee development occurred at this time. In most of the American colonies the older English committee traditions were continued and the use of standing committees increased. However, in Britain the struggle for power between Parliament and the Crown and the development of the cabinet system caused the decline of independent standing legislative committees.[14]

In British colonies founded earlier than South Carolina, the use of the committee system varied greatly. Most New England colonies had no standing committees until the American Revolution. Thus, almost all committee activity was restricted to ad hoc or sessionary legislative bodies dealing with investigations, writing bills, or auditing records.[15] Although certain committees appear in session after session, they were ad hoc or select bodies with different members, although they often dealt with similar problems.

In the Southern frontier colonies and in Pennsylvania, the pattern of committee organization was different. The two oldest Southern mainland colonies, Virginia and Maryland, both used committees extensively, and Virginia was perhaps the most advanced of all colonies in the use of standing committees. By the 1660s Virginians were employing extrasessionary committees and additional committees on finance, petitions, appeals, grievances, and countless other subjects. Even the small island colonies of Jamaica and Barbados had assemblies with committees at work. In the Quaker colony, William Penn's "Frame of Government" of 1682 provided for a division of the Pennsylvania Council into four committees. However, this provision was altered because of the small size of that legislative body. The assembly of Penn's proprietary colony modeled itself on the British House of Commons and therefore had many standing committees.[16]

[12] Jameson, "Standing-Committee System," pp. 252–53, 255–56.
[13] Ibid., pp. 257–59.
[14] Harlow, *Legislative Methods,* pp. 117–19.
[15] Ibid., pp. 64, 111.
[16] Jameson, "Standing-Committee System," pp. 262, 265–67.

In contrast to Pennsylvania and the Southern provinces, the other middle colonies were slow to develop a standing committee structure. The small New York Assembly did not utilize permanent committees until the 1730s, and New Jersey was without standing committees until 1771.[17]

Both the example of committees at work in other colonies and the earlier precedent set in seventeenth-century Great Britain provided the precedent for the committee system in South Carolina. Throughout the entire colonial period and especially after 1721, when South Carolina became a royal colony, Carolina traders and immigrants brought ideas as well as goods from other parts of the British empire.[18] Correspondence between governors and the Board of Trade illustrates this fact. Even in the 1720s, the first decade of royal rule, when the frontier line was only a few miles from Charles Town, the provincial executives wrote that the elected assembly was using precedents from Virginia and Barbados as justification for its actions. Governor Sir Francis Nicholson of South Carolina complained of "commonwealth ideas" being spread from Massachusetts.[19]

An example of transmission of ideas from one colony to another is found in the voluminous correspondence of an eighteenth-century South Carolina merchant, Colonel Henry Laurens. Laurens was a frontier landowner and a prominent member of the province's Commons House of Assembly. His correspondence with businessmen in other provinces about political as well as commercial matters indicates how readily the drift of intercolonial political and institutional ideas occurred.[20] His correspondents included merchants in London, Philadelphia, Pensacola, New York, and Georgia, as well as associates in frontier trading posts. By the last decade of colonial history, the combination of a variety of committees of correspondence, better roads, and improved postal services resulted in better intercolonial communication on political problems.[21]

[17] Ibid., pp. 266–67.

[18] Carl Bridenbaugh's *Cities in the Wilderness* and *Cities in Revolt* show the interrelation of business and political leaders in New York, Boston, Philadelphia, and Newport with those in Charles Town.

[19] Governor Robert Johnson to Board of Trade, 26 March 1731, British Public Record Office, Colonial Office, 5/406 (hereafter cited as PRO CO). Johnson wrote that previous Governor Sir Francis Nicholson allowed the practice and the Assembly claimed the practice was used in Barbados, Virginia, and other colonies. See Nicholson to Board of Trade, 18 June 1724, PRO CO 5/406.

[20] Henry Laurens, "The Correspondence of Henry Laurens," *South Carolina Historical and Genealogical Magazine* 28 (1927): 141–50, 207–12; 29 (1928): 97–105, 193–200. The original Henry Laurens' Letterbooks are at the South Carolina Historical Society in Charleston.

[21] Bridenbaugh, *Cities in Revolt*, pp. 54–55.

Many aspects of this exchange of ideas were to have important implications in the growth of the legislative committee system in South Carolina. Carolinians developed leadership and a sense of direction for political affairs. Able, informed assembly members, experienced in legislative and committee matters, helped to develop an efficient legislative committee system. Committee members over a period of fifty-five years (1721–1776) provided legislative leadership which led to the independence of South Carolina from England.

To understand the internal forces which influenced South Carolina's legislative committee system during the royal period, it is necessary to examine developments in the colony's era of proprietary government (1663–1719). This fifty-six-year period formed the basis for nearly every phase of later provincial development.[22]

Proprietary developments really began in 1663 when Charles II granted land and a charter to a group of his friends who had been steadfast supporters during his years of exile and restoration.[23] The grant of land included the area occupied by the modern states of Georgia, North Carolina, and South Carolina and extended westward to the Pacific. In this immense area, the king gave the eight owners the right to be "lords and proprietors." This charter enabled the proprietors "to enact and publish laws or constitutions they judged proper and necessary to the public state of the province, with the assent, advice and approbation of the freemen of the colony." It also gave them the authority "to erect courts of jurisdiction, and appoint civil judges, magistrates and officers, to erect forts, castles, cities, and towns, to make war; to levy, muster, and train men to the use of arms. . . ." In addition, the charter provided religious liberty for the colonists. The proprietors were required by the charter to allow an assembly of freeholders the right to make laws necessary for the government and maintenance of peace.

[22] The best primary materials are Dr. Alexander Hewatt, "Historical Account of the Rise and Progress of the Colonies of South Carolina and Georgia," in Bartholomew Rivers Carroll, ed., *Historical Collections of South Carolina*, 1:xxi–533; and John Oldmixon, "Accounts of Carolina," in ibid., 2:391–462. The most comprehensive secondary works are David Duncan Wallace, *A History of South Carolina*, vol. 1; and Edward McCrady, *The History of South Carolina under the Proprietary Government, 1670–1719*. More recent and valuable contributions on this period have been written by the late M. Eugene Sirmans in *Colonial South Carolina*. Also see John Andrew Doyle, *The English Colonies in America*, vol. 1, *Maryland, Virginia and the Carolinas*, pp. 374–80. This older work contains one of the best descriptions of the implications of the proprietary period and the revolution of 1719 for later colonial history.

[23] Hewatt, "Account of South Carolina," pp. 43–47.

The major restriction placed upon the proprietary assembly was that it could not pass legislation "repugnant to the laws and statutes of England."[24]

Besides royal charter provisions and proprietors' instructions, there was yet another major constitutional influence in the early provincial period. This was *The Fundamental Constitutions of Carolina of 1669* which was later modified a number of times. This controversial document, attributed to John Locke, had 120 separate articles; though none specifically mentioned committees, several dealt with the assembly and influenced the development of the legislative committee system in South Carolina. Article 71 was significant because it contained provisions for a provincial parliament. This legislature was to consist of proprietors or their deputies, landgraves, "cassiques," and one freeholder from each precinct. "They shall sit all together in one room, and have every member one vote."[25] However, nothing was to be proposed in this parliament until approved by the proprietor-dominated "Great Council." It appears that Locke, if he was the author of this document, envisioned a two-chambered governmental body.[26]

The thirty-seventh article stated that the Speaker in Parliament and President of the Grand Council, the two men who appointed committee members, were to be proprietors or their deputies.[27] This provision, which reinforced executive authority, was in force until the 1690s, when the lower house gained greater freedom of action.

Article 51 gave the power to prepare all legislation to the Grand Council: "Nor shall any matter whatsoever be prepared in parliament, but what hath first passed the Grand Council, which after having been read three several days in the parliament, shall by majority votes be passed or rejected." Thus, in theory, the seventeenth-century legislature had only a negative role in colonial government.[28]

Articles 72 through 79 were concerned with freemen elected to the lower house. A fifty-acre property requirement was established for voters. Each representative in parliament was required to own five hundred or more acres of land. This property restriction established a precedent of electing members of the landed, planter aristocracy to the popular chamber and restricting

[24] Ibid.; Sirmans, *Colonial South Carolina*, pp. 7–16, 37–38, 43–44, 67.

[25] "Fundamental Constitutions of Carolina," in Carroll, ed., *Historical Collections of South Carolina*, 2:361–90.

[26] Ibid., pp. 371–72, 375, 380–83. According to discussions at the Anglo-American Historical Conference in London, summer, 1965, editors of the Locke correspondence question his authorship of this document. Interview with Dr. Wilbur R. Jacobs, 3 May 1966.

[27] "Fundamental Constitutions," pp. 371–72.   [28] Ibid., p. 375.

the political activity of the frontier settlers. The requirement remained in force throughout the eighteenth century. Other provisions dealt with quorums (one-half the members), dates of elections, length of terms of office (two years), and ratification of bills by the proprietors.[29]

The Fundamental Constitutions thus provided an institutional basis from which later royal political and constitutional developments grew. Often this growth was toward greater self-government and was expressed as a rejection of the proprietors' rule. In spite of such conflicts, the province gradually moved toward more self-government. In 1693, Carolina was divided in two parts, and the name South Carolina was used for the first time for that region south of Cape Fear. This division of the colony provided an opportunity for the thirty-man lower house to gain a greater voice in public affairs.[30]

The role of committees in the development of the provincial legislature can best be observed by examining some of the most important events of the last thirty years of proprietary rule. Taking advantage of the usual lack of interest of the absentee proprietors, the frontier assembly in 1693 appointed a committee to examine the charter and make recommendations concerning the role of the legislature. The report of this committee stressed the need for more home rule. Reaction to the report was recorded in the proprietors' journal of April 12, 1693:

We take notice that there is a committee appointed to draw up what they would have for a system of government for the future. . . . Since they have so disrespectfully refused that excellent system we offered in our constitution, we have thought it best both for ourselves and them to govern by all the powers granted to us by our letters patent from the Crown.[31]

Although displeased with the assembly's course of action, the proprietors regretfully allowed the South Carolina legislature to gain more power. In the thirty years after 1690, the Commons House records show that the colonists continued their freedom of action in local matters in spite of proprietary criticism.

This growth of self-government during the proprietary period did not always result in judiciously considered legislation. Between 1692 and 1710, legislative activity was sometimes obstructive and caused factionalism and

---

[29] Ibid., pp. 380–83; see also Sirmans, *Colonial South Carolina,* pp. 7–16 passim.

[30] Hewatt, "Account of South Carolina," p. 113; David Duncan Wallace, *South Carolina: A Short History, 1520–1948,* pp. 45–57; and Doyle, *English Colonies in America,* 1:362–63.

[31] Quoted in Wallace, *Short History,* p. 46.

rivalry. Part of this confusion may be traced to the fact that most legislators of this era were pioneer planters who had limited education and political experience. For example, there were virtually no British-trained lawyers to provide leadership in the colony until the late 1690s.

An illustration of this legislative immaturity was a disruptive factionalism based upon religious and sectional animosities. Three elements or "parties" worked at cross purposes in the South Carolina assembly and Council.[32] One powerful faction represented the tidewater Berkeley County (including Charles Town), which was settled largely by high church Anglicans, immigrants from Barbados and England, merchants, and planters. These colonists supported an aggressive policy against the Spaniards and Indians and restriction of political offices to members of their own church. A second faction was made up of dissenters, largely settled in Colleton County, whose prime interests were freedom of conscience, elimination of religious qualifications for public office, and better treatment for less prosperous planters. The other element was composed of the newly arrived Huguenot immigrants who desired freedom of religion and absence of discrimination. The high point of this three-way internal struggle was an act of 1703 which temporarily excluded all but Anglicans from holding seats in the legislature.[33]

The outcome of this religious struggle was that the dissenting element within the assembly formed an unofficial party committee or junto. In 1706, this group sent its own agent, Joseph Boone, to petition the British House of Lords to set aside the South Carolina Religious Test Law of 1703. Queen Anne disallowed the act and the dissenter element continued to have a voice in South Carolina's government.[34]

Important as it was in the development of colonial civil liberties, this action also established certain precedents. One was recognition of the right of unofficial committees to organize a minority of legislators to win parliamentary battles. Committees were now able to correspond with colonial agents in England. Neither of these gains was unnoticed by the members of the lower house, who used them effectively in the remaining years of proprietary government and thereafter.

Besides being involved in the controversies over sectional, religious, and constitutional issues, legislative committees took part in other struggles before 1719. Some of these grew out of Indian affairs, conflicts with the

[32] Hewatt, "Account of South Carolina," pp. 117–77 passim; and Wallace, *Short History,* pp. 58–80.

[33] Oldmixon, "Accounts of Carolina," p. 430.

[34] McCrady, *Proprietary Government,* pp. 425–28; Sirmans, *Colonial South Carolina,* pp. 75–100.

Spaniards, and monetary policy. Other significant issues revolved around increasing the power of the Commons House of Assembly and the ouster of proprietors from governing the colony.[35]

As was the case in most newly established colonies, South Carolina's economic growth depended upon commerce with the Indians. Indian trade, particularly with the Cherokee, formed the foundation for many of the earliest fortunes of Carolinians. This Indian commerce was considered a proprietary prerogative until the 1690s, when the colonists assumed greater control through their legislature. The colonists' zealous and sometimes unethical activities (particularly the enslavement of Indians) enraged the natives. The result was the Indian attack on the colony in 1706 during the bloody Tuscorora War. Later, from 1715 to 1717, the Spaniards gave supplies to hostile Indians during the Yamassee conflict when South Carolina was nearly destroyed.[36]

Because almost everyone suffered during these wars, the importance of improving Indian relations was obvious to most South Carolinians. The legislative answer to the problem was establishment of a Board of Commissioners for Indian Affairs in 1710. The Board was a committee made up of members of the assembly and the Council. The commissioners attempted to regulate Indian traders. They also tried to cope with problems before they became overwhelming by acting as a kind of sounding board for Indian grievances. This body eventually became one of the self-regulating committees outside of the South Carolina General Assembly.[37]

Besides the threat of Indian attack, the colony was exposed to danger from hostile Spaniards who viewed South Carolina as part of their territory. The potential danger of a Spanish assault was to shape Carolina attitudes and policies throughout this later colonial period. South Carolina legislative committees used the Spanish menace as full or partial justification for policies which otherwise probably would not have passed the scrutiny of British officials. For example, the Commons House of Assembly, led by

[35] Hewatt, "Account of South Carolina," pp. 144–87.

[36] Howard H. Peckham, *The Colonial Wars, 1689–1762*, pp. 7, 14, 20, 61, 65–66, 82; Verner W. Crane, *The Southern Frontier, 1670–1732*, pp. 162–90.

[37] Hewatt, "Account of South Carolina," pp. 195–201, 203–4; McCrady, *Proprietary Government*, pp. 546–47; and Wallace, *Short History*, p. 90. The technique the Commons House of Assembly used to obtain power in governmental matters was twofold. It began to claim the same rights and privileges as the British House of Commons and it hindered important legislative matters concerned with provincial defense until it got its way with money bills. Also see South Carolina, Board of Commissioners for Indian Affairs, *Journals, September 20, 1710–August 29, 1718*, in *The Colonial Records of South Carolina*, for a fuller treatment of this subject.

Nicholas Trott, an English barrister and assembly leader in the early 1700s, used fear of the Spaniards to gain the right to originate money bills.[38] In order to cope with military expenses, the lower house issued paper money for the first time in 1702. A legislative committee drafted the first of a series of slave codes because the Spaniards were said to be instigating Negro desertions and insurrections. Petitions to the crown for annexation of South Carolina as a royal colony in 1709, 1717, and finally in 1719, stressed the inability of the proprietors to provide assistance against Spanish and Indian attack.[39] Thus the presence of a Spanish military force in St. Augustine, Florida, was not always a matter of despair for political manipulators in Charles Town.

Throughout these conflicts the legislative committee system slowly grew in strength and vigor. The thirty-man Commons House used committees more and more frequently toward the end of this era. Committees in the period from 1692 to 1719, while occasionally taking the lead in suggesting reforms, were nevertheless dominated by the legislative leadership of the governors and Council.[40] Most of the committees of the Commons House and the Council in this era were ad hoc committees. Committees of the lower house were primarily concerned with modifying bills from the Council, investigating petitions, or approving governmental expenditures.[41]

The significance of the Commons House legislative accomplishments during the proprietary years seems to have been overlooked by the clerk of the assembly. In the *Journals of the Commons House of Assembly* for these years, events of the greatest importance rated only a line or two from his

[38] This fear of Spanish attack was particularly strong during the period of King George's War and the War of Jenkins' Ear (1739–1748) when Lt. Governor William Bull I and Governor James Glen mentioned threatened attacks in some of their letters to the Board of Trade. See Abstracts of Correspondence between South Carolina Governors and the Board of Trade, 1721–1764, PRO CO 5/406; and Hewatt, "Account of South Carolina," pp. 129–30.

[39] James Glen, "A description of South Carolina: Containing many curious and Interesting Particulars relating to the Civil, Natural, and Commercial history of that Colony," in *Historical Collections of South Carolina*, ed. B. R. Carroll, 2:163–65, 180, 189–90, 192; Wallace, *Short History*, p. 90; Richard P. Sherman, *Robert Johnson: Proprietary and Royal Governor of South Carolina*, pp. 15–29; and Sirmans, *Colonial South Carolina*, pp. 101–28.

[40] This progression in committee activity can be observed by examining *JCHA* (Salley) for the following sessions: September 1692; 23 February–10 March 1697; 10–12 November 1697; 4 February–1 March 1701; and 22 October 1707–12 February 1707/08.

[41] Ibid., February–March 1697, pp. 5, 6, 9–20; February–March 1701, pp. 3–8; and 22 October 1707–12 February 1707/08, pp. 51–53, 62–63, 69, 70.

pen. The clerk briefly mentions committee control of the receiver general (treasurer), tax bills and the budget, and the right to correspond with South Carolina's agent in Great Britain. These were a few examples of the transfer of authority to the assembly during the proprietary period. Indeed, proprietary vetoes of proposals for colonial legislative reforms, often developed by committees, helped bring about the revolution of 1719 that ended proprietary rule.[42]

This bloodless revolution was the first step in South Carolina's becoming a royal colony. From 1719 to 1721 the people of the colony waited for a royal decision as to their colonial status. In retrospect, it appears that this period was one of real significance in committee development, because in these years the legislature and its committees actually governed the colony.[43]

In 1721 a form of government emerged which was designed to meet the needs of the frontier colony. Original expression of the new framework for government was the South Carolina Provincial Charter of 1721. Later modifications came in crown instructions to governors.[44]

South Carolina's royal governmental structure closely resembled that of England. Government was vested in a legislature and a governor.[45] As in other royal colonies, the members of the Upper House were appointed by the crown upon recommendation by governors and the Board of Trade.[46] The

[42] Hewatt, "Account of South Carolina," pp. 219–24; Sirmans, *Colonial South Carolina*, pp. 69–70, 69 fn.

[43] Governor James Moore and the Committee on Correspondence to the Board of Trade, 11 August 1720; and two petitions and memorandums, n.d. (ca. 1720) and 29 September 1720, PRO CO 5/378; Journals of the Commons House of Assembly, South Carolina Archives Department, March–May 1720, pp. 426–66 [hereafter cited as JCHA (Arch.)]. There are limited records of the Commons House of Assembly in the period from 10 June 1718 to 3 February 1720. See also McCrady, *Proprietary Government*, pp. 633–75; Wallace, *Short History*, pp. 99–105; and Sherman, *Robert Johnson*, pp. 50–54.

[44] Leonard Woods Labaree, *Royal Government in America*, pp. 421–48; and Wallace, *Short History*, pp. 106–19.

[45] Sir Egerton Leigh, Bart., *Considerations in certain transactions of the Province of South Carolina*, pp. 1–90. Valuable as a detailed account of a political appointee of the crown. Also see Glen, "Description of South Carolina," pp. 201–20. South Carolina's "constitution" was similar to that of other Southern royal colonies. It was the unique internal political and institutional development, fostered in large part by the committee system, that made its government dissimilar.

[46] M. Eugene Sirmans, "The South Carolina Royal Council, 1720–1763," *William and Mary Quarterly*, 3d ser., 38 (1961): 373–75. Here, as throughout the book, I am using "Council" and "Upper House" interchangeably. It should be understood that the two bodies had different functions and a different set of journals was kept for each body, but the personnel was the same.

lower house of the legislature, the Commons House of Assembly, was elected by the freeholders of the province.[47] The governor was considered a kind of third branch of the legislative department as well as the royal executive in the colony. The governor, his appointed officials,[48] and the twelve-man Upper House, when it acted in the capacity of His Majesty's Council, completed the royal administrative machinery of provincial government.

The colony's judiciary was also closely related to other departments of the provincial government. As an example, those members who served in the Upper House, or Council, also functioned as the justices of the colony's highest tribunal, the Court of Chancery. Other judges in South Carolina often had elective posts in local or provincial government. Usually the colony's chief justice and attorney general were members of the Council.[49] Many of the assistant judges were members of the assembly in Charles Town, which was the site of both the capital and the main courts in the province. Judicial cases as well as legislative and executive decisions were, at least in theory, reviewed by British officials in England to protect the King's prerogative.[50]

The person chiefly responsible for supervision and operation of this

[47] Article 12 of Governor James Glen's instructions, quoted in Mary F. Carter, "Governor James Glen: A Study in Colonial Administrative Policies" (Ph.D. dissertation, University of California, Los Angeles, 1951), pp. 154, 325–26; and William A. Schaper, "Sectionalism and Representation in South Carolina, A Sociological Study," *American Historical Association Annual Report,* 1900, 1:324, 349–50. The voting requirements in the first years of the royal colony were fifty acres of land and a small amount of taxes paid each year. The property qualifications for assemblymen were 500 acres and a larger tax payment. These qualifications were altered several times during the royal period. The revisions normally increased the suffrage standards, but the upward movement of property qualifications was offset by the general and prolonged prosperity of the colony after the 1730s. By the eve of the Revolution in 1774, nearly all planters, merchants, and reasonably successful artisans could qualify to vote.

[48] Some of the more important of these officials were the clerks of the Commons House and the Upper House of the General Assembly, colonial agent, chief justice, commissary general, surveyor general, provost marshall, customs officials, and collectors of quit rents.

[49] The Chancery was the highest appeal court in the colony. Prominent chief justices are cited in Edward McCrady, *The History of South Carolina under the Royal Government,* 1719–1776, pp. 114–18.

[50] Assistant judges did not have to be legally trained. Their appointments were sometimes a matter of political patronage. *JCHA* (Salley), 15 November 1726–11 March 1726/27, pp. 69–70, 162, 197; Wallace, *Short History,* pp. 115–19; and Richard Maxwell Brown, *The South Carolina Regulators,* pp. 64–111.

complex and sometimes unwieldy governmental machinery was the royal governor. None of the governors found this post an easy assignment. They faced growing internal legislative opposition to the royal prerogative, external threat of war, and the continuing menace of slave insurrections.

A brief examination of the list of eleven royal governors between 1721 and 1775[51] indicates no special criteria used by British officials to pick the most qualified candidate for the job. Some were political appointees, a few were veteran colonial servants, and others were provincials. The first two royal governors, Sir Francis Nicholson and Robert Johnson, had been governors of other Southern colonies before coming to South Carolina. They were followed by two local council presidents, William Bull I and Thomas Broughton, who took over on the death of the regularly appointed governor who preceded them.

The most outstanding governor, in terms of both accomplishment and length of service, was James Glen, a Scotsman who had previously been an attorney and sheriff. He was followed by two mediocre executives, William Henry Lyttleton and Thomas Boone, who were chosen largely because of family connections. Lieutenant Governor William Bull II was perhaps the most durable and one of the ablest of the executives. He held the governorship with reasonable success five different times. Sandwiched between the terms of William Bull II were the last royal governors, Lord Charles Greville Montagu and Lord William Campbell. Few scandals discredited these South Carolina executives. The majority were respected by the powerful planter-merchant oligarchy of the province.[52]

[51] In colonial South Carolina, the term governor was only used if the chief royal official of the colony came from England. Lieutenant governors were either South Carolinians officially designated to lead the colony by the Board of Trade, the Privy Council, and the King, or Englishmen who assisted the governor when he was in the colony. If there was neither a governor nor a lieutenant governor in the colony, the next highest ranking official in the province, the president of the Council, ruled as acting governor.

The royal governors of South Carolina were: Sir Francis Nicholson, 1721–1725; Arthur Middleton, president of the Council, 1725–1730; Robert Johnson, 1730–1735; Thomas Broughton, lieutenant governor, 1735–1737; William Bull I, president of the Council and later lieutenant governor, 1737–1743; James Glen, 1743–1756; William Henry Lyttleton, 1756–1760; Thomas Boone, 1761–1764; William Bull II, lieutenant governor, 1760–1761, 1764–1766, 1768, 1769–1771, and 1773–1775; Lord Charles Greville Montagu, 1766–1773; and Lord William Campbell, 1775. See PRO CO 5/406 to understand just what pressure they were under.

[52] John Richard Alden, *John Stuart and the Southern Colonial Frontier*, p. 57. Also see Clarence J. Attig, "William Henry Lyttleton: A Study in Colonial Administration" (Ph.D. dissertation, University of Nebraska, 1958); Hellen Kohn Hennig,

The duties and responsibilities of these men were outlined in their royal instructions and gubernatorial commissions. Both documents were often formidable in length. Indeed, the instructions alone sometimes ran to more than one hundred paragraphs. These official documents, totaling as many as eighty pages, contained administrative directions from the Lords Commissioners of Trade and Plantations, or Board of Trade. This crown agency had the general responsibility for supervising the work of governors and for making the final recommendations on important colonial matters to the King's Privy Council.[53]

In addition to following directives of the Board of Trade, provincial governors often had to work closely with the Commissioners of the Admiralty and Treasury of the mother country.[54] Colonial executives also were expected to cooperate with neighboring governors and to support military and naval operations during the long Anglo-French conflict in the eighteenth century.

The governor of South Carolina was equipped with an imposing set of titles; Captain General of the Province and Vice Admiral of the Provincial Navy were two of the most impressive.[55] He also had certain political powers to protect the royal prerogative. For instance, in dealing with the assembly, governors could and did convoke and reconvoke, dissolve and prorogue the assembly, and call new elections.[56]

The power of the governor was further bolstered by veto power, by selection of the seat of colonial government, and by privileged communications with the Board of Trade.[57] In theory, he also enjoyed the political

---

Great South Carolinians, from Colonial Days to the Confederate War, pp. 73–80; Sherman, *Robert Johnson;* Thomas Jefferson Wertenbaker, *The Old South: The Founding of American Civilization,* pp. 339–43; and David Ramsay, *Ramsay's History of South Carolina,* 1:69.

[53] Carter, "James Glen," pp. 190–370.   [54] Ibid., pp. 9–10.

[55] His other duties and powers were the collection of quit rents, mustering the militia, responsibility for moral and religious activity in the province, and coordinating military and naval forces in the colony.

[56] James Glen to Commons House of Assembly, June 1756, quoted in *The South Carolina Gazette* (microfilm, hereafter cited as *SCG*), 5 June 1756, South Carolina newspapers collection, Charleston Library Society.

[57] Carter, "James Glen," p. 14; Herbert Levi Osgood, *The American Colonies in the Eighteenth Century,* 4:142; Charles McLean Andrews, *The Colonial Period in American History,* 4:420–22; and Board of Trade to colonial governors, 15 May 1761, PRO CO 5/216. The governors were the only officials allowed to communicate directly with the Board. Letters were considered confidential and governors were criticized if they shared privileged communications with the assembly. Board of Trade to James Glen, 20 December 1748, and 1 December 1749, quoted in Carter, "James Glen," p. 12.

support of the councilors. All these factors would make it appear that South Carolina royal governors should have been masters of their province.

Yet the powers of the governor were often inadequate to cope with the determined drive for greater self-government expressed by South Carolina legislators. Provincial executives often complained to the Board of Trade about the independent conduct of the assembly and its committees.[58] For example, the assembly once imprisoned the colony's surveyor general and attempted to jail the provincial chief justice against the governor's wishes. One of the more popular governors, James Glen, was threatened by an assembly committee with having the province's half of his £1,000 yearly salary withheld and the rental allowance for his mansion, "Belvedere," revoked.[59]

Thus we see how provincial executives often found their powers limited by legislative action. The power struggle was complicated by a protracted constitutional and fiscal rivalry between the assembly and the governor's council. The basic issues at stake were control of taxes, the liberties and privileges of the Commons House of Assembly, and the lower house's continued stress on home rule. Colonial South Carolina legislators took their traditional British liberties seriously. The governors, faced with instructions from superiors in England on one hand and the tight-fisted assembly on the other, were often very frustrated.[60]

Governors, of course, often profited by advice from able provincials who were members of the Council. This body, it will be recalled, met as the Upper House of the South Carolina General Assembly. Members of the Council viewed their responsibilities as those of a miniature House of Lords. Although the Council's powers were not detailed by the colonial charter of

---

[58] Glen to Board of Trade, 6 February 1744, PRO CO 5/370; for a comprehensive examination of this matter see Jack P. Greene, *The Quest for Power.* Glen complained of the assembly using the ballot as a "vile Venetian juggle" and claimed it "unhinged government." He was concerned over the Council's inefficiency and the Commons' reluctance to vote money for his projects. Robert Johnson wrote about his detractors in the Commons, who were complaining about him to his superiors in London. Francis Nicholson was concerned with the growth of "commonwealth ideas" from Massachusetts. These examples are a few of many contained in PRO CO 5/406, abstracts of correspondence between governors of South Carolina and the Board of Trade, 1721–1756.

[59] *SCG*, 27 June 1748; and Wertenbaker, *Old South*, pp. 342–43.

[60] Board of Trade to Glen, 20 December 1748 and 9 December 1749, PRO CO 5/372, quoted in Carter, "James Glen." This observation, of course, is an inference drawn from governors' speeches to the assembly and executives' official correspondence with British officials.

1721, for over a decade the Council functioned as the Upper House of the legislature.[61]

The role of the Upper House in colonial South Carolina's affairs is thus often difficult to follow because of its complex work and responsibilities.[62] A sketch of the Council's part in the major political events of the colony illustrates the complexity of the problem.

If the political history of South Carolina as a royal colony were divided into three sections,[63] the councilors' part in the first period, from 1721 to the mid-1730s, was one of constructive leadership. The membership represented various political factions. Some were former members of the proprietary council. Others were backers of the 1719 revolution and supporters of the King's interest.[64] These legislative leaders helped guide the colony in the period of transition from proprietary government to royal status. They also played an important part in the development of strategy in the threatened Anglo-Spanish War of the 1720s. In addition, the councilors helped shape Indian policy. The Council also attempted to create a sound monetary policy and to cope with problems growing out of the sale of public lands. In most of these matters, the councilors' legislative programs were more conservative than those of the Commons House of Assembly.

During the second phase of South Carolina's colonial history, from the mid-1730s to the end of the French and Indian War, the Council's position of leadership was under attack by the governors and assembly. There were several causes for this thirty-year political struggle. In part, the conflict was a continuation of prior struggles of the proprietary regime. Another factor was that, as the population of the South Carolina backcountry increased rapidly in the 1750s and 1760s,[65] the councilors no longer represented the interests of the majority. Since the Council's membership continued to be frozen at twelve, many able South Carolinians were not eligible for membership. These talented colonists instead served in the Commons House of Assembly. To Commons members, proud of the growing power of their chamber, the condescending or sometimes hostile statements made by councilors tended to

[61] Sirmans, "South Carolina Council," pp. 373–80; Leigh, *Considerations in certain transactions,* pp. 1–90. See note 67, this chapter.

[62] The Council played three different roles—legislator, judge, and executive. Confusion was also caused by the fact that the councilors' responsibilities were poorly defined by British colonial officials.

[63] I selected these three divisions arbitrarily to show the gradual decline of the Council's political importance.

[64] Sirmans, "South Carolina Council," p. 379.

[65] See the population estimates from colonial documents in Wallace, *Short History,* appendix 33, p. 709.

widen the gap between the two houses. More friction between the representatives of the Upper House and the Commons House of Assembly resulted from the Board of Trade's policy of appointing merchants and non-resident British "placemen" to the Council.[66]

Governors in this middle thirty-year period of the colony's history were periodically at odds with members of the upper chamber for various reasons. An intermittent battle was fought over the governor's right to meet with the councilors when they acted as an Upper House.[67] When new British governors arrived in the colony, they sometimes criticized their predecessors, the provisional lieutenant governors, who often still remained active as councilors. Governors who had heavy military responsibilities to maintain frontier defenses sometimes believed that the councilors' narrow interpretation of their Council duties hindered cooperation between the two houses. In this three-way struggle for leadership between governors, councilors, and assemblymen, the councilors usually won their skirmishes with the governors. At the same time, the Council often lost in the struggle with the popularly elected house.[68]

The final chapter of the Council in South Carolina colonial history is from 1763, the end of the French and Indian War, to 1775. In these years, the councilors ceased to be a major political force in provincial affairs. The crown policy of rewarding needy British politicians with appointments to the Council further divorced this body from the people of South Carolina. Finally in the 1770s, the purging of Council member William Henry Drayton (one of the chief advocates of South Carolina self-government) by a clique of British appointees in the colony, marked the nadir of the upper chamber.[69]

---

[66] Edmund Atkin, "Journals of the Upper House of Assembly and His Majesty's Council," 13:173, South Carolina Archives Department; Sirmans, "South Carolina Council," pp. 376–77, 385–86. Atkin was a wealthy Charles Town councilor and merchant. He later became well known for his work as Superintendent of Indian Affairs for the Southern colonies. In this instance, Atkin was chairman of an Upper House committee which wrote a lengthy report on the Council's relationship with the governor and the lower house. Councilor Atkin and his committee members warned the Commons House of the dangers of losing the support of the Upper House in financial affairs. He stated that "men of LITTLE ESTATES may get in the [lower house] who will have it in their power to oppose the BEST."

[67] Glen to Board of Trade, 17 July 1750, PRO CO 5/406. Upper House committee report "to enquire into the constitution, state, and practices of the Legislature of this province," "Journals of the Upper House," 13 (7 May 1745): 118–74; and Sirmans, "South Carolina Council," pp. 385–86.

[68] Sirmans, "South Carolina Council," pp. 381–88.

[69] The growth of Commons House status can be estimated by several methods. One was the attitude of provincial leaders to serving in the lower house. Examples of

The twelve councilors, when serving as the Upper House of the legislature, followed the pattern of the British Parliament in the use of committees. The small size of the upper chamber, often reduced by absenteeism or conflicting governmental responsibilities, sometimes caused the body to have only a bare quorum of three to consider legislation. When such a condition existed, the Upper House acted as a committee of the whole house. If more members were present, they were appointed to sessionary or ad hoc committees. Because the Council had only twelve members, an individual councilor had more committee assignments than had a Commons member. In the Council, committee assignments were more equitably shared and committees were smaller in size than those of the lower house.[70]

Council-Commons joint committee assignments were important in maintaining the councilors' role as a check upon the assembly. But cooperation in legislative business was also made possible by the use of such joint bodies.[71] Joint committees were used throughout the entire eighteenth century.

One of the reasons for the Upper House's role as legislative leader early in the royal period was that it usually had equal representation on conference, joint sessionary, and extrasessionary committees.[72] This meant that Upper House members would often dominate or obtain compromise decisions in joint or conference committees.

An example of the decline of councilors' power on joint committees in the late colonial period can be seen in the committee on correspondence.[73]

---

men who refused Council seats to serve in the Commons House were Henry Laurens and William Wragg. Commons prestige can also be estimated from articles in contemporary newspapers. Also see Sirmans, "South Carolina Council," pp. 381–88, and William M. Dabney and Marvin Dargan, *William Henry Drayton and the American Revolution*, pp. 50–51, 63–64.

[70] Some of the Council's committees were Indian affairs, trade, religion, correspondence, budgetary matters, and petitions and accounts. Generally speaking, there was a companion Upper House committee for every one in the Commons House. The average Upper House committee had from two to four members. It was not unusual to have a subject committed to a one-man committee.

[71] Nicholson to Commons House, 17 June 1724, *JCHA* (Salley), 2 June 1724–16 June 1724, pp. 15, 38, 43; and *JCHA* (Salley), for the session beginning 23 February 1724/25, pp. 18, 37. Governor Nicholson urged members of both houses to work together and took the lead in suggesting the use of joint committees. When the two chambers worked closely, legislation was initiated and passed with rapidity.

[72] *JCHA* (Salley), 1724, pp. 64, 68.

[73] Prior to 1775, the function of this committee was to carry on official correspondence with the colonial agent, other colonies, and crown officials. After the 1730s, this committee met between normal sessions due to the increasing press of business. Ella Lonn, *The Colonial Agents of the Southern Colonies*, pp. 44, 248–49, 254–56, 259–65.

This joint committee, which first came into existence in the proprietary period, was responsible for official correspondence sent to royal officials in Great Britain or to other colonies. Originally, in the 1720s, this body had nearly 30 percent of its membership from the Upper House.[74] By 1763 the committee on correspondence, after several decades of "packing" by the lower house, had grown in membership from twelve to twenty-two. The breakdown of membership in the 1760s was eighteen assemblymen and four councilors. Such a change in committee membership indicates how completely the assemblymen dominated this key committee. Since the number of committee members from the lower house was high, assemblymen could actually conduct business without the presence of representatives from the Upper House.[75]

[74] Jack P. Greene, "The Gadsden Election Controversy and the Revolutionary Movement in South Carolina," pp. 479–80; *JCHA* (Salley), 1724/25, p. 70.
[75] Greene, "Gadsden Election," pp. 479–80.

CHAPTER II

The Development of Legislative Committees in the Commons House of Assembly

In the frontier province of South Carolina, the Commons House of Assembly was the only governmental body responsible to the electorate. The gradual acquisition of greater power by the assembly was therefore one of the most important political trends in eighteenth-century South Carolina.[1] By 1763, the assembly was so well entrenched in power that it could virtually stop governmental operation when it wished to do so.

The Commons House legislators generated the ideas, administered the finances, and guarded the public's interest through the legislative committee system. As the colony grew and legislative responsibilities increased, committees were assigned new roles. When the legislature was operating at its peak efficiency, during the years from 1737 to 1760, the size, number, and types of committees increased to meet new problems of frontier politics. By 1763, the Commons House had committees or commissions (appointed, self-regulated boards which administered certain governmental responsibilities, such as Indian trade, repair of roads, construction of fortifications, and fire protection of Charles Town) for nearly every phase of its activity.

Specialization in committee assignments grew as the number of members and of committees was enlarged. The Speaker of the Commons House, who made committee assignments, thus had considerable power over the functioning of the legislative process. In the period after 1721, the Speaker seems to have given the most desired posts to the ablest legislators, those with greatest seniority, and those who were generally favored with wealth and political influence.[2]

The Journal of the Commons House of Assembly illustrates how important committees were in the legislative process. The first normal activity of each session was to select a temporary committee chairman to initiate business. The opening weeks of the several legislative sessions which met each year were largely devoted to committee assignments. Appointments were matters of real concern to individual assemblymen.[3] Normally in each year a legislator might serve on one or more of the twenty to twenty-five assembly committees. In 1721, at the start of the royal period, seventeen committees were at work. Fifty-five years later the number was not much greater. Yet a quantitative measurement of this sort does not reveal the changes that were occurring. One trend was the gradual establishment of six standing committees. These replaced sessionary and a variety of ad hoc legislative bodies. Standing committees were preferred because they provided continuity of operation.[4]

[1] This theme has been stated by many colonial historians but has not been related to the committee system. The first expression of this idea is found in Justin M. Winsor, ed., *Narrative and Critical History of America,* 4:338; and the most recent in Jack Philip Greene, *The Quest for Power;* Robert M. Zemsky, "Power, Influence, and Status: Leadership Patterns in the Massachusetts Assembly, 1740–1755," *William and Mary Quarterly,* 3d ser., 26, no. 4 (October 1969): 502–20; and M. Eugene Sirmans, *Colonial South Carolina.*

[2] See committee assignments listed in Appendix II (pp. 131–81) or the original journals with tax returns for the colony in PRO CO 5/1324 (South Carolina Miscellaneous); and genealogical articles in the *South Carolina Historical Magazine* (see *South Carolina Historical Magazine Subject Index,* p. 703).

The Speakers of the Commons House of Assembly during the royal period were: Joseph Moore, Jr., 1721–1724; Thomas Hepworth, Jr., 1724; Thomas Broughton, 1725–1727; William Dry, 1728–1729; John Lloyd I, 1731 and 1731–1732; William Dunning, 1731; Robert Hume, 1732–1733; Paul Jenys, 1733–1736; Charles Pinckney, 1736–1740; William Bull II, 1740–1742, 1744–1747, and 1748–1749; Benjamin Whitaker, 1742–1744; Henry Middleton, 1747 and 1754–1755; Andrew Rutledge, 1749–1752; James Mitchie, 1752–1754; Benjamin Smith, 1755–1763; Rawlins Lowndes, 1763–1765 and 1772–1775; and Peter Manigault, 1765–1772. See Sirmans, *Colonial South Carolina,* pp. 56–58, 92, 116–19; Robert Luce, *Legislative Assemblies,* pp. 20, 278, 396–97; and idem, *Legislative Procedures and the Course of Business in Framing of Statutes,* pp. 14, 26; JCHA (Salley), 1696, p. 6; see also Salley, other proprietary *Journals of the Commons House of Assembly;* and JCHA, manuscript V, South Carolina Archives Department, Columbia; Ralph Volney Harlow, *A History of Legislative Methods in the Period before 1825,* pp. 3–9, 57; and Greene, *Quest for Power,* p. 38; JCHA (Salley), 1725–1726, pp. 75–76.

[3] *JCHA* (Jenkins), reel 16, 19 November 1755; and *JCHA* (Easterby), 6:570–72; 7:586–89; and vols. 1–4, 8–9, passim. *JCHA* (Salley), 15 March 1726–11 March 1726/27, indicates that forty-three committees functioned during this period.

[4] *JCHA* (Arch.), 5, passim; *JCHA* (Jenkins), reel 17, unit 2, passim; Herbert Levi Osgood, *The American Colonies in the Eighteenth Century,* 4:142; and

Another important factor in committee organization was the establishment of extrasessionary, or recess, Commons House committees. These groups were created to perform legislative or sometimes executive tasks when the legislature was not in session. Examples were committees on correspondence and on Indian affairs.[5] Other types of committees in the assembly included extraordinary committees, committees of the whole house, major committees, and routine committees.[6]

We have seen that standing committees and committees of the whole house can be traced to the British House of Commons. The first such English committees were those formed to consider certain legislative subjects, such as privileges, elections, religion, and grievances. Later, Parliament instituted committees of the whole house on trade and courts of justice.[7]

Equivalents of these British committees of the whole house functioned in the South Carolina Commons House as standing committees.[8] The technique of forming the assembly into a committee of the whole house was employed for important or controversial measures so that all members could have a voice in the decision. Under this procedure, members were freed from formal rules of parliamentary procedure and encouraged to debate. This practice also enabled the Speaker to participate in debates. The legislature often used this device when they wished to maintain secrecy, because the comments of assemblymen were not recorded in the Commons House records,[9] as they would be at other times.

Another type of committee was the "extraordinary committee." These committees determined matters of broad policy for the house, especially in regard to internal affairs of the province and to relations with the mother country. They differed from other committees in that they did not necessarily deal with specific legislation. They were particularly active during the years of crises after 1763.[10] The most influential members of the forty-eight-man Commons House were usually named by the Speaker to these extraordinary committees. The most significant of the extraordinary committees was that

---

William Roy Smith, *South Carolina as a Royal Province, 1719–1776,* p. 11. Smith and Osgood agree that there were standing committees. Smith lists these as: religion, privileges and elections, grievances, trade, and courts of justice. Harlow, *Legislative Methods,* p. 18 and 18 fn., disagrees with Smith. My own research supports the fact that there were more than two standing committees in the Commons House. See also John Franklin Jameson, "The Origin of the Standing-Committee System in American Legislative Bodies," p. 247.

[5] Greene, *Quest for Power,* p. 463.   [6] Ibid.
[7] Jameson, "Standing-Committee System," pp. 247–55.
[8] Smith, *Royal Province,* p. 11.
[9] Harlow, *Legislative Methods,* pp. 92, 94–95, 101.
[10] Greene, *Quest for Power,* p. 463.

on the state of the province, which examined major problems, such as economic depression or Indian attack.

There were two additional types of assembly committees. One handled major legislation and the other was concerned with routine business. Major legislative committees were ad hoc groups which drafted legislation, considered claims, or computed the annual budget. The duties of routine committees included checking the number and condition of muskets stored in the attic of the State House and investigating the quality of gunpowder in the provincial magazines.[11] Some additional routine assignments were to check the constitutionality and possibility of legal conflicts in newly drafted bills and to carry messages to the Council room or governor's mansion.

Key committee assignments, made by the Commons House Speaker, usually went to veteran legislators, acknowledged leaders, or assembly members with special knowledge of the problems to be considered. Representatives from Charles Town and low-country parishes, or members with advantageous family and business connections also were favored with better committee appointments.[12] Those who did not obtain key committee assignments from the Speaker were newly elected assemblymen, representatives from frontier parishes who actually lived in the backcountry, or legislators outside the higher social strata.

The careers of four members of the Commons House illustrate how the wealthy, aristocratic class tended to monopolize key committee assignments.

Peter Timothy was one of the few artisans to serve in the Commons House of Assembly in the 1750s.[13] But Timothy's background would lead a modern observer to believe he would be a superior legislator. He was a member of the exceptionally able Huguenot community of the colony and was printer of the most influential newspaper in the province, *The South Carolina Gazette.* Then, too, his father's former position as provincial printer, newspaper owner, librarian of the Charles Town Library Society, and partner of Benjamin Franklin, should have been helpful. Timothy himself had acquired slaves and land. His combined income from the

[11] These responsibilities fell upon members of the armory and powder receiver's accounts committees.

[12] After the 1730s the old resentment between planters and merchants began to decrease. The two groups cooperated on most issues except those dealing with cheap money. See Jack Philip Greene, "The Gadsden Election Controversy and the Revolutionary Movement in South Carolina," *Mississippi Valley Historical Review,* 46 (1959): 472–73; and see the appendixes of this book for a fuller treatment.

[13] Richard Walsh, *Charleston's Sons of Liberty: A Study of the Artisans, 1763–1789,* pp. 18–21.

newspaper, land speculation, his deputy postmaster position for the Southern colonies, and private printing made him a respected citizen. Yet he received so few important committee assignments that his brief career in the Commons House, 1755–1757, cannot even be considered of second-rate importance. Perhaps a combination of inexperience, Timothy's overenthusiastic nature and his occupation stigmatized him in the eyes of his aristocratic colleagues.[14]

A decade later, Charles Cotesworth Pinckney's career in colonial politics, 1769–1775, presents another example of the difficulty of a newly elected member in obtaining important committee assignments. In this case it was not Pinckney's occupation or social background which hindered his rapid progress up the Commons House ladder of political standing. The young legislator's father, Charles Pinckney, was a successful lawyer and rice planter, had been speaker of the Commons House, Councilor, Chief Justice of the colony, and South Carolina's agent in London. Pinckney's mother, Eliza Lucas Pinckney, was the daughter of the governor of Antigua and won colony-wide respect for her discovery of the first techniques of growing indigo profitably in the province. In addition two influential members of the house were closely related cousins, Charles Pinckney and Charles Cotesworth. Furthermore, Charles Cotesworth Pinckney was an exceptionally bright, industrious graduate of Oxford and an accredited lawyer trained in the Middle Temple of the Inns of Court in London.[15] Yet, with all of these favorable credentials, Pinckney, in the eyes of Speaker Peter Manigault, still must have seemed untried because of his lack of legislative experience.

How, then, did Pinckney achieve his later success in the Commons House and in the national period to follow? First of all he accepted the routine drudgery of the first three years in the assembly. He did a creditable job in his routine committee assignments—carrying messages, auditing records, determining the nature and extent of public land in Charles Town, and preparing the "Schedule of Charges." This period was really a time of apprenticeship in governmental administration, finance, and the mechanics of legislation.[16]

---

[14] Hennig Cohen, ed., *The South Carolina Gazette, 1732–1775,* pp. 230–45; Peter Timothy, *Letters of Peter Timothy, Printer of Charleston to Benjamin Franklin,* passim; and Walsh, *Sons of Liberty,* pp. 24–28, 64. Timothy was one of the few assemblymen who was not supported by the rest of the Commons when he was insulted during the middle of a legislative session in the 1750s.

[15] Marvin Ralph Zahniser, "The Public Career of Charles Cotesworth Pinckney" (Ph.D. dissertation, University of California, Santa Barbara, 1963), pp. 2–20.

[16] Ibid., p. 26.

In Pinckney's case, it appears that his activities outside the Commons House may have been equally important in the advancement of his political career. In his legal profession, he demonstrated his competence, a fact not to be missed by the power bloc dominating the assembly committee assignments in the 1760s. Other factors contributing to his success were his activities in charitable, Anglican, and social circles, where he met and impressed provincial leaders. His marriage to Sarah Middleton, the daughter of a respected councilor and exceptionally wealthy planter, certainly did not hurt his cause in family-conscious South Carolina. Thus young Pinckney, for a variety of reasons, became a successful legislator and eventually held a number of key committee posts that were denied him when he first joined the Commons House of Assembly.[17]

Committee service was often denied representatives from frontier parishes despite their ability. Moreover, the difficulty faced by a frontiersman in winning an assembly seat further diminished his chances of being a dominant force on committees. The cases of Captain James St. John and Dr. Thomas Cooper indicate the difficulty outsiders had in being accepted as active members of the Commons House of Assembly. Thomas Cooper was a leader of a group of smaller frontier planters who protested a land swindle by Commons leaders and Governor Robert Johnson in the early 1730s. James St. John was the provincial surveyor-general who refused to cooperate with the General Assembly and the governor in land matters.

Cooper and St. John unilaterally decided to resurvey the land grants distributed by Governor Johnson and the legislature. Their purpose was to unmask fraud and they hoped to take the matter to the English royal courts for resolution. When the low-country clique of assembly leaders learned of their activities, the legislators found the two men guilty of contempt of the Commons House and arrested them. They were jailed without being allowed the constitutional right of *habeas corpus*.[18] While in jail, Cooper and St. John were elected as protest candidates to the Commons House. The

---

[17] The power bloc in the Commons House at the time consisted of: Benjamin Smith, Isaac Mazyck, Thomas Middleton, William Wragg, Robert Pringle, William Roper, Rawlins Lowndes, Charles Pinckney, Peter Manigault, James Parson, and Peter Taylor. See Zahniser, "Charles Cotesworth Pinckney," pp. 20–35. The South Carolina Commons and Upper houses were filled with so many relatives of blood and marriage that even the most skilled genealogist would find it difficult to trace all the relationships. It is obvious that family qualities and connections were second only to business relationships in explaining the interstructure of the power blocs at work in South Carolina colonial politics.

[18] Thomas Jefferson Wertenbaker, *The Old South*, pp. 341–43. Also see Sirmans, *Colonial South Carolina*, pp. 172–82; and Richard P. Sherman, *Robert Johnson*, pp. 143–52, for different interpretations.

members of the lower house committee on privileges and elections refused to seat them for several months and their names are obvious omissions from any list of legislators with important committee assignments.[19]

The experiences of Dr. Cooper, Captain St. John, Charles Cotesworth Pinckney, and Peter Timothy underscore the difficulty certain assemblymen had in obtaining superior committee assignments.

Considered superior among the committees in the South Carolina Commons House throughout the fifty-four years of royal rule were those which protected the liberty, self-government, or self-interest of the people of the colony. The standing committees, particularly those on grievances, trade, courts of justice, petitions and accounts, and privileges and elections, had great prestige, as did joint and conference committees staffed by leading members of both chambers. Another important group was the sessionary committees, which dealt with vital provincial matters, such as frontier defense and intergovernmental relations. Although less prestigious than these powerful long-term committees, routine, ad hoc committee assignments occasionally resulted in the most important legislative activity of the entire assembly.[20]

An illustration of a standing committee on which veteran, able legislators served was the committee on grievances. Most South Carolinians looked to the Commons House of Assembly as the ultimate protector of their liberties and rights,[21] and this legislative role was the primary responsibility of the grievances committee. Grievances of anyone except slaves were considered, but the problems of legislators usually received first consideration. Petitions dealing with grievances of individual South Carolinians were either referred to this committee by the Speaker or presented directly to this body in publicly advertised open hearings.

Another standing committee, the committee on petitions and accounts, was concerned with parallel problems of public welfare. This committee considered special problems, such as monetary claims against the government or requests for assistance in solving local problems. Often these petitions came from frontier sections of the colony seeking monetary assistance for needed improvements. Bills were frequently drafted to resolve

---

[19] Greene, *Quest for Power,* pp. 475–88.

[20] Luce, *Legislative Assemblies,* pp. 186–87. An example of a routine ad hoc committee assignment which became exceptionally important was the message committee of two who carried an announcement to Lt. Governor William Bull II in an early hour before the opening of the current assembly. Bull, still in bed, was persuaded to open the Commons before he was fully aware of what he had done. See Chapter VIII below.

[21] *JCHA* (Salley), 1724, p. 47; 1726/27, pp. 69–70.

the problems. The influence of individual petitions in shaping legislation was greatest in the first two decades of the royal period. After 1740 the committees began to take the lead in drafting bills rather than merely reacting to problems brought to their attention.

Petitions, when viewed over a long period of time, were significant in another way. They probably were the South Carolina citizen's best method of indicating his opinion and influencing the political process between triennial elections.[22] Many of these petitions dealt with minor considerations, such as clearing a creek for navigation, constructing a frontier church, paying the Speaker for rental of a house in which the assembly met, or constructing a path through Reverend Alexander Garden's glebe.[23] Other petitions were concerned with major provincial problems and might be signed by hundreds of subjects, such as the appeals to the provincial government by the backcountry Regulators in 1767 and 1768.[24]

The general record of the committee on petitions and accounts indicates that problems of Commons House members received first consideration. Usually their claims were resolved by governmental expenditures of tax monies. In matters of an altruistic nature (widows' pensions, petitions for new church facilities, etc.) the committee record was noteworthy. When it came to problems of frontiersmen, mechanics, or people of the "meaner sort," the committeemen were less likely to act. Normally such petitions required a ground swell of public opinion before legislators would consider them.[25]

An additional standing legislative committee, that on trade, assisted the commercial interests of the province. South Carolina was one of the North American colonies which prospered under the British mercantile system.[26] The committee on trade was in part responsible for this state of affairs. Its members recognized how important trade was to South Carolina in general and particularly to its provincial capital, Charles Town. There was no lack

[22] Harlow, *Legislative Methods*, p. 111. Robert Eldon Brown and B. Katherine Brown, *Virginia, 1705–1786: Democracy or Aristocracy?* pp. 233–34, state that a similar pattern existed in Virginia.

[23] *JCHA* (Easterby), 6:247; and *JCHA* (Salley), 1724, pp. 53–54, and 1726/27, pp. 178–79. This was not the famous South Carolina botanist and naturalist.

[24] Richard Maxwell Brown, *The South Carolina Regulators*, pp. 145–48.

[25] Frederick Dalcho, M.D., in his *An Historical Account of the Protestant Episcopal Church in South Carolina*, points out on a parish-by-parish basis how the assembly met church needs. For a fuller treatment of this problem, see Charles Woodmason, *The South Carolina Backcountry on the Eve of the Revolution*, and Brown, *South Carolina Regulators*.

[26] Lawrence Henry Gipson, *The British Empire before the American Revolution*, vol. 2, *Southern Plantations*, p. 150.

of local business leaders to serve on this committee.[27] The membership of this committee and the Upper House, when it acted as a committee of the whole on trade, reflected the dominance and concern of planters and merchants dealing with products for overseas consumption.

Activity of the Commons House committee on trade can be traced from the beginning of the royal period. Scarcely weeks after South Carolina was admitted as a provisional colony by the crown in 1721, correspondence reached London from Charles Town asking that trade restrictions on the colony's chief staple, rice, be removed from the enumerated list. In the late 1730s, the assembly's concern about trade was aroused, almost to the point of armed conflict, by Georgia's interference with South Carolina Indian trade along the Savannah River. In this altercation, members of the committee on trade led an aggressive legislative response to the problem.

Another example of this body's work was the assistance it gave to South Carolinians in their recovery from the economic recession of 1739–1747. The committee secured a royal bounty on South Carolina's new commercial crop, indigo. This helped to create a profitable staple crop which provided new opportunities for South Carolina planters to profit from the use of their large slave population.[28]

Such examples show the highlights of the committee's work. However, it was the routine, session-by-session activity which must in part explain South Carolina's preeminence in colonial trade. This prosperity was not achieved without opposition from other colonies and sometimes from British authorities. Although South Carolina's geography made it relatively easy to produce valuable plantation and forest products and to profit from the interior Indian trade, other provinces had similar natural advantages. The less affluent neighboring colonies of Georgia and North Carolina desired a greater share of colonial trade. Faced with the problem of reconciling the different economic interests of many colonies, the Board of Trade tried to resolve the issue by presenting lengthy trade instructions to royal governors.[29]

[27] A survey of the occupations of committeemen (listed in the appendixes) indicates that the majority were planters, with a significant minority of merchants and lawyers.

[28] Petition from the South Carolina General Assembly to the Board of Trade, n.d. (ca. 1720), PRO CO 5/382; Lt. Governor Thomas Broughton to Board of Trade, 6 August 1736, PRO CO 5/406; and *JCHA* (Easterby), 7:193; 8:ix–x; and Gipson, *Southern Plantations*, p. 135.

[29] Harry Roy Merrens, *Colonial North Carolina in the Eighteenth Century*, pp. 108–42, 173–81; Mary F. Carter, "Governor James Glen" (Ph.D. dissertation, University of California, Los Angeles, 1951), p. 192; and Leonard Woods Labaree, *Royal Government in America*, pp. 7, 420–49.

Some of these directives, of course, were to the liking of the Commons House of Assembly, but others were viewed as restrictive. The committee on trade and other legislative bodies took the lead in suggesting improvements, changes, or noncompliance with British commercial policy.

Except in the case of such problems as the Stamp Act and the Tea Act (discussed in Chapters VI and VII), the representatives of the lower and upper houses worked together on trade matters, perhaps as a result of shared business interests.[30] Royal governors occasionally vetoed trade measures that conflicted with their instructions, but generally favored those drafted by assembly committees.

Perhaps as important as the trade committee was the standing committee on privileges and elections.[31] In the Commons, this body was primarily concerned with protection of the power, privileges, and political independence of the assembly and its members. Councilors on their committee, on the other hand, seemed to be primarily interested in protecting the royal prerogative.

Although the Commons committee on privileges and elections met irregularly, it usually dealt with problems relating to legislative powers claimed by the governor. Some of the sharpest clashes between the governor and both houses during this fifty-four-year period were over matters of internal privilege, particularly the judging of assembly elections. The committee also concerned itself with the election of the Speaker and quarrels over the selection of officers and employees of the legislature. The actions of the committee often tested the relative strength of the royal governors' power. The governors learned that each time this committee won even a minor victory, another precedent was established leading toward more self-government. As a consequence, the Speaker of the Commons House appointed members with legal talent to this committee. Such talent, concentrated in one committee, often was enough, as later chapters will show, to win in controversies with governors.[32]

[30] Councilors' qualifications were defined by the Board of Trade as "men of good life and well affected to our government and good estates and abilities and not necessitous persons or much in debt." Leonard W. Labaree, ed., *Royal Instructions to British Colonial Governors, 1670–1776*, 1:55, quoted in M. Eugene Sirmans, "The South Carolina Royal Council, 1720–1763," p. 373, 380, 392.

[31] Smith, *Royal Province*, p. 103; and Harlow, *Legislative Methods*, pp. 18, 111.

[32] *SCG*, 5 February 1763; *JCHA* (Salley), 1725, pp. 103–5, 107, 109; and 1725–1726, pp. 19, 92; Greene, "Gadsden Election," pp. 472–73, 476–77; idem, *Quest for Power*, pp. 205–22; Osgood, *Eighteenth Century*, 4:143, 273; and Carter, "James Glen," p. 157. Internal privileges meant the rights and privileges of

Joint committees of both chambers played an important role in South Carolina government. Particularly in the 1720s, most of the important legislation was drafted by such joint committees. One of these was the powerful joint committee on correspondence, mentioned earlier, whose members drafted most official communications. This committee also controlled the colonial agency in London. Many of its members lived in Charles Town because they worked both in and out of the normal legislative session.[33]

Another key joint committee was that on Indian affairs. Relations with the powerful Southern Indians were always of crucial concern in South Carolina before 1763 because of the threat they posed.[34] A constant threat from the French, the Spaniards, and their native allies further emphasized the importance of maintaining friendly relations with the Indians. The divisive squabblings with South Carolina's neighbors over Indian policy also was a major concern of this joint body.[35]

This committee differed from many others in composition and was probably most representative of the entire colony.[36] Its members took bold measures to resolve Indian problems. They recommended the appointment of the Commissioners of Indian Affairs, wrote the governors' speeches to the Indians, and gave minute instructions to their Indian agents in the field.[37]

The basis for the legislature's power in Indian affairs was the principle of legislative responsibility for the public welfare. A more practical reason for the legislature's interest was that the conduct of Indian affairs was usually

---

members of the legislature. Such matters as freedom of debate, freedom from arrest or insult during legislative sessions, and freedom to determine the qualifications of their membership were considered particularly important.

[33] *JCHA* (Salley), 1724, pp. 4, 6, 14; 1724–1725, pp. 15–16, 18, 130; 1725–1726, pp. 25, 60–62; Ella Lonn, *The Colonial Agents of the Southern Colonies,* pp. 142–56. Comparison of the dates of correspondence in the Charles Garth Letterbook, South Carolina Archives Department, with the dates of the sessions of the assembly, verifies this statement. Greene, *Quest for Power,* pp. 465–66.

[34] John Richard Alden, *John Stuart and the Southern Colonial Frontier,* p. 6.

[35] Carter, "James Glen," pp. 65, 78, 100, 103. Biographies of other Southern colonial governors are helpful, particularly Desmond Clarke, *Arthur Dobbs, Esquire, 1689–1765;* and Louis Knott Koontz, *Robert Dinwiddie.*

[36] See committee assignments in the appendixes.

[37] See John Herbert, *Journal of Colonel John Herbert, Commissioner of Indian Affairs,* pp. ii, 5–7; and *JCHA* (Jenkins), reel 16 (9 January 1756); *JCHA* (Salley), 1724, pp. 12–13, 16, 19; 1724–1725, p. 75; 1725–1726, pp. 89–90; 1726–1727, pp. 15–17, 27–28, 63, 102, 142; and *JCHA* (Easterby), 3:493; 4:439; 5:173.

financed from the provincial treasury. According to royal instructions to the governors, the Commons House had a voice in public expenditures.[38]

The Upper House also expressed concern about Indian relations. Perhaps this interest was due to the substantial investments in frontier land and Indian trade of many of the councilors.[39] Little wonder that individuals from the upper chamber were as active in the joint committee on Indian affairs as were commoners.

Two legislative leaders who at different times represented the upper and lower houses in the Indian Affairs Committee were Colonel James Moore and Edmund Atkin. Colonel Moore was a surveyor, planter, and well-known militia leader. He was a hero in the province for his successful frontier campaigns against the Spaniards and Indians. Moore thus brought a good deal of practical experience as well as a unique governmental background to committee meetings. He was one of the two South Carolinians who had been Speaker of the Commons House, lieutenant governor, and acting governor. The Indian Affairs Committee was the only committee Moore attended when he was Speaker of the Commons House in the early 1720s, an indication of its importance.

An equally concerned member of the committee was Councilor Edmund Atkin. A successful merchant originally from England, Atkin took his committee duties very seriously in the 1740s and 1750s. In fact, so interested was Atkin in Indian affairs that he wrote a famous report and plan concerning the Southern Indians. As a result of this plan, Atkin, and later another South Carolinian, John Stuart, were asked to coordinate British Imperial Indian policy in all the Southern colonies. Clearly the work of this committee and its members was of real importance.

Probably the most crucial joint committees were those on taxes and the estimate. Early in the royal period, the lower house cooperated with the Upper House in developing the final tax bill the governor was to sign.[40] By the late 1730s, however, the divergent tendencies of the three elements of

[38] Article 35 of the governor's instruction, quoted in *JCHA* (Salley), 1725–1726, pp. 75–76; Enabling Act of 1721 (Royal Charter), in South Carolina Documents, Miscellaneous, PRO CO 5/1326; Merrill Jensen, ed., *English Historical Documents: American Colonial Documents to 1776*, pp. 121–25; and David Duncan Wallace, *South Carolina: A Short History, 1520–1948*, p. 106.

[39] A committee of any three councilors could authorize the sale of public land. William M. Dabney and Marvin Dargan, *William Henry Drayton and the American Revolution*, pp. 121–25; and Alden, *John Stuart*, p. 22.

[40] *JCHA* (Salley), 1724–1725, pp. 18, 68; 1725–1726, pp. 9, 36, 60–64; and Sir Francis Nicholson to Board of Trade, 4 December 1723, PRO CO 5/406.

the colony's legislature (governor, Upper House, and Commons House) became noticeable in struggles over passage of the yearly tax bill.[41]

Perhaps the cream of the legislature was involved in the committees dealing with taxes.[42] Planters and merchants who served on these committees sometimes acted as if taxes were a threat against their liberty and property. Legislative proposals from governors demanding considerable expenditures of funds were often looked upon with disfavor and ignored by lower house tax committees.[43] Thus committees came very close to using the modern legislative technique of "pigeonholing" key bills and thereby creating pressure upon the other branches of government.

Such obstructionistic tactics by various Commons House tax committees were a deliberate effort to reduce the power of the governor. Committee members and the assembly at large supported the principle of low taxes and minimal executive power in government. The tactical advantage that commoners gained in other legislative struggles was therefore often due to the fiscal pressure tactics of their committees.

Assemblymen had a personal interest in this whole problem of taxation. Tax records indicate that, other than councilors, commoners were the largest taxpayers in the province.[44] The financial holdings of their members obviously influenced the outcome of tax measures considered by lower house committees.

Nearly equal in importance with the joint and standing committees were the sessionary committees. These were appointed for one session, often about eight weeks in length, to consider public problems or the writing of bills and resolutions. Throughout the royal period, most bills were drafted by sessionary committees of the lower house. The committees, normally of about six members each, were dominated by low-country representatives.[45] Member-

---

[41] In the late 1740s and after 1763, the two houses disagreed over the control of tax measures. The upper chamber ended with little voice in fiscal affairs. Sometimes during these struggles, several years would go by without payment of public debts, but the discontented merchants and mechanics usually supported the Commons.

[42] See the appendixes.

[43] The technique used by committees was to fail to report unpopular expenditures to the entire Commons House prior to the close of the session. The other basic method was to reserve the money in such a way that it could not be appropriated.

[44] James Glen, quoted in Osgood, *Eighteenth Century,* 4:142, 263, 268–69, 273; Sirmans, "South Carolina Council," pp. 385–86; and South Carolina Miscellaneous Records, Tax Rolls, PRO CO 5/1356 passim.

[45] Greene, *Quest for Power,* pp. 464–66; Harlow, *Legislative Methods,* pp. 15–16, 22; *JCHA* (Jenkins), reel 17 (19 May 1760); *JCHA* (Salley), 1726–1727, pp. 11–47, 56 fn., 172–82; and *JCHA* (Easterby), 1:581.

33

ship on sessionary committees was often expanded when emergencies brought sudden demands for quick action.[46]

Each committee had a chairman who usually reported to the entire Commons House when legislative drafts were prepared or when the committee needed direction. These committees used a variety of sources of information in drafting legislation.[47] Certain sessionary committees had the power to subpoena individuals. Failure to appear might mean punishment for contempt of the Commons House. Legislators on sessionary committees dealing with controversial issues were protected from arrest, as were all other legislative committee members, by an act of the General Assembly.[48]

The work of ad hoc committees (temporary committees which were assigned specific tasks) was much less complex than that of other committees. Ad hoc bodies were usually small, ranging from one to five members, and their life was usually short. When the assigned task was completed, the committee was dissolved. Members were occupied with special investigations or routine tasks, such as counting the muskets in the armory and making audits.

Although the sheer volume of committee appointments and reports dominates the pages of the Commons House *Journals* and the Council records, little evidence of what occurred within committee meetings exists today.[49] An occasional disgruntled member with a minority view indicated his displeasure in *The South Carolina Gazette*. Once an entire Upper House committee broke the precedent of privacy and publicly stated its position in the *Gazette*. This occurred during the nearly annual quarrel over taxes between the councilors and their Commons counterpart committee.[50] Until the 1750s such public statements were infrequent.

Throughout the eighteenth century, committees of both houses operated

---

[46] *JCHA* (Salley), 1726–1727, pp. 60, 63, 99, 162. Other times when committees were expanded were during the Stono slave massacre of 1739, during the Regulator disturbances of 1768, and during threatened Indian attacks.

[47] *JCHA* (Salley), 1724, pp. 8–9; 1725–1726, pp. 55–57, 70; 1726–1727, p. 4; *JCHA* (Easterby), 1:27. The entire Commons House had to vote certain powers of investigation to committees.

[48] *JCHA* (Salley), 1726–1727, pp. 9, 13.

[49] The two best sources are the Charles Garth Letterbook, South Carolina Archives Dept., and the letters of colonial leaders in the *South Carolina Historical and Genealogical Magazine*. See the *South Carolina Historical Magazine Subject Index*, pp. 688–733, for specific examples.

[50] William Bull II was responsible for the letter in the *South Carolina Gazette*, quoted in Edward McCrady, *The History of South Carolina under the Royal Government, 1719–1776*, pp. 288–91.

less formally than those of modern legislative bodies.[51] Few official records were maintained. Procedural transcripts, minority reports, roll call votes, names of witnesses, and extensive committee staffs, all part of modern legislative operation, were not officially recorded. Instead, provincial lawmakers, with only a clerk at best to serve them, apparently had a great deal of freedom in their operation and procedures.[52]

This lack of formal structure sometimes created difficulties for South Carolinians whose views differed from the majority in the Commons House or the Council but who had no official recourse.[53] Committee "packing" by the Speaker was commonplace, particularly after 1762.[54] An example of this occured when a low-country junto, led by Speaker Peter Manigault, frustrated provincial authority for long periods in the early 1770s and nearly stopped the provincial legislative process. A similar case was a clique of British "placemen" who dominated Upper House committees and the entire Council in the 1760s and 1770s.[55]

The general lack of committee records obliges the researcher to emphasize external features of committee organization. Nearly fifty years ago, Ralph Volney Harlow, in a pioneer study of the committee system, stated that it appeared primarily to be dry, institutional history. Yet human interest was certainly present in colonial committee chambers. Legislators of the eighteenth century by no means lacked an understanding of devious methods, and assemblymen undoubtedly devised many clever projects and schemes in their committee meetings. Complaints by the Council, and governor, and disallowals by the Board of Trade and Privy Council illustrate the political craftiness of the astute committeemen of the South Carolina Commons House of Assembly.[56]

An atmosphere of propriety was not strictly maintained by committee members. Josiah Quincy, Jr., a Massachusetts visitor in the 1770s, attested to this lack of decorum in the Charles Town Commons chamber when he

[51] Harlow, *Legislative Methods,* pp. 2–3, 23, 104, 112, 115–16.

[52] Clinton Ivan Winslow, *State Legislative Committees: A Study in Procedure,* pp. 12, 15–17, 19, 26, 31–32, 35, 140; and *JCHA* (Salley), 1724–1725, p. 30. Even the Council ran short of clerks when the General Assembly was busiest near the close of sessions.

[53] *JCHA* (Salley), 1725–1726, pp. 89, 92; and 1726–1727, p. 22; Wallace, *Short History,* pp. 107–9; and Wertenbaker, *Old South,* pp. 340–45.

[54] *JCHA* (Salley), 1726–1727, pp. 62, 162; Greene, "Gadsden Election," pp. 479–80; and *JCHA* (Easterby), 6:189.

[55] Dabney and Dargan, *William Henry Drayton,* pp. 11–12, 28–29, 50–51.

[56] Harlow, *Legislative Methods,* pp. 103–4; and McCrady, *Royal Government,* pp. 281–82.

observed the entire assembly in session in 1773. Quincy wrote in his journal that the members "conversed, lolled and chatted, much like a friendly jovial society." They "sat with their hats on, uncovering only when they rose to speak."[57] This informality gave way to excitement and emotion during committee debate in the hot, overly humid South Carolina summer.

Reflecting an awareness of this free atmosphere, the correspondence of South Carolina governors sometimes touched upon controversial legislative committees. Committees did not keep minutes of their meetings and governors seeking information on committee activity had to rely upon the lower house *Journals*. These *Journals* were poorly indexed and usually gave only the names of committee members and the text of their final report to the Commons plenary meetings. Indeed, Governor James Glen complained about this problem in one of his reports to the Board of Trade. Glen stated, "I turn over with great labor most of the old Journals of the Council and Assembly and as they have no Indices I was obliged to submit to the drudgery of reading many of them—a sort of study in which there is neither Entertainment nor Instruction."[58]

The primitive character of the *Journals* was but one of many problems indicating that South Carolina's committee system faced operating difficulties not present in British parliamentary committees. Another was the problem of staffing clerical positions. Selection of these legislative appointees was a problem common to all royal colonies. Although few in number by modern standards, legislative clerical positions were considered desirable, and competition for them was keen. They were of prime importance to the functioning of the committees and of the entire legislature. Such appointments also constituted a form of political patronage which will be discussed later.

Important appointments, such as the colonial agent, were nominally controlled by royal officials, but in reality were dominated by legislative committees on correspondence and governmental finance.[59] Other appointments to lesser posts, such as committee clerks, messengers, the colonial printer, and the provincial treasurer, were dominated by the Commons

[57] Josiah Quincy, Jr., "Journal of Josiah Quincy, Jr., 1773," *Massachusetts Historical Society Proceedings* 49 (1915/1916): 452; and Carter, "James Glen," p. 5.

[58] See Abstracts of Correspondence between South Carolina Governors and the Board of Trade, PRO CO 5/406; Harlow, *Legislative Methods*, pp. 104–5; and Glen to Board of Trade, "An attempt towards an Estimate of the value of South Carolina," March 1751, South Carolina Public Records, 24:303–4, quoted in Sirmans, *Colonial South Carolina*, p. 361.

[59] Greene, *Quest for Power*, pp. 205–14, and 210 fn.

House. Officials who held these posts acted as the administrative agents of the lower house committees.

A lack of adequate physical facilities for committee meetings also created difficulties in this frontier province until the completion of the provincial State House in Charles Town in 1759.[60] Before construction of a permanent seat of government, legislators of both chambers met in rented quarters during governmental sessions.[61] If private homes proved inadequate, committees were appointed to seek other quarters. Modern authorities on group dynamics stress the importance of an adequate meeting place as a prerequisite for effective committee operation.[62] Considering the fact that many meetings of early South Carolina legislative committees were held in home studies, inns, taverns, public houses, and armories, the quality and speed of their legislative work is truly impressive.

When the red brick capitol on Meeting and Broad streets in Charles Town was completed in 1759, committees met in second-floor offices.[63] Committee members left the main chamber on the first floor in the afternoons and worked in their upstairs offices. In times of emergency, committees met in the evenings and members' attendance was waived during the normal morning sessions of the Commons House.[64] By the 1760s the system had developed to such a degree that the speed of their deliberations matched that of modern legislatures.

[60] A committee developed the plans for the Provincial State House, which was completed twenty-four years later. See *JCHA* (Salley), 1724–1725, and Alexander Samuel Salley, *State Houses of South Carolina, 1751–1936*, p. 12–22.

[61] The Commons House often met at Colonel Brewton's home in the 1720s. The Indian Affairs Committee met at Colonel George Chicken's inn. The Council also convened in private homes until the 1730s.

[62] Audrey Trecker and Harleigh B. Trecker, *Committee Common Sense*, pp. 85–104; and Edward Eyre Hunt, *Conventions, Committees, and Conferences, and How to Run Them*, pp. 40–49.

[63] *JCHA* (Salley), 1765, passim. The opening hour for lower house meetings was set at the start of each session. It was actually 8, 9, or 10 A.M. The Commons could alter the opening hour at any time by agreeing to a new hour before adjournment.

[64] *JCHA* (Easterby), 2:319; and *JCHA* (Salley), 1724–1725, p. 16.

CHAPTER III

The Legislative Committee System in the Early Royal Period, 1719–1725

In the early years of the royal period, members of the South Carolina Commons House of Assembly established a number of committee precedents. By May 1725, the end of the administration of the first royal governor, Sir Francis Nicholson, the legislative committee system had become well entrenched, due in part to Nicholson's support. As a result, it was difficult after 1725 to curb the power of a number of legislative committees.[1]

This was an important period in the development of the legislative committee system. Although the colony was not officially at war, the legislature was still concerned with the threat of armed conflict. Before the settlement of Georgia in 1732,[2] South Carolina was British North America's southernmost frontier, flanked to the west by numerous Indians of questionable loyalty.[3] Furthermore, a diplomatic contest was being carried on between South Carolina, Spanish Florida, and the southern French outposts for the support of the Southern Indians.[4] Indeed, in 1715–1716 the colony was nearly eliminated by the Yamassee Indians, and the colonists continued to feel the effects of that conflict until the early 1730s.[5]

The uncertainty of future relations with the Southern Indians was also complicated by a quest for profits from Indian trade. South Carolinians on legislative committees were well aware that nearly 20 percent of the total provincial income was derived from the Indian trade.[6] Therefore, reports of committees dealing with Indian matters were considered important enough to be carefully examined by both houses of the General Assembly.[7]

Related economic problems of the 1720s concerned immigration, currency, and land development. Similar problems existed in other colonies. Commons House committees attempted to find adequate capital to finance internal development and recommended measures to increase the amount of provincial money in circulation. Moreover, the assembly expanded the volume of "currency" by authorizing the use of rice as a form of legal tender. This inflationary program brought about some of the sharpest political clashes of the decade. Directly or indirectly, the monetary program of Commons committees caused economic unrest and dissension within the branches of provincial government.

In the 1720s, legislative committees gave special attention to methods of improving the colony's frontier economy by encouraging immigration. Committee reports stressed that more white settlers meant greater prosperity and that the presence of immigrants would increase the value of Carolina plantations by reducing the threat of Indian attacks from without or slave uprisings from within. Yet, in order to attract settlers, South Carolina needed the right inducements—land and opportunities for trading and investment. Legislative committees periodically discussed this subject until the mid-1730s. Numerous assembly, joint, and conference committees also struggled with problems related to irrigation, selection of new crops, and land distribution in an attempt to stimulate the economy of the colony.

Since many of the problems faced by legislative committees were carried over from the proprietary period, one may ask why the inhabitants of South Carolina chose to solve their problems under crown control rather than under the proprietary government. The answer is that many colonists felt

[1] Governor James Glen to Board of Trade, 10 October 1748, *Collections of the South Carolina Historical Society*, 2:302.

[2] In 1731 the new colony was created out of the southern part of South Carolina by royal instructions.

[3] See James Adair, *History of the American Indians*, pp. 235–401; and Chapman James Milling, *Red Carolinians*, pp. 157–285 passim.

[4] Verner W. Crane, *The Southern Frontier, 1670–1732*, pp. 108–17; Milling, *Red Carolinians*, pp. 273–75; Lt. Governor Thomas Broughton to Board of Trade, 15 July 1737, PRO CO 5/406; and Glen to Board of Trade, 2 May 1746, 20 April 1747, 14 April 1748, and 26 July 1748, PRO CO 5/406.

[5] Crane, *Southern Frontier*, p. 112.   [6] Ibid., p. 115.

[7] *JCHA* (Jenkins), reel 3, pp. 277, 364. Also see *The South Carolina Indian Books*, ed. William L. McDowell; Robert Lee Meriwether, *The Expansion of South Carolina, 1729–1765*; Edmund Atkin, *Indians of the Southern Frontier: The Edmund Atkin Report and Plan of 1755*, pp. xx, 17–38; and John Richard Alden, *John Stuart and the Southern Colonial Frontier*, pp. 5–19, 28–56, 76, 108, 130.

they were unjustly treated by the proprietors. The colonists, it will be re-called, after nearly fifty years of proprietary rule, finally rejected the proprietors in a bloodless revolution in 1719. It is important to note that this revolution was organized by a group of men acting as a convention or extralegal committee.[8]

The members of the extralegal revolutionary committee capitalized on the colonists' grievances against the proprietors. A significant cause of the 1719 revolution was a series of proprietary vetoes of South Carolina reform legislation which later became the heart of the legislative program of the revolutionary party leaders.

Moreover, the proprietary favoritism shown to Chief Justice Nicholas Trott and his brother-in-law, Colonel William Rhett (both members of the Council), angered members of the revolutionary committee.

One angry committee member was Alexander Skene, a recent immigrant from the West Indies. He brought a good deal of political experience to the colony, having been council secretary of the colony of Barbados. Skene immediately became active in the South Carolina proprietary government and was soon named to the Council. After a few months in this post, Skene was removed by the proprietors. Evidently this was due to Trott's influence in England. Skene was immediately elected to the lower house as a kind of protest, and was understandably unhappy about the proprietors' action. He became a leader in the anti-Trott faction in the Commons and later in the extralegal, revolutionary committee.

As we can see in Skene's case, Trott and Rhett held a good deal of power in South Carolina government, derived from their connections in England and their dominance of key Upper House committee posts. The absentee proprietors in England often relied upon their reports and overlooked those of the governor.[9] Prior to the revolution in 1719, Trott was accused of a number of questionable practices in the administration of his judicial posi-tion. Many legislators felt that Trott and Rhett had brought about the unpopular vetoes of acts to promote immigration, to occupy vacant Indian lands, and to prevent fraud in government. Trott, for example, was sup-ported by the absentee proprietary council in London, even though a memo-rial of thirty-one "articles of complaint" was signed against him by all the

[8] Alexander Hewatt, "Historical Account of the Rise and Progress of the Colonies of South Carolina," *Historical Collections of South Carolina,* ed. Bartholomew Rivers Carroll, 1:224; and Francis Yonge, "A Narrative of the Proceedings of the People of South Carolina in the Year 1719," in ibid., 2:165–66.

[9] Hewatt, "Account of South Carolina," pp. 186, 206–7, 214.

attorneys of the colony. This memorial was supported by a Commons House committee, a majority of the Council, and even the governor. The proprietors' response to the memorial was to dissolve the lower house and remove the anti-Trott faction in the Council.[10]

A Commons House election in the summer of 1719 returned the nucleus of the assemblymen who opposed not only Trott and Rhett but the entire proprietary system of government. At the same election many of the councilors, previously dismissed by the proprietors, were elected to the lower house. These new commoners received key committee assignments and gave direction to the discontented forces in the legislature who opposed the proprietors. Legislators on committees particularly disliked the fact that, although South Carolina was a proprietary colony, Carolinians had to observe royal tax and commercial regulations. Many felt that the colonists should have the advantages of a royal colony, namely, British military and naval protection, since they were paying royal taxes.[11]

Meanwhile, in the fall of 1719, the South Carolina frontier government was faced with the threat of a Spanish invasion fleet from Havana. Governor Robert Johnson hastily called a joint session of councilors and newly-elected assemblymen to prepare for the threatened invasion. Johnson asked the legislators, then sitting as a committee of the whole house, to form a voluntary association to contribute their private funds to rebuild the fortifications of Charles Town, there being no tax monies available in the treasury.[12] In the debate that followed, Chief Justice Nicholas Trott's inflammatory remarks about submitting to proprietary rule broke up the meeting. As Councilor Francis Yonge put it, "They chose to hazard the loss of the Country to the *Spaniards* rather than to submit to acknowledge a Right in the *Proprietors* of repealing their laws." Governor Johnson then decided to activate the militia to prepare for the enemy.[13]

Prior to the militia muster, on the night of November 17, 1719, several leaders of the colony met and formed the extralegal revolutionary committee whose members subscribed funds for the repair of Charles Town's fortifications. They also agreed to an association or compact to overthrow the proprietary government.[14]

The leaders of this revolutionary committee were Alexander Skene, Speaker Arthur Middleton, Colonel George Logan, and Major William

[10] Ibid., pp. 214–19.

[11] Ibid., pp. 182–92, 200–205; Yonge, "Narrative of 1719," pp. 144–51.

[12] Hewatt, "Account of South Carolina," pp. 224–25; and Yonge, "Narrative of 1719," pp. 162–63.

[13] Yonge, "Narrative of 1719," p. 164.   [14] Ibid., pp. 164–65.

Blakeway.[15] Although this committee constituted a minority of the assembly, they sensed public opinion well enough to know that they could achieve their objective of separation from the proprietors before resistance could form.

The leaders of the revolutionary committee made every attempt to give the revolt a respectable appearance in order to win crown support.[16] They organized their bloodless revolution skillfully. The committee members contacted the chief militia officers and won their support before the militia muster. Then they contacted Governor Johnson, who was apparently completely surprised when they offered him the reins of the interim revolutionary government until royal pleasure was known.[17] Johnson, however, remained loyal to the proprietors, and although he lacked troops, he threatened hostile action against the members of the revolutionary committee. It was at that time, on December 21, 1719, that the governor dissolved the Commons House of Assembly, which represented the center of the revolutionary leadership.[18]

Major William Blakeway, one of the leaders of the revolution, was in many ways representative of the men who took over the government in 1719. Blakeway was a militia officer and one of the most prominent attorneys in the frontier colony. Although his appointment as powder receiver had been rejected by the Commons House in 1717, he apparently felt no ill will toward his colleagues. Like the other leaders he actively disliked the authoritarian power of Trott and Rhett. Blakeway also apparently was adversely affected by the depression following the Yamassee War. He must have realized that their gamble in the revolution might mean a high political office in the royal period that would follow. As will be seen, Blakeway did profit greatly by the events of 1719 and was appointed to the Council.

The events that followed Governor Johnson's dissolution in December 1719 indicate that the leaders of the revolutionary committee and the whole General Assembly had planned further action. The thirty Commons House members, now temporarily without official status, retired to a tavern to drink punch and plan strategy. After a sprightly session, the commoners formed themselves into a "Convention," and claimed the power to represent the public's wishes.[19] This body then elected a temporary governor, Colonel

[15] Hewatt, "Account of South Carolina," pp. 225–26. Skene, Logan, and Blakeway were all assembly leaders. See their assignments in Appendix I, below.

[16] Yonge, "Narrative of 1719," pp. 164–65.

[17] Hewatt, "Account of South Carolina," pp. 226–27.

[18] Ibid., pp. 227–28; and Yonge, "Narrative of 1719," pp. 167–69.

[19] Hewatt, "Account of South Carolina," pp. 228, 235.

James Moore, Jr., and the other major appointive officers in the colony.[20] Among these officials were commissioners of correspondence, who were appointed to compose memorials explaining the action of the revolutionary body to authorities in England.

During this shift of power, Governor Johnson was not inactive. He tried to rally public opinion behind him by reminding the colonists of the oncoming Spanish fleet. However, the Spaniards were defeated about this time by the British naval forces in the waters of the Bahama Islands.

The ousted governor then verbally challenged the power of the revolutionary committee but was unsuccessful. On each occasion the committee's leaders had anticipated the governor's actions and won over the remaining proprietary supporters. In fact the revolutionaries were so successful that by the end of the revolution there were only three provincial leaders who remained loyal to Johnson.[21]

In the eighteen months that followed the revolution, the province was governed by legislative bodies which had no official authority. The colony's government at this time consisted of the elected Commons House, which was assisted by an Upper House, and officials appointed by the revolutionary leaders. The chief objective of the interim government was to secure the support of the royal authorities. To accomplish this goal, the South Carolinians sent several colonial agents to London to deliver the petitions and memorials drafted by the South Carolina commissioners of correspondence.[22] These documents show astute appreciation for diplomatic technique. Their ten-page memorial of February 25, 1720, for example, stressed the commercial value and military importance of South Carolina in the British Empire. This approach seems to have been more effective than constitutional arguments in justifying the revolt against the proprietors.[23]

The revolutionary government's request for royal status for the colony was finally approved in 1720, although their request to retain Moore as their governor was rejected. Because British officials were reluctant to have a governor of untested loyalty, the Board of Trade appointed Sir Francis Nicholson, who had been a loyal servant of the crown and had served as governor in Virginia and several other colonies. The members of the legislature were not displeased at Nicholson's appointment for they knew of

[20] Ibid., p. 258.   [21] Yonge, "Narrative of 1719," pp. 180–88.
[22] Memorial of Colonel John Barnwell to Royal Officials, 7 February 1720, in Barnwell Papers, South Carolina Historical Society.
[23] South Carolina Commissioners of Correspondence to Board of Trade, 14 February 1719/20, PRO CO 5/382.

his reputation as a competent governor and frontier military leader.[24] The general approval of the assembly was echoed by members of a special committee which expressed thanks to the royal officials.

Thus South Carolinians in 1719–1720 completed a successful revolution against the proprietors. Their attempt to retain their own revolutionary governor indicates their desire for self-government. The success of legislative committees in resolving political problems was not soon forgotten. The spirit of the 1719 revolution persisted and reappeared in full force fifty-six years later.[25] It was no accident that in the American Revolution of 1776, South Carolina assemblymen again formed revolutionary extralegal committees which dominated the colony's government.[26] In 1719–1721, the Speaker and eight other revolutionary leaders completely dominated the committee activity of the South Carolina Commons House of Assembly.[27]

The impact of these political developments was not lost on South Carolina observers in the 1720s. One of these was former councilor Colonel William Rhett, who was temporarily discredited in the revolution. Although Rhett was no longer active in legislative committees, he managed to remain active in governmental affairs. In return for not leading his militia regiment against the revolutionary committee of 1719, Rhett was rewarded by the new government with the profitable position of commissioner of fortifications. While he solidified his political position in Charles Town, Rhett secretly corresponded with his old associates in London.[28] In a letter written in November 1719 to one of the proprietors, Rhett summed up the new leadership in a critical but prophetic observation in which he stated, "I must tell you, sir, if the much greater part of the most substantial people had their choice, they would not choose King George's government." A month later Colonel Rhett restated his view in another letter to London in which he wrote that: "[if their] revolt is not cropt in the bud, they will set up for themselves against his majesty." Rhett seems to have been convinced that frontier South Carolinians actually wished to rule themselves as a kind of commonwealth.[29]

---

[24] Ibid., 29 September 1720.   [25] Hewatt, "Account of South Carolina," p. 256.
[26] See Chapter VIII below. Also see John Andrew Doyle, *The English Colonies in America,* 1:390. (Doyle provides the best comparison of the Revolution of 1719 and the American Revolution.)
[27] *The State Records of South Carolina: Extracts from the Journals of the Provincial Congresses of South Carolina, 1775–1776,* ed. William Edwin Hemphill and Wylma Ann Wates, pp. xvi, xvii, xxi, xxiii, xxvi.
[28] Hewatt, "Account of South Carolina," pp. 239, 244, 247.
[29] Rhett to the Lords Proprietors, 1720, *Collections of the South Carolina Historical Society,* 2:237; and Justin M. Winsor, ed., *Narrative and Critical History of America,* 5:328 fn.

Yet the Commons House of Assembly gave Sir Francis Nicholson a cordial welcome when the new royal governor arrived in Charles Town in May 1721.[30] Though South Carolina was suffering a temporary economic depression at that time from the destruction of crops and plantations during the Yamassee War of 1715–1717, assemblymen did their best to impress Nicholson.[31] A joint committee of the revolutionary General Assembly planned and carried out a gala reception for the new governor at the home of Colonel Alexander Parris, a rich Charles Town legislator.[32] This affair established a tradition of demonstrating hospitality for new royal governors.

Nicholson himself appeared anxious to please the colonists and soon showed his good will by generous contributions to schools, churches, and charities. His "honeymoon" with the South Carolina legislature and its committees lasted until 1723. The first few months of his administration were marked by significant accomplishments by both houses of the General Assembly. Through the use of joint legislative committees, assemblymen drafted legislation to improve both fortifications and Indian relations. Representatives also drew up bills to create new churches and a free school in Charles Town.

Francis Nicholson's administration succeeded because of at least two factors. Obviously, one of these was the governor's own ability and extensive experience. Another was the assemblymen's close cooperation. Both Nicholson and the members of legislative committees knew the danger to the colony from potential French, Spanish, and Indian attack. Only three years had passed since the end of the bitter Yamassee War.[33]

In all legislative matters the new governor worked closely with the Upper House. The governor's first official business was to summon the Council on May 29, 1721.[34] During the opening ceremonies, the councilors swore oaths of allegiance to the crown and Nicholson presented his official commissions to govern. The twelve councilors who attended this opening meeting had been selected by Nicholson and the Board of Trade. As for their political

---

[30] Commissioners of Correspondence to South Carolina's Colonial Agent, Joseph Moore, PRO CO 5/358, n.d. (ca. 1721).

[31] Hewatt, "Account of South Carolina," p. 257.

[32] *JCHA* (Jenkins), reel 2, p. 473.

[33] See the leading authorities on this period: William Roy Smith, *South Carolina as a Royal Province, 1719–1776*, pp. 108–10, 123, 192, 234–41; Edward McCrady, *The History of South Carolina under the Royal Government, 1719–1776*, pp. 34–68; M. Eugene Sirmans, *Colonial South Carolina*, pp. 134–37; David Duncan Wallace, *A History of South Carolina*, 1: 275–93; Stephen Saunders Webb, "The Strange Career of Francis Nicholson," *William and Mary Quarterly*, 3d ser., 23, no. 4 (1966): 513, 546–48.

[34] Account of the first Council session, 8 July 1721, PRO CO 5/358.

background, they were a mixture of revolutionary leaders, reliable royalists, and holdovers from the proprietary Council.[35] All were long-time South Carolina residents with experience on legislative committees. With the governor's approval they chose Arthur Middleton, former proprietary Speaker and a revolutionary committee leader, as their president.

During the first twelve meetings of this Council, important appointive officeholders were interviewed. Councilors, acting as a committee of the whole house, evaluated qualifications of the various applicants. New governmental commissions for provincial offices were issued.[36] A variety of other matters were covered in the 8:00 A.M. to 5:00 P.M. meetings held in a Charles Town private home. Governor Nicholson and the councilors initiated a survey of the colony's economy. They also took steps to improve the fortification of the southern boundary of the province. The enthusiasm of the members of the Upper House was evidenced by their excellent attendance. All the councilors attended every meeting of the session, with the exception of the provincial secretary, Charles Hart, who had an attack of gout. Nicholson was cooperative in his dealings with the councilors, but he always took care to comply with his instructions from the Board of Trade.[37]

One of the first acts of the new governor and Council, scarcely ten days after Nicholson's arrival in Charles Town, was to call for the election of a new Commons House of Assembly, which was to meet in July. After the election was completed, the bicameral structure of the General Assembly was reestablished. At their initial meeting, members of the lower house appointed the first legislative committees of the royal era. These included committees on correspondence, on Indian affairs, and on petitions and accounts. Many of the representatives who served on the legislative committees were planters who were in debt to English and Charles Town merchants. A minority of the committeemen, on the other hand, were merchants and attorneys.[38] Most of the revolutionary leaders of the period from 1719 to 1721 were elected to the Commons House and formed a majority of the assemblymen.

Governor Nicholson encouraged the use of committees in the assembly, and their use continued after he left for England in 1725. From 1719 to

---

[35] M. Eugene Sirmans, "The South Carolina Royal Council, 1720–1763," *William and Mary Quarterly,* 3d ser., 38 (1961): 373, 381–82.

[36] Alexander Samuel Salley, ed., *Journal of His Majesty's Council,* 29 May–10 June 1721, pp. 1–9.

[37] Nicholson to Board of Trade, 13 June 1721, PRO CO 5/406.

[38] *JCHA* (Jenkins), reel 2 (27 July–15 August 1721), pp. 497–535; also see the appendixes, below.

1725, committees grew in size, in total number, and in permanency. In the first session of the lower house, July–August, 1721, there were twenty committees upon which the thirty-six members of the Commons House might serve.[39] Of these, only one was designated a standing committee. Eleven more were either ad hoc or joint committees. Many of these were formed at the request of the governor or Council.[40]

The growth of the committee system can be seen by comparing records of the 1721 session with those of another session sixteen years later. In 1737 there were ten standing committees and a total of seventy-three other committees at work. Nearly all of the 1737 committees had a larger membership than those of 1721. A further comparison indicates that of the seventy-three additional committees in 1737, only five were new joint committees with the Upper House.[41]

The decline in the use of joint committees, noted above, was indicative of the first attempts of the Commons legislative committees to gain greater political power. During the 1720s the Speaker of the assembly refused to allow lower house conference committees to meet in the Council's chamber.[42] After this issue was settled, conference meetings were normally held in private quarters. In 1725 the Speaker demanded that Upper House committees no longer amend money bills nor hold conferences on financial subjects, but the Council refused to bend to his will on this point.[43]

Other conflicts between the Council and the assembly during this period resulted from the initiative of Commons committees in drafting bills and in conducting investigations. Assemblymen even began to criticize Upper House committee members for not attending joint committee meetings. Despite the notably high quality of Commons committee work, Sir Francis Nicholson's successor, Assembly President Arthur Middleton, on one occa-

---

[39] *JCHA* (Jenkins), reel 2 (27 July–15 August 1721), pp. 497–535.
[40] The technique for forming a joint committee is illustrated in the following message from Commons Speaker James Moore, Jr., to Governor Nicholson, 29 July 1721:

> According to your Excellency's desire which we highly approve of, we shall appoint a committee of our house to confer with a committee of his Majestys Council for the dispatch of business, for better cultivating and preserving a good correspondence between the both Houses, which must be of the utmost advantage to the interest of his Majesty and his subjects in this place.

JCHA (Jenkins), reel 2, pp. 16, 505.
[41] *JCHA* (Easterby), 1 passim.   [42] *JCHA* (Salley), 1726–1727, pp. 54–57.
[43] *JCHA* (Jenkins), reel 3, unit 2, pp. 31–39, 248, 327; Smith, *Royal Province*, pp. 290–91; David Duncan Wallace, *A Constitutional History of South Carolina, 1725–1775*, pp. 51–52.

sion reflected the growing political friction of the 1720s by complaining of Commons House "low wit" in marginal notations on a committee report.[44]

In 1722, a struggle developed over an assembly bill authorizing the printing of paper money. The assembly at this time was dominated by planter interests favoring an expansion of credit and the continued printing of paper money. The merchants, on the other hand, opposed the bill and complained that South Carolina paper money already in circulation was only worth one-seventh the value of British sterling.[45] Twenty-two Charles Town merchants, including six members of the Commons House, composed a memorial opposing the paper money bill and the general policy of allowing provincial paper money to be accepted as legal tender.

So incensed were the assemblymen at this challenge to their authority that the Commons, acting as a committee of the whole house, condemned the merchants' memorial as "false and scandalous . . . destructive to the true interest of this Province . . . an indignity to the present General Assembly." The assembly then passed a resolution empowering a special investigative committee to "inspect further into the aforesaid memorial" to see if it violated any laws. The same assemblymen, now acting as a legislative body, accepted the committee's report, which was critical of the merchants, and ordered the arrest and imprisonment of the memorialists in the Charles Town gaol.[46] This move increased the power of the lower house and cowed other opponents of the bill into submission. It is not surprising that Governor Nicholson finally decided to approve the currency bill even though members of his own Council opposed it.

With this victory, the lower house established a precedent for future extensions of its power. From this time on, and especially in the later 1720s and the 1730s, the assembly continued to cause the arrest and imprisonment of individuals on the recommendation of special committees in order to quell opposition. Violations of commoners' "privileges" (such as making derogatory remarks about individual assemblymen, failing to look after an assemblyman's horse, or threatening legal action against legislators) were reason enough for committee recommendation of imprisonment without trial.[47] Nevertheless, in session after session of the early 1720s, the legislators were able to do their work without jailing their opponents. No doubt

[44] *JCHA* (Easterby), 1:72–157, 278.
[45] *JCHA* (Jenkins), reel 2 (6 November–18 December 1722), pp. 99–105.
[46] Ibid., pp. 113–14.
[47] Ibid., reel 2 (1 October–21 December 1723), pp. 348–49; and Jack Philip Greene, *The Quest for Power*, p. 214 fn., citing JCHA, 6 April 1733, PRO CO 5/433.

many of those who would oppose the assembly were intimidated by the example of others who had challenged its authority. There was one person, however, the assemblymen could not arrest and imprison, and that was Governor Nicholson.

Let us turn, then, to a detailed examination of assembly committee activity during Nicholson's governorship to see how committees operated and how they dealt with controversial problems that sometimes involved the governor. In a fourteen-day session, from June 13 to June 27, 1724, for which the extant records are full and adequately recorded, we can see specifically how committees functioned as workshops of legislative activity. The following is a kind of "case history" of legislative committees.[48]

The assembly session opened on June 13, 1724, a date set by Governor Nicholson. Since this session occurred before the construction of the two permanent homes of the Commons (the brick armory and later, in 1756, the provincial State House), members attended meetings in a house rented from the provincial powder receiver, Colonel Miles Brewton.

The meeting opened in the traditional fashion of the British House of Commons with the presentation of the official mace. Major Thomas Hepworth, Jr., was selected as Speaker. He wore a wig and gown. Other house officers were also dressed in English parliamentary garments.[49] Because this was not the first session of the year, members did not spend time selecting standing committees or drafting rules of legislation. After seven members arrived, "the house was formed." However, these members could conduct only informal meetings until nineteen or more representatives were present. When the nineteenth person arrived, a committee of two, the traditional number for delivering messages, informed Governor Nicholson that the lower house was in session.[50] The officers of the assembly were announced at this time. That afternoon any members who were attending the legislature for the first time were sworn into the Commons House of Assembly.

After these formalities, the real business of the legislative session began. The provincial secretary, Charles Hart, delivered to the Speaker of the Commons House the accumulated correspondence and petitions collected by the governor, Council, and committee on correspondence since the last session. In this case, most of the correspondence dealt with Indian affairs,

---

[48] *JCHA* (Salley), 1724, pp. 41–54.

[49] An eye-witness description of the opening of the Commons House of Assembly in 1773 was recorded by Josiah Quincy, Jr., in "Journal of Josiah Quincy, Jr., 1773," *Massachusetts Historical Society Proceedings* 49 (1915–1916): 451–52, 454–55.

[50] *JCHA* (Salley), 1724, p. 3.

with relations with the French, and with official matters from British governmental agencies. The Secretary also summoned the Commons members to the Council chamber to hear the governor's opening message of the session. In this address, Nicholson discussed the situation of the province in regard to the threat of Spanish and Indian attack. He described the legislative program he desired and called for harmony within the General Assembly. As we have seen, Francis Nicholson was well aware of the functioning of legislative committees. In this case, he suggested the formation of joint committees to report upon crucial problems.[51]

One of the new joint committees appointed by the Speaker on the following day was the committee on Indian affairs. This committee of six (three more were added the next day) was to consider a petition from a French sea captain who wished to dock his ship in Charles Town but who was suspected of being a secret agent from Mobile. It was feared the captain might discover the location of the deep water passage through the sand bar that protected Charles Town harbor. The committee refused the captain's petition to land.[52]

Also on June 14, the Speaker appointed a special committee to draft a "Bill to Qualify Protestant Dissenters in this Province to Sitt in the Commons . . . according to the form of their professions."[53] The timing and title of such a bill indicate Carolinian toleration for religious minority groups. At the same time, it was a move of parliamentary strategy. The assembly members had been engaged in an intermittent battle with Governor Nicholson over the seating of certain Presbyterian dissenters in the legislature. The formation of this committee indicated that the harmonious relationships which previously existed between the executive and the commoners were now somewhat strained. The governor, however, in an unusual show of tact in this time of controversy, thanked the members of the lower house for appointing the committee, but recommended that the assembly occupy itself with Indian affairs.[54]

On June 15, the third day of the session, the Speaker appointed a committee to consider amendments to the slave code or "Negro Act." The low-country of South Carolina had a large slave population which labored on the rice plantations. Contemporary legislative records show that in the 1720s the whites were usually outnumbered by Negroes, who were ruled by a harsh slave code. It is not surprising that many of the planter-assemblymen feared the threat of a slave uprising, and in nearly every Commons session

[51] Ibid., pp. 3, 4, 5, 9, 14, 15, 38, 43.   [52] Ibid., pp. 3–4.
[53] Ibid., p. 5.   [54] Ibid.

there was at least one committee concerned with the control and discipline of Negro slaves.

On June 15 another committee reported that South Carolinians were not complying with an act of the previous session that "obliges people to ride armed on Sundays." The committee members recommended that the law be sent to all church wardens for posting.[55] This report was another step in the planters' program to impress their power on the slaves.

The afternoon of June 15 was filled with more committee activity. A committee was appointed to draw up a resolution that a new armory be built. Still another committee reported on French and Indian diplomacy. The afternoon closed with the governor's second message of the day in which he discussed the use of bills of credit for legal tender.

The next nine days followed a similar pattern, with a total of twenty committees at work. Messages from the governor and Upper House to the Commons and the assemblymen's replies kept the legislative clerks working full time. From the opening of the assembly at 8:00 A.M. to adjournment late in the afternoon, except for a luncheon period, many Commons members were tied up in committee meetings to discuss the governor's proposals for legislation. On June 15, after the Commoners rejected one of Governor Nicholson's financial proposals, he actually accused them of being disloyal to the crown.[56]

Committees played a part in an uproar that occurred with the governor at this time. The Commons House voted to disband its colonial agency in London and temporarily ended its committee on correspondence. This unilateral action angered Governor Nicholson. His rage increased when a Commons House ad hoc committee sent a letter in reply to one of Nicholson's speeches without consulting with the Council. Governor Nicholson wrote "that [he] took it as high Presumption and Unparliamentary to give your answers without a committee of both Houses as proposed and this was less than arbitrary." He further accused the assembly of trying to undermine his position as governor and of being malicious.[57] Yet, the Commons committees continued to write to the governor despite his complaints and from that time the number of joint committees with the Upper House began to decrease.

It was little wonder that Nicholson wrote the Board of Trade on June 29, 1724, two days after the end of this session, that the behavior of the assembly was "bad!" He further stated that "the spirit of commonwealth principles increaseth daily," a factor which he attributed to visiting New

[55] Ibid., p. 7.   [56] Ibid., p. 43.   [57] Ibid., pp. 38–43, 49.

Englanders. He also declared that the "people are very variable in their politics."[58]

This detailed account of committee activity shows how the assembly consolidated its authority and did not hesitate to oppose the royal governor. In 1724 to 1725, Nicholson managed to deal with the assembly and its headstrong committees without coming to open hostility.[59] Actually, before he departed for England on May 18, 1725, Nicholson had mended his fences with the Commons House, whose members expressed gratitude for his work as governor. The Commons House had reason to appreciate Nicholson's work, for he was the first royal governor to take office in the colony, and he had demonstrated a willingness to work with assembly committees and to use them in the legislative process so necessary to the operation of the imperial governmental system. Sir Francis Nicholson left behind him a legacy of colonial governmental growth and a maturing legislature aware of its power through the use of committees.

[58] Nicholson to Board of Trade, 18 June 1724, PRO CO 5/406.
[59] See appendixes below for committee leaders.

CHAPTER IV

The Legislative Committee System in a Period of Western Expansion, 1727–1737

The departure of Governor Sir Francis Nicholson in 1725 marked the start of a new chapter in South Carolina history. There were several problems—Indians, Western land, and the economy—which plagued both the legislature and the three governors who followed Nicholson. Legislative attempts to deal with these problems were complicated by friction between the upper and lower houses of the General Assembly.[1]

The Commons House often relied on legislative crises to further its drive toward greater self-government, but the acting governor in the years 1725 to 1730, Arthur Middleton, staunchly opposed the growth of legislative power. The result of Middleton's policy was a clash of wills which caused a near revolution.[2] Robert Johnson was more successful in his governorship, from 1730 to 1735. His success was in large part due to his conciliatory tactics and a rapid turnover of Commons Speakers. During Johnson's administration internal problems resulting from a frontier land scandal temporarily helped to bring about a cessation of friction between the three branches of the legislature.[3] After Johnson's death in 1735 the administration of Lt. Governor Thomas Broughton (1735–1737) was marked by relative legislative harmony and growing prosperity.[4] Throughout the period from 1725 to 1737, the balance of political power continued to shift to the assembly. The Commons took the opportunity to propose legislation that would increase its power whenever the governor appeared likely to bend to its will.

The year 1727 provides an illustration of a recurring tendency of the assembly to press for greater self-government. The acting governor and president of the Council, Arthur Middleton, reached a crisis in his relations with assembly committees that year.[5] Middleton's plight was partly a result of his attempt to halt the commoners' growing determination to have their own way in legislative matters. Indeed, because of this rivalry, Middleton prorogued and dissolved the Commons over ten times in his five-year administration.[6] His relations with the Commons House were especially touchy in 1727 because the colony was plagued by a continuing economic recession resulting from the slow recovery from the damages of the Yamassee War.[7]

During Middleton's administration the key economic problem facing legislative committees was the shortage of colonial currency. It will be recalled that the 1722 arrests recommended by Commons House committees were a device to control those who opposed paper money bills. In 1727, the addition of newly elected members to Commons committees evidently increased the determination of the lower house to issue more paper money. In a sense, the desire of commoners to increase the volume of currency was similar to modern inflationary techniques used to combat depressions. The Board of Trade was generally opposed to such expansions of colonial paper money, but several legislative committees continued to recommend measures, subject to lower house approval, that would increase the amount of currency in circulation. The legislators finally devised a method that would

[1] Dr. Alexander Hewatt, "Historical Account of the Rise and Progress of the Colonies of South Carolina and Georgia," *Historical Collections of South Carolina,* ed. Bartholomew Rivers Carroll, 1:269–325.

[2] Middleton to Board of Trade, 19 December 1728, and South Carolina Council to Board of Trade, n.d. (ca. 1728), PRO CO 5/406. See *JCHA* (Salley), 1 November–30 April 1726/27; and *JCHA* (Jenkins), reel 3 (1727–1730) passim.

[3] Hewatt, "Account of South Carolina," pp. 284–311; Gugielma Melton Kaminer, "A Dictionary of South Carolina Biography during the Royal Period, 1719–1776" (Masters thesis, University of South Carolina, 1926), pp. 41–42; Jack Philip Greene, *Quest for Power,* p. 460; and Richard P. Sherman, *Robert Johnson: Proprietary and Royal Governor of South Carolina,* passim.

[4] Hewatt, "Account of South Carolina," pp. 311–25; *JCHA* (Easterby), 1:1–347, passim; Broughton to Board of Trade, 6 May 1735, 6 and 16 August 1736, PRO CO 5/406; and M. Eugene Sirmans, "The South Carolina Royal Council, 1720–1763," pp. 382–84.

[5] Kaminer, "Dictionary of South Carolina Biography," pp. 56–57.

[6] Hewatt, "Account of South Carolina," pp. 271–75.

[7] Ibid., pp. 269–73; also see Verner W. Crane, *The Southern Frontier, 1670–1732,* for a fuller treatment of Franco/Spanish frontier relations with South Carolina before 1732.

satisfy both their need for money and the British authorities. They established a "sinking fund" in their treasury which was used to redeem certain bills of credit which circulated as currency. This "sinking fund" evidently seemed to the legislators who served on the Commons committees to be the best way out of the colony's financial difficulties.[8]

Middleton had trouble with other Commons House committees. As we have seen, the grievances committee's traditional role was to protect the rights of citizens, particularly members of the assembly.[9] Legislators took their rights extremely seriously, and in 1727 when a well-known member of the Commons was arrested, the assemblymen caused a near revolution. The assemblyman, Landgrave Thomas Smith, a former councilor and respected planter, was an outspoken critic of the Council and an ardent supporter of the assembly's financial programs, such as those on paper currency.[10] When he was arrested for his criticism of Governor Middleton and the Council, the assembly committee on grievances became involved. The committee reported that the persons (the colony's chief justice and provost marshall) who had issued the writ to arrest Smith were guilty of a breach of the assembly's privilege and were subject to arrest; a majority of the lower house accepted the report. The Commons House thus attempted to turn the tables on Governor Middleton, the Council, and the chief justice. At this time the commoners sent the messenger of the Commons House, one Mr. Brown, to arrest the chief justice even though he was a member of the Council.[11]

The Commons messenger twice attempted to capture the chief justice in the Council's chamber. The first time Brown was denied entrance to the Council meeting room. On the second try he managed to slip in by an unguarded entrance, but before he could arrest the chief justice, Brown was captured by the angry Governor Middleton. After calling the Commons messenger a "saucy rogue," Middleton and his councilors threw Brown bodily out of the upper chamber. Governor Middleton then dissolved the Com-

---

[8] Oliver Morton Dickerson, *American Colonial Government, 1696–1765,* pp. 13, 160, 174, 248, 252–53, 317–20; interview with Dr. Charles Lee, state archivist, South Carolina State Archives Department, Columbia, S.C., 10 August 1965; and Curtis Putnam Nettels, *The Money Supply of the American Colonies before 1720,* pp. 11–14, 45–66, 155–56, 162–283.

[9] *JCHA* (Salley), 17 November 1726–11 March 1726/27, pp. 4, 5, 21, 37, 45–46, 65–66, 70–71, 83, 87–88, 91, 98, 118, 124, 130, 166.

[10] Edward McCrady, *The History of South Carolina under the Royal Government,* pp. 80–87.

[11] *JCHA* (Jenkins), reel 3, unit 1 (1727), pp. 5, 20–25, 517–19; unit 2, pp. 601–2.

mons House before the assemblymen could take further action against the chief justice.[12] This matter was not forgotten by the commoners, and the lower house committees on taxes retaliated against the Upper House by not drafting tax bills for several months.

Later, in 1729, Acting Governor Middleton tried to heal the differences between himself and the legislature by inviting members of both houses to a social engagement held in the Council's chamber. An official charged with the seating arrangements placed the assemblymen at the foot of the table and the councilors in the seats of honor. Upon seeing the seating arrangements, the commoners became irate. The next morning, a disgruntled lower house ordered a special committee to investigate this breach of etiquette. The committee wrote an aggressive, ringing denunciation of the Council in their report to the Commons House. The committee report was promptly approved by the entire lower house and was sent to Governor Middleton and his Council. After receiving the report, the Governor took the unprecedented step of apologizing to the Commons House.

An additional example of Commons' aggressive behavior occurred in the early 1730s in a land speculation scandal. Governmental land sales had been stopped since 1719 because the former proprietors were contesting the right of the crown to revoke their charter. During this period of dispute, the validity of new land titles granted by royal officials was subject to question by proprietary claimants. Finally in 1729, the crown bought out the claims of seven of the eight remaining proprietors, thereby clarifying the fact that South Carolina was a royal colony. Land sales were resumed in 1731. The stage was thus set for provincial politicians, including some leaders in assembly committees, to engage in frontier land speculation.[13]

The impetus behind western land speculation originally came from London rather than from Charles Town legislative committees. Robert Johnson, the able South Carolina governor from 1730 to 1735, while residing in England in the late 1720s, proposed to royal officials a program of westward expansion. The heart of this program was the creation of a series of eleven townships located in frontier areas. Johnson envisioned these territorial units as self-contained communities of small freeholders producing agricultural products (silk, wheat, hemp, and naval stores) and cottage industrial products for local provincial use. These townships were to protect the frontier and bring diversity to South Carolina's chronically depressed economy of the

[12] Ibid., unit 1, pp. 521–23.
[13] Hewatt, "Account of South Carolina," pp. 274–75.

1720s. Some of the products of the proposed communities were to be sent to England.

This program caught the eye of the Board of Trade and made Robert Johnson appear to be the man needed as the next royal governor of South Carolina.[14] Moreover, Acting Governor Middleton's apparent lack of success in dealing with the assembly and its committees indicated the need for an able successor. The Board of Trade's selection of Johnson as governor delighted most South Carolinians. And indeed, Johnson's administration, although not free of problems, marked the beginning of one of the longest periods of cooperation between the governor and the Commons House committees in South Carolina's colonial history.[15]

During this period, Governor Johnson's land program helped to bring a return of prosperity to South Carolina. Johnson's township program called for more acreage for crops and a greater diversity of agricultural products. It also called for new settlers who would strengthen the military security of the province. Of course, better military security and increased population in the hinterland would help Charles Town merchants, who envisioned profits from a greater volume of trade and increased value for their unoccupied town lots.[16]

Thus there were high expectations for increased land sales when Governor Johnson arrived in Charles Town on December 15, 1730. In the implementation of the public land program, the power of Commons committees is again apparent.[17] Members of the Commons House committees on grievances, privileges and elections, and special investigative committees were involved in solving problems growing out of land sales. The entire body of legislators, acting as a committee of the whole house, also helped to formulate policies dealing with the opening of the unoccupied and frontier regions of the public domain.[18]

Although the new governor and committee members of the General

[14] Ibid., pp. 284–87, 296–300; Robert Lee Meriwether, *Expansion of South Carolina, 1729–1765*, pp. 17–118 passim; and Sherman, *Robert Johnson,* pp. 107–18.

[15] Johnson to Board of Trade, 27 December 1730, 26 March 1731, and 15 December 1732, PRO CO 5/406; *JCHA* (Jenkins), reel 4, units 1–3 (1730–1733) passim; *JCHA* (Salley), 8 November 1734–7 June 1735, passim; *SCG,* 10 May 1735; and McCrady, *Royal Government,* pp. 167–68.

[16] Hewatt, "Account of South Carolina," pp. 284–87; and Meriwether, *Expansion of South Carolina,* pp. 1–26.

[17] Hewatt, "Account of South Carolina," pp. 277–300, 311.

[18] See *JCHA* (Jenkins), reel 4 (1732–1733) passim.

Assembly had high expectations for the land program, there were others who opposed the method of sale. Chief among the critics were royal officials such as Surveyor General James St. John and his deputies, and Chief Justice Robert Wright. St. John and Wright criticized the method of awarding land titles because it encouraged profiteering.[19] According to St. John and his associates, much of the unoccupied acreage which was open for sale was claimed by holders of vague proprietary land patents. These claimants, including members of both houses of the legislature, demanded first choice of new lands. The land speculation schemes of members of both houses appeared to undercut the original goal of the small freeholders. By 1737, many thousands of township acres had become the holdings of the governor, councilors, and members of the lower house.[20]

What was the role of legislative committees in this land program? Committeemen occupied themselves in drafting laws to implement British instructions regarding land sales for the benefit of the people of South Carolina and, primarily, of themselves. Subject to Commons House approval, committees also took action against critics of the land program. Committees investigating the operation of the surveyor general's office reported that St. John himself was guilty of mismanagement and profiteering. Other special committees reported that St. John was guilty of a breach of the privilege of the Commons for slandering the commoners in a public place. As a result of these reports, St. John and his assistants were arrested by the messenger of the lower house and were imprisoned.[21] When the St. John case came to the attention of Chief Justice Wright, he issued several writs of *habeas corpus* to free the imprisoned surveyors and their sympathizers, some of whom had also been arrested. The Commons House committee dealing with executive salaries retaliated by refusing to approve Wright's salary for several years.[22]

In 1733 other aggressive measures were taken by legislative committees as a result of the St. John case. Commons committees actually prevented

[19] Ibid., pp. 875–1160 passim.

[20] Hewatt, "Account of South Carolina," pp. 277–79, 311; McCrady, *Royal Government,* pp. 149–63; and Sherman, *Robert Johnson,* pp. 143–82 passim.

[21] *JCHA* (Jenkins), reel 4 (16 November–20 December 1732), pp. 811, 813; (9 January–17 March 1733), pp. 892–93, 895–96, 902–3, 915–16, 920–23, 928–29, 932, 939–40, 942, 946–47, 957–58, 962–63, 981, 988; (13 April–9 June 1733), pp. 990–91, 1000–1002, 1007, 1017, 1021–25, 1040, 1075.

[22] Ibid. (3 April–9 June 1733), pp. 1000–1003, 1012–13, 1060, 1068, 1070, 1079, 1082, 1085–86.

attorneys of the imprisoned surveyor from freeing their clients from custody. Indeed, many of the lawyers themselves were jailed for so-called breaches of the privilege of the Commons House.[23] It was several months before all the lawyers and surveyors were released from prison. Committees were even involved in the release of prisoners. Before a prisoner could be released, he had to petition a special Commons committee. The petitioner promised to pay a fine to cover the costs of his imprisonment and begged forgiveness for his action. If the committee approved his petition, the prisoner had to pay another fine to the Commons House messenger and then appear before the bar of the Commons House. At this time the Speaker required that the offender kneel before all the Commons members and beg forgiveness. The Speaker then delivered an official reprimand before the individual was released from custody.

Such high-handed behavior by the commoners caused resentment in colonists who did not agree with the land policy of the lower house. Some of the dissidents managed to win elections to the Commons in 1732, 1733, and 1734. These protest candidates, many of whom were frontiersmen sympathetic to Surveyor General St. John, were in some cases denied their Commons seats by the members of the committee on privileges and elections who, it will be recalled, had the power to judge all elections. The actions of this committee and the others involved in the land scandal were obviously questionable, but such a boldfaced show of committee power undoubtedly made the colonists reluctant to oppose the will of the Commons in the future.[24]

Aside from this scandal, Governor Johnson's administration was marked by unusually harmonious relationships between legislative and executive branches of government. Committees functioned much as they had under Governor Nicholson. Indeed, the only political problem of any consequence dealt with the right of the commoners to select their own clerk.

The contest with Governor Johnson over selection of the clerk was more than just a matter of political patronage. The clerk was the most important employee of the lower house. He maintained the assembly's records, kept the Commons *Journals,* helped draft bills and committee reports, and coordinated legislative activity between the Commons sessions. Moreover, the

[23] Ibid. (9 January–17 March 1733), pp. 940, 949; (13 April–9 June 1733), pp. 992–93, 996, 998–99, 1008, 1011, 1013, 1030.

[24] *JCHA* (Salley), 8 November 1734–7 June 1735, p. 33. See Sherman, *Robert Johnson,* pp. 143–82, and M. Eugene Sirmans, *Colonial South Carolina, A Political History, 1663–1763,* pp. 164–82, for different interpretations.

clerk's work was vitally important to the operation of legislative committees because either the clerk or one of his assistants often acted as secretary to various committees. The commoners recognized the significance of this post and fought hard to maintain the right to select their own candidate for the position. However, after several months of controversy with the governor, the assemblymen settled for a compromise solution that lasted until the revolutionary war. The compromise provided that the legislature could suggest the name of the clerk and the governor had the right to accept or reject the commoners' candidate.[25]

Another difficulty of the mid-1730s which concerned legislative committees was the unclear boundary line between North Carolina and South Carolina. The line between the provinces had never been surveyed and both colonies claimed the area south of the Cape Fear River. In the 1730s, this disputed frontier area became a haven for criminals and tax-dodging planters. In an attempt to solve these problems, Governor Johnson appealed to the Board of Trade for action. The governor suggested a boundary line to be run thirty miles south of the Cape Fear River and parallel to it. So persuasive was Johnson's appeal that the Board approved South Carolina's land claims. Johnson and the governor of North Carolina, Gabriel Johnston, were ordered to form a joint commission to survey the boundary line.[26]

The governor referred the selection of the boundary commissioners to both houses of South Carolina's General Assembly. The Upper House promptly recommended men for the job. The commoners referred the matter to a legislative committee for action. Because of their concern over the land scandal, weeks passed before the committeemen finally suggested men for the boundary commission. They selected fellow members of the lower house, even though they lacked surveying experience. When the names of these assemblymen were sent to the Upper House, the councilors refused to approve them. Months passed before a conference committee worked out a compromise.

The North Carolina governor took advantage of this delay to present his colony's case to the Board of Trade. The members of the Board reversed their earlier decision, favorable to South Carolina, and awarded thousands of acres

---

[25] *JCHA* (Jenkins), reel 4 (9–23 January 1731), pp. 610–32; (7 November–16 December 1732), p. 851; and *JCHA*, PRO CO 5/432, 18 February 1731, pp. 4–8, 10–11, cited in Greene, *Quest for Power*, pp. 209–10.

[26] Marvin Lucas Skaggs, *North Carolina's Boundary Disputes Involving Her Southern Line*, pp. 26–46. Also see Alexander S. Salley, "The Boundary Line between North Carolina and South Carolina," *South Carolina Historical Bulletin*, no. 10, South Carolina Historical Commission, Columbia, 1930, pp. 1–23.

to North Carolina. In this instance, the delay caused by dilatory Commons committee tactics undid the work of Governor Johnson and was damaging to the welfare of the colony.[27]

During the administrations of Governors Johnson, Middleton, and Broughton (1725–1737), Commons committees gradually grew in size, as did the total membership of the house. This growth improved the bargaining position of the commoners when they met their counterparts in the Council. In joint or conference committees, assemblymen could often outtalk or outvote the councilors. Because Commons members controlled the clerk of the lower house, assembly committee reports were recorded in such a way that members of the Upper House, members of the Board of Trade, and even the governor did not know the full activities of committee members. Accounts of victories won in skirmishes with the Upper House were carefully preserved in the Commons *Journals* for use in future battles with the Council.[28] Probably the lower house would have accomplished even more in these years had there not been such a rapid turnover of Speakers due to illness and personal "hardship." Speakers throughout the royal period received no salary for the many hours they worked both in and out of the legislative sessions.

The pattern of legislative activity of the early 1730s continued after Governor Johnson's death in 1735, when the office devolved on Johnson's brother-in-law, Lieutenant Governor Thomas Broughton. Broughton was experienced and likeable, and had been a councilor. He was best known for his leadership in Indian campaigns and in the revolution of 1719.[29] His administration enjoyed the prosperity initiated under Johnson. Broughton did not oppose the activities of the lower house. Indeed, he had more pressing interests in questionable land dealings, and by the time of his death in 1737 he had helped himself to thousands of acres of public lands. Broughton was not alone in this practice because members of both houses, who served without pay, were also compensating themselves with profitable lands. Yet during Broughton's administration, the Commons House also quickened the growth toward greater colonial self-government.[30]

During the administrations of all the governors between 1725 and 1737,

[27] *JCHA* (Jenkins), reel 4 (3 April–4 June 1733), pp. 1087, 1092, 1098.

[28] Precedents recorded in past journals were researched by special ad hoc committees of the lower house to improve the bargaining position of the Commons House with the Upper House. Greene, *Quest for Power*, pp. 9–10, 14–16.

[29] Hewatt, "Account of South Carolina," pp. 310–11.

[30] *JCHA* (Easterby), 1:9–11, 249–52, 254–55, 269–71, 276, 278–83, 384, 744, and passim; Sirmans, *Colonial South Carolina*, pp. 182–91.

certain committees had a particularly important part in the legislative process. In these years South Carolinians developed something akin to modern "steering committees" in their committees "on what bills are needed" and "on acts expired or near expiring."[31] Most bills initiated by Commons legislators in this period were suggested by these two committees, although other bills were suggested by the governor, by private citizens, or by local governmental agencies. Other committees became significant in the legislative process, specifically, extrasessionary or recess committees, such as the committee on Indian affairs, the committee on correspondence, and the committees "on what bills are needed next session." These recess committees acted as the legislature's spokesmen between sessions and helped promote greater home rule by the lower house.[32]

In the 1730s, legislators had opportunities for a great deal of contact with the people of the province. The ratio of thirty-six assemblymen to the white population of 30,000 made personal contact with constituents very likely.[33] The white citizens of South Carolina looked upon the representatives as their voice in colonial government. To encourage contact with South Carolinians, legislative bodies, such as the committee on petitions and accounts, publicly advertised some of their meetings. Announcements of these meetings appeared in the *South Carolina Gazette* and on bulletin boards in public buildings and Anglican churches. Citizens who had performed special services, had sustained property losses, or wanted to suggest improvements for the colony often sent memorials to the Commons. Their cases would be considered by either a special committee or the committee on petitions and accounts.[34] After study, the committee would recommend an amount of money to be presented to the individual or approval of a special project, subject to the Commons' approval. The committee's suggestions were usually accepted by the entire house.[35] Important committees were given

---

[31] Both committees were ad hoc bodies. The committee "on what bills are needed" usually met between sessions or during the first few days of a session. The committee "on laws expired or near expiring" was also usually appointed in the opening days of a new session.

[32] According to the South Carolina Election Act of 1721, the Commons House had to meet twice a year. During most years the assembly met at least four times. JCHA (Arch.), 7 (1726): 554.

[33] David Duncan Wallace, *South Carolina: A Short History, 1520–1948*, p. 709.

[34] *JCHA* (Salley), 15 November 1726–14 March 1726/27, p. 12. Also see Hennig Cohen, ed., *The South Carolina Gazette, 1732–1775*, pp. 9–10, 13–14, for examples of advertising.

[35] An understanding of the work of the committee on petitions and accounts can be drawn from *JCHA* (Salley), 15 November 1726–14 March 1726/27. Of the

power to subpoena persons, papers, and records pertinent to their investigations.[36]

One of the important committees in this period was the joint committee on correspondence. It will be recalled that this body was originally formed during proprietary days and operated briefly as a "commission," a quasi-executive committee, during the 1719 revolution. In the 1720s its members were evenly distributed between the two chambers.[37] However, by 1737, the commoners had gained a clear numerical supremacy.[38] With the exception of a brief period in 1724, the committee was responsible for correspondence with the colonial agent in England.[39] After 1731, the committee regularly met both in and out of legislative sessions.[40] The colonial agent, often a prominent London-based South Carolinian with influential governmental connections, was kept informed of governmental matters in South Carolina. The committee made suggestions to the agent concerning provincial laws he should support in England and those British policies he should oppose. In return, the agent provided information which the committee on correspondence passed on to the governor and the Upper House and Commons House.[41]

The committee on correspondence met throughout the year and actually accomplished the work of many special committees. Other special Commons committees met periodically throughout the period from 1725 to 1737 and their endeavors were important to the colony's development. Legislators on a Commons committee were responsible for bringing the first provincial printer and his newspaper to the colony in 1732.[42] In Robert Johnson's administration, the first comprehensive compilation of printed laws appeared as a result of the combined efforts of the former chief justice, Dr. Nicholas Trott, and several lower house special committees.[43]

174 pages of the journal, 34 pages alone are concerned with the committee on petitions and accounts. Seven other ad hoc committees dealt with other petitions.

[36] *JCHA* (Jenkins), reel 4 (12 February–3 June 1731), p. 619, is one of many examples in the records.

[37] *JCHA* (Jenkins), reel 2 (6–20 September 1721), n.p.; (25 January–10 March 1722), p. 23.

[38] *JCHA* (Easterby), 1:25, 40.

[39] Nicholson to Board of Trade, 18 June 1724, PRO CO 5/406.

[40] See the Charles Garth Letterbook, South Carolina Archives Department; parts of the Garth correspondence are published in *The South Carolina Historical and Genealogical Magazine* 28–31, 33 (1927–1933).

[41] Ella Lonn, *The Colonial Agents of the Southern Colonies*, pp. 21–47.

[42] *JCHA* (Jenkins), reel 4 (12 February–3 June 1731), p. 664; (18 January –20 March 1731/32), pp. 833–34, 837, 840, 842; and Cohen, *South Carolina Gazette*, pp. 3–4.

[43] *JCHA* (Easterby), 1:330.

Citizens living in Charles Town were well aware of the work of special ad hoc committees. Indeed, Commons special committees and commissioners appointed by the legislature conducted the government of that unincorporated town. All laws dealing with Charles Town were drafted by special committees of the two houses of the legislature.[44] The committees' work was implemented by commissioners, constables, and the night watch.

A closer look at the duties of committees during this period shows that most special committees of both houses met and normally completed their business in a few days. During most sessions, committees of the two houses compromised their differences in a joint conference committee and passed new laws. But special Commons committees could delay legislation for a matter of months or even years by obstructionistic or dilatory tactics. An example was the Swiss immigration plan proposed by Colonel John Peter Pury of Charles Town. Colonel Pury requested permission from the assembly to bring in Swiss immigrants to settle a frontier township. It took Pury several months of committee hearings to obtain legislative approval and financial support for his plan. When the immigrants arrived, the commoners were so deeply involved in other matters that the legislative committees assigned to assist the Swiss did not fulfill their commitments. This neglect caused many of the settlers to become dissatisfied and leave the province.[45]

A man who was particularly active on many of the most important special and standing committees of this era was Charles Pinckney. Pinckney was the father of Charles Cotesworth Pinckney, an assembly leader of the late 1760s and 1770s and the Federalist candidate for president of the United States in 1804. Charles Pinckney was the son of a West Indian privateer who turned to merchandizing when he migrated to Charles Town. His father amassed a considerable fortune and sent Charles to England for his higher education. The future Speaker returned from London as a British-trained attorney. This legal background practically insured him a successful practice among the South Carolina planters. Pinckney began his long career as a member of legislative committees in 1731 when he was elected to the Commons House from Christ Church parish. That same year he was appointed provincial attorney general.[46]

[44] Carl Bridenbaugh, *Cities in the Wilderness*, pp. 7–8, 14–15, 66, 144–45, 160–61, 193, 212, 218–19, 304, 318–19, 327–28, 351–52, 371–72, 377–78. Bridenbaugh is highly critical of the legislature's performance in ruling Charles Town.

[45] Meriwether, *Expansion of South Carolina*, pp. 33–41.

[46] Kaminer, "Dictionary of South Carolina Biography," p. 64; *JCHA* (Jenkins), reel 4 (12 February–3 June 1731), p. 613; (5 November–31 May 1734), p. 1;

Charles Pinckney's success as a committee chairman and legislative leader can be attributed to his superior political ability and interest in governmental matters. The young lawyer's career was advanced when he inherited a considerable fortune which he further increased by his own effort. Pinckney was a brave militia soldier and was rapidly promoted to the rank of colonel. Most important of all, he had caught the eye of the Council leader, Colonel William Bull I. Bull, a wealthy planter and later lieutenant governor from 1737 to 1743, supported Pinckney's political career.[47] Bull sponsored Pinckney's membership in the "best" social organizations in Charles Town. The contacts the attorney made through the Masons, Ubiquarians, and St. Cecilia Society all helped him rise rapidly in political circles.[48] He was thus an exception to the Commons tradition of attaining legislative seniority before receiving appointments to important committees.

In the 1730s, the routine of Charles Pinckney and his colleagues on committees of the Commons House ran about as follows. The working day began at nine in the morning when the bell of St. Philip's Anglican church rang a special call for the opening of the Commons House. Pinckney attended Commons meetings regularly, and his rare absences to attend to private business were always previously cleared with the Speaker. (Absentees were liable for fines of twenty to forty shillings a day as well as the fees of the messenger to call them to attend sessions.) If it was not a special occasion or the weekly church session, Pinckney's morning would open when the clerk of the Commons read the previous day's minutes or special communications. Debates on bills, committee reports, and special committee assignments by the Speaker followed until about "eleven of the clock." At that time the Speaker "ordered committees out" to attend to their business.

Because of Pinckney's legal expertise, he was often assigned as a "committee of one" to draft private or exceptionally difficult bills.[49] For this work he was paid a special fee if his petition for remuneration was approved by the committee on petitions and accounts.

---

also see Mabel L. Webber, "The Thomas Pinckney Family of South Carolina," *South Carolina Historical and Genealogical Magazine* 39 (1938): 15–35, 174–75.

[47] Sirmans, "South Carolina Council," pp. 378–79.

[48] St. Cecilia Society Founders, South Carolina Historical Society; Bridenbaugh, *Cities in the Wilderness*, pp. 417–18, 440–41; *SCG*, 1733–1737 passim; also see Harriet Horry Ravenal, *Eliza Pinckney;* and Marvin Ralph Zahniser, "The Public Career of Charles Cotesworth Pinckney" (Ph.D. dissertation, University of California, Santa Barbara, 1963).

[49] *JCHA* (Salley) (8 November 1734–7 June 1735), pp. 124, 151–52, 160, 178.

Charles Pinckney's legislative ability, judging from the Commons *Journals,* was notable. Before the end of his first year in the assembly, he no longer performed routine committee tasks, such as checking Commons bills against engrossed final copies to be signed by the governor, auditing the powder receiver's accounts, and carrying messages to the governor or Council. Instead, Pinckney was appointed to such important standing committees as correspondence and petitions and accounts. As a member of important special committees, he was sometimes assigned to write messages to the governor. Often more than one committee of which he was a member met at the same time. From extant Commons records it is apparent that he sometimes even skipped meetings of committees of which he was chairman in order to attend others that seemed more important to him.

At noon Pinckney and other committee members usually took a two-hour luncheon recess. The legislators reconvened at two, when they were again summoned by the tolling of bells in St. Philip's soaring steeple. Afternoon meetings were often entirely devoted to committee affairs. Pinckney actively participated in these sessions, judging from the number of reports he presented to the Commons House. Often he served on conference committees and joint committees with members of the Upper House. In the 1730s, these meetings were held in private quarters or taverns rather than in either the Upper House or lower house chambers.[50] Committee meetings usually ended around four or five o'clock in the afternoon. One reason for this closing time was that the Charles Town social season was at its peak when the assemblymen were in town. The members of both houses and their wives often maintained an active social schedule in the evening. Charles Pinckney was sometimes an exception; he was recorded as serving on at least one committee that was busy at night.

This crowded schedule was repeated six days a week during an average legislative session, which lasted anywhere from two weeks to three months. Every year there was a minimum of two such sessions. For this hectic activity, members received no pay. Yet they enjoyed the personal and intangible benefits of personal service and on some occasions very real profits in land dealings. Indeed, certain assemblymen repeatedly ran for office.

In Pinckney's first term he was paid the high honor of being publicly commended for a committee report.[51] In 1736, after only one full term, he was elected Speaker by the required majority of Commons members. As

[50] *JCHA* (Easterby), 1:185–86.
[51] Ibid., p. 152.

Speaker, it will be recalled, he was responsible for all committee assignments. In his service as Commons Speaker, Pinckney strengthened the position of the lower house by improving the operation of its committees. For instance, he refused to allow Commons committees to meet with Council committees on monetary subjects, thereby increasing the power of lower house monetary committees. During his tenure, there was a reduction in the number of recommittals for slipshod committee work. He carefully selected committee members and as a result decreased the number of times he had to hurriedly add more members when committees could not meet their deadlines.[52] Pinckney served as Speaker until he was appointed a councilor in 1741.

Typical of the aristocratic class of his day, Charles Pinckney continued his public service until his death in 1758. Judging from his successful later career as a councilor, chief justice of the colony, and then as a colonial agent, he had learned valuable lessons in Commons committee meetings.[53]

Pinckney's career serves to illustrate the importance of service on legislative committees. Indeed, Pinckney's work on legislative committees was partly responsible for his rapid rise in South Carolina politics. As Speaker, Pinckney increased the effectiveness of the committee system, indicating his recognition of its importance to South Carolina government. The committees upon which Pinckney and his colleagues served provided a form of political apprenticeship in which assemblymen grew in political acumen.

[52] Ibid., pp. 4, 622–24, 689, 695–704, 717–24, 727, 758, 762; Greene, *Quest for Power,* pp. 55–60; and Sirmans, *Colonial South Carolina,* pp. 202–7.

[53] Kaminer, "Dictionary of South Carolina Biography," pp. 65–66; and McCrady, *Royal Government,* pp. 173–76, 181, 246, 279–81, 465, 470, 473–75, 495, 533, 795.

CHAPTER V

The Legislative Committee System in Peace and Frontier Conflict, 1737–1748

From 1737 to 1748, South Carolina was embroiled in intercolonial war. Fortunately for the colony's welfare in this troubled period, South Carolinians were led by two governors of genuine ability, William Bull I (1737–1744) and James Glen (1744–1756).[1] In these years, the work of the legislative committees stimulated growth toward increased self-government despite intercolonial strife.

South Carolina was actively involved in the conflict with Spain during the War of Jenkins' Ear (1739–1744).[2] When this struggle expanded into the third of the major intercolonial wars, King George's War (1744–1748), Carolinians found themselves part of an imperial struggle against Spaniards, French, and Indians. Legislative committees had to shoulder many of the costs, plans, and responsibilities of South Carolina's part in both wars.[3]

Conflict in the colonial South imposed many responsibilities upon the South Carolina legislature and its committee system. Committees either planned or approved the military strategy, and bore the burden of recommending financial measures to pay for wartime expenses.[4] Committee members even drafted the legislation to activate the militia when Carolinians fought in Spanish Florida or on the frontier.

A host of other responsibilities devolved upon committees during this period, such as attempting to solve an economic depression caused by a decreased international rice trade, the result of interference with shipping by the Spaniards and French.[5] Committees recommended the introduction of new crops, such as hemp, wheat, silk, and indigo to diversify the agriculture of the colony. Moreover, military conflict caused committees to consider a host of petitions and memorials from persons making claims against the provincial government. At least once a year, Carolinians involved in the war effort presented vouchers of their expenses (use of slaves, providing food or supplies, repair of military equipment, etc.). These requests had to be investigated by committee members prior to the final committee report, which made a recommendation for payment.[6]

Perhaps the most important of all the legislative committees of this era were the joint committees on Indian relations. These committees played an important part in formulating Indian policy, as has been previously mentioned. Military success in the sparsely settled Southern colonies, such as South Carolina, often depended upon persuading Indian allies to attack one's enemy or upon neutralizing a potential Indian foe by skillful diplomacy.[7] To help accomplish this goal, committees composed governors' and agents' speeches to be delivered at Indian conferences. Committees even recommended men for the post of Indian agent.[8] In Governor James Glen's

[1] *JCHA* (Easterby), 4: x; Gugielma Melton Kaminer, "A Dictionary of South Carolina Biography during the Royal Period, 1719–1776" (Master's thesis, University of South Carolina, 1926), pp. 11–12; and Helen Kohn Hennig, *Great South Carolinians, from Colonial Days to the Confederate War*, pp. 33–37. Also see Mary F. Carter, "Governor James Glen" (Ph.D. dissertation, University of California, Los Angeles, 1951); and M. Eugene Sirmans, Jr., "Masters of Ashley Hall" (Ph.D. dissertation, Princeton University, 1959).

[2] This conflict was named for Robert Jenkins, an English master mariner whose ship was captured by the Spaniards in 1731. In the engagement Jenkins's ear was cut off. Seven years later the incident was brought to the attention of the House of Commons and led to war in 1739.

[3] See Alexander Hewatt, "Historical Account of the Rise and Progress of the Colonies of South Carolina and Georgia," *Historical Collections of South Carolina,* ed. Bartholomew Rivers Carroll, 1:311–14, 321, 326–40; Howard H. Peckham, *The Colonial Wars, 1689–1762,* pp. 88–95; and Lt. Governor William Bull I to Board of Trade, 20 April 1738, 5 October 1739, 3 and 28 July 1740, and 27 May 1741, PRO CO 5/406.

[4] *JCHA* (Easterby), 2:227–28, 235, 237–38, 240–47, 250–52, 257, 302–6, 397, 402, and many others.

[5] Henry Laurens, "The Correspondence of Henry Laurens," *South Carolina Historical and Genealogical Magazine* 29 (1928): 290.

[6] *JCHA* (Easterby), 2:164–66, 210–11, 352–53, 391, 468, 503–4; 3:43–44, 114–15, 204, 262, 264–65, 277, 321–22; 4:38–39, 515; many more examples can be found.

[7] See Chapman James Milling, *Red Carolinians,* passim; John Richard Alden, *John Stuart and the Southern Colonial Frontier,* pp. 3, 8, 14–15, 17–18, 25–29, 34, 44, 55–56, 66–67, 76, 83, 113–14, 123, 130–32; and Peckham, *Colonial Wars,* p. 20. See also Wilbur R. Jacobs, *Diplomacy and Indian Gifts,* pp. 5, 11–45.

[8] *JCHA* (Easterby), 2:313, 315, 326, 528–29, 547; Carter, "James Glen," p. 159; and South Carolina Public Records, 22:287–88, cited in Robert Lee Meriwether, *The Expansion of South Carolina, 1729–1765,* p. 194.

administration, legislative committees went so far as to select individual gifts and go in the field to observe his meetings with Indian leaders and sometimes attended meetings with Indians when they visited Charles Town.[9] Committees drafted detailed regulations for Indian traders who distributed goods among the natives. The lower cost of British trade goods was a vital factor in explaining Indian loyalty during intercolonial wars.[10]

The South Carolina–Georgia campaign against the Spaniards in Florida at this time also involved committees. The man responsible for military operations in the two colonies was Major General James Oglethorpe, the governor of Georgia. In 1739 Oglethorpe was ordered to attack and destroy the center of Spanish power, the fortress capital of St. Augustine.[11] This strategy in itself was not new; Carolina militia had twice before crippled the Florida pueblo and its fort, San Marcos. But they had not been able to destroy it.[12] General Oglethorpe required a sizeable force of colonists and Indians supported by British sea power to overwhelm the enemy. He also needed the element of surprise.

For his project to succeed, the Georgia governor knew he had to have the support of the South Carolina Commons House. Carolinians had to provide both manpower and money to finance the expedition. The need for funds meant that the entire operation had to be approved by the committees of the Commons House, because by 1739 the Commons claimed the authority to originate all bills dealing with governmental finance. When the St. Augustine expedition proposal was referred to the Commons House by Lieutenant Governor William Bull I, the commoners, as one might expect, referred it to a committee for consideration. The committee at this time apparently overlooked its animosity toward the upper chamber and readily conferred with the Council on the subject.[13]

The subject of the St. Augustine expedition continued to reappear frequently until 1741, when a legislative committee rendered a critical final report about the failure of the expedition to accomplish its mission.[14]

An examination of committee reports shows the detailed supervision by

[9] *SCG*, 6 May 1745; *JCHA* (Easterby), 3:240–41; and Meriwether, *Expansion of South Carolina*, pp. 193–94.
[10] Meriwether, *Expansion of South Carolina*, pp. 185–91.
[11] Hewatt, "Account of South Carolina," p. 334.
[12] *JCHA* (Easterby), 3:78–247; and Peckham, *Colonial Wars*, pp. 89–90.
[13] *JCHA* (Easterby), 2:161.
[14] "Joint Committee of the South Carolina General Assembly on St. Augustine Affair Report," *Historical Collections of South Carolina*, ed. Bartholomew Rivers Carroll, 2:347–61; and *JCHA* (Easterby), 3:78–247 (the entire report).

commoners in this military matter. On November 19, 1739, the first of some fourteen different legislative committees connected with the St. Augustine expedition met. The Speaker appointed a special committee on that date after Lt. Governor William Bull informed the lower house that royal officials had alerted him that a British attack on St. Augustine was likely. The Commons special committee of November 19 was joined by a similar Upper House committee to become the first of many joint committees on the St. Augustine expedition. The first joint committee stated that South Carolina should support General Oglethorpe's expedition with public funds. This committee report was debated by the entire Commons House without any real action. Thirty-nine days later, on December 18, another message from the governor on the same subject was debated.[15] The result of the second committee's report on December 18 was that the Commons House voted to repair and supply gunpowder to Ft. Frederick on the Altamaha River at the Georgia border.[16]

The next day Speaker Charles Pinckney asked the Upper House to confer with the lower house to consider ways of improving General Oglethorpe's plan for attacking St. Augustine. Three days later, the chairman of this second joint committee, Chief Justice Benjamin Whitaker, reported that the committee needed more time to come to a conclusion.[17] The next morning, a Commons member of that committee, Andrew Rutledge, submitted a draft of the committee's report to the entire lower house. The report stated that it would be advantageous to destroy the fort at St. Augustine. The committee-men further recommended to Lieutenant Governor Bull that the Commons House should thoroughly examine General Oglethorpe's plan for the military expedition before taking any further action. This report was approved in an amended form by both houses of the General Assembly. A conference committee then ironed out differences between the upper and lower chambers and sent the final report to the governor.[18] Yet the implicit reservations in the report reflected the commoners' reluctance to finance a campaign in Florida until they had a more complete idea of the entire operation.

Nearly a month later, on February 10, 1740, Bull forwarded to the Commons House a letter from General Oglethorpe describing his logistical and personnel requirements for the expedition.[19] When Oglethorpe's letter was read to the Commons, Speaker Charles Pinckney immediately appointed

---

[15] *JCHA* (Easterby), 2:86–88, 91.   [16] Ibid., pp. 88–89, 95.
[17] Ibid., p. 100.   [18] Ibid., pp. 100, 102, 106, 116.
[19] Ibid., pp. 159–61; and M. Eugene Sirmans, *Colonial South Carolina*, pp. 210–21.

a third committee on St. Augustine. Its membership included the original committeemen and eight new assemblymen. Pinckney then requested that a committee from the Upper House join this Commons committee to consider the subject of Oglethorpe's letter. The councilors quickly agreed.[20]

This joint committee must have burned the midnight oil, for on February 16 its members reported an estimate of the cost of the entire expedition as £100,000, South Carolina currency. The report was sent to both houses of the General Assembly. The Council, after considering it, sent a message to the lower house asking if there were sufficient funds in the treasury to finance Oglethorpe's project. Speaker Pinckney reacted in his usual manner to requests for large expenditures. He postponed a reply to the Council until more information could be gathered, since the cost of the expedition would exhaust the provincial treasury and result in higher taxes.[21] This action illustrates a reluctance of the Commons House to expend public funds and to increase taxes. Moreover, as we will see, commoners used their position of power in shaping the cost estimates of the St. Augustine expedition to gain tactical advantage in other conference committees which were concurrently negotiating with the Council such issues as money bills.

The threat of war was stimulating a great deal of other committee work. The committee on the armory, which normally met only once or twice a year, became exceptionally active after the start of the War of Jenkins' Ear. The members of the armory committee had to check the weapons in the public armories and they arranged for the repair of arms which were not operational. Special committees were appointed to examine South Carolina's inadequate forts and magazines. Other committees investigated and proposed improvements in the militia and the Charles Town watch.[22] Several committees dealing with Indian matters were busy as well. For example, Andrew Rutledge's joint committee on securing Indian support for the colony reported the need for Indian agents to serve in native villages.[23]

Lieutenant Governor Bull sent an important written message to the Commons House on February 13, 1740, which stimulated more committee activity. Bull commented on the importance of Indian trade in keeping pro-British natives steadfast in South Carolina's interest. In the same message Bull expressed concern about procurement of ordnance for the Florida campaign.[24] Bull's letter closed with an estimate of the costs of the St. Augustine expedition which he had obtained from General Oglethorpe. This

---

[20] *JCHA* (Easterby), 2:162.   [21] Ibid., p. 164.
[22] Ibid., pp. 186–87.   [23] Ibid., pp. 164–65.
[24] Ibid., pp. 172–73. Bull also discussed a threat of a slave revolt.

message was referred to the joint committee considering the expedition. The committee chairman, Andrew Rutledge, reported on February 14 that Oglethorpe's estimate of costs for South Carolina's part of the expedition, £209,492 in South Carolina currency, was unrealistically high. Instead, the legislators, who knew South Carolina was paying for the greater share of the expedition, stated that they were willing to spend only £120,000 (South Carolina currency) of the public funds.[25]

On February 20, the Commons members of the committee, acting this time as a lower house committee of "ways and means for the St. Augustine expedition," presented its plan for raising the £120,000. This was a great deal of money for the colony to raise at this time because of the reduced international market for its rice.[26] So the commoners considered it impossible to appropriate the entire amount in tax monies in one year. Instead, the Commons committee suggested that only £40,000 be paid immediately and that the remainder be financed through issuing an eighteenth-century equivalent of modern war bond certificates, provincial "certificates of debt." It will be recalled that these certificates were considered unofficially as a form of tender in South Carolina.[27]

Ostensibly this suggestion was a reasonable course of action to support a patriotic cause. It appears, however, that the proposal was an attempt by the lower house to increase the volume of provincial currency. Even though the Board of Trade and Council opposed this inflationary program, the commoners insisted upon its passage. After a brief dispute with the Upper House in 1740, the Commons passed the bill to issue the paper debt certificates.[28]

By the afternoon of February 20 the report of the third Commons committee on St. Augustine was ready for further consideration by other legislative committees. A two-man message committee carried the completed draft of the report, as well as a request for a fourth joint committee, to the Council for its consideration. Then the councilors formed their own committee on ways and means, who immediately agreed to meet their companion committee in the lower house.[29]

By the next day, the fourth joint committee on St. Augustine, acting as a committee on ways and means, had completed its conference and had prepared a detailed report on how the money was to be allocated. This three-page document contained salaries of officers and enlisted men, costs of

[25] Ibid., p. 179.   [26] Meriwether, *Expansion of South Carolina*, p. 188.
[27] *JCHA* (Easterby), 2:190.
[28] Jack Philip Greene, *The Quest for Power*, pp. 109–10.
[29] *JCHA* (Easterby), 2:194, 198.

contracted slave labor, gifts to Indians and supplies for one thousand natives, and munitions. The report also included an estimate of the costs of military supplies, medical equipment, provisions for the colonial troops, and transportation from Charles Town to St. Augustine.[30] The assembly was then adjourned for two weeks and this fourth joint committee report was sent to Lieutenant Governor Bull. Bull, in turn, forwarded the report to General Oglethorpe in Georgia.

Oglethorpe no doubt was disappointed when he read the joint committee report. Not only had nearly £100,000 been cut from his original request, but four months of valuable time had passed and the South Carolina legislature's deliberations were far from complete. Legislative committees still had to approve South Carolina military leaders, plan further strategy, and help negotiate agreements for military supplies. A further delay occurred, because it was nearly a month (April 6) before Bull forwarded General Oglethorpe's reply to the Commons. In this letter, Oglethorpe urged the Carolinians to act quickly. He further offered to ride from Augusta to Charles Town to consult personally with the third joint St. Augustine committee.[31]

While Oglethorpe awaited a reply from the assembly, Speaker Charles Pinckney wrote to Bull asking for a fourth joint committee to confer on a different subject. Pinckney wanted to discuss the matter of general Indian war which he believed threatened South Carolina.[32] Knowing the desire of General Oglethorpe and Governor Bull to initiate the St. Augustine expedition, Pinckney used this side issue of Indian war for his own advantage. His apparent objective at this time was to resolve certain problems in the Indian trade to which South Carolina assemblymen objected. For instance, the leaders of the Commons believed that Georgians were obstructing South Carolinians' route to the interior tribes along the Savannah River.[33] Moreover, assemblymen desired to limit some of the malpractices of Indian traders by bringing about a tighter regulation of Indian trade by governmental Indian agents.[34] These proposed regulations generally ran counter to the Council's interest, since several councilors were deeply involved in the profitable Indian trade, and favored the status quo of loose regulation.[35] Hence a conflict of interest divided the third St. Augustine committee.

[30] Ibid., pp. 195–97; Meriwether, *Expansion of South Carolina*, pp. 186–88. Also see Edmund Atkin, *Indians of the Southern Frontier*, pp. 9–10, 30; and Jacobs, *Diplomacy and Indian Gifts*, pp. 5, 11–28, 36–38, 42–60.
[31] *JCHA* (Easterby), 2:258.   [32] Ibid., pp. 258–59.
[33] Ibid., 1:72–157.   [34] Ibid., 2:200.
[35] Meriwether, *Expansion of South Carolina*, pp. 186–87, 202.

However, the councilors reluctantly approved Speaker Pinckney's request for a joint committee meeting. This meeting was held on the evening of April 6. The next day, the *Journal for the Commons House of Assembly* indicated that a heated argument had occurred between two committeemen during the previous night's conference. The participants were the Commons committee chairman, Andrew Rutledge, and Councilor Edmund Atkin, who maintained that he was insulted.[36] Although the exact nature of the altercation was not stated, it was serious enough to cause the Speaker to apologize to the Upper House the next day. The controversy between Atkin and Rutledge threatened to explode into a real breach between the two houses. The Council implied that Rutledge should be disciplined, and the President of the Council at first even refused to accept Pinckney's apology.[37]

This uproar wasted another day, but finally on April 8, 1740, Oglethorpe met with the joint committee, and an agreement was reached on the details of the expedition. The committee gave the general four months to accomplish his objective, allocating salaries for only that period of time.[38] In a rare display of speed, the report was approved the same day by both houses of the General Assembly.[39]

Even after the vote was taken, details of the campaign were still studied by several other special committees.[40] By April 15, one result of the planning was the selection of a commander for the South Carolina forces, Colonel Alexander Vander Dussen. Vander Dussen was a member of the Commons committee which had been so deeply involved in the military planning. His selection was representative of the interrelationship between legislative planning and the actual military leadersip of the St. Augustine campaign by key members of Commons committees. That same day a legislative committee presented its final draft of the bill to pay for the expedition. The commoners had inserted certain provisions in the bill which solified the primacy of the lower house in monetary matters. The assemblymen attempted to deny the right of the Upper House to amend this or future money bills.[41]

The actual history of the St. Augustine expedition is well known. The British and Indians under Oglethorpe reached Florida on May 20, 1740.[42]

---

[36] *JCHA* (Easterby), 2:263, 264; see Atkin, *Indians of the Southern Frontier*, pp. xvi–xx.
[37] *JCHA* (Easterby), 2:265.   [38] Ibid., pp. 273–75.
[39] Ibid., p. 275.   [40] Sirmans, *Colonial South Carolina*, pp. 211–12.
[41] *JCHA* (Easterby), 2:278–79, 288–90, 294–95, 302, 309–10.
[42] See Meriwether, *Expansion of South Carolina*, pp. 188–89, for a brief account of the expedition; Hewatt, "Account of South Carolina," pp. 326–29.

The Spaniards had learned of the attack and were prepared to resist. James Oglethorpe's leadership, at least according to contemporary South Carolina writers, was inadequate. He alienated his Indian auxiliaries and the South Carolina volunteers. The heat and humidity undermined the efficiency of the invaders. The British attacked the town and made several attempts to breach the Spaniards' Fort San Marcos. The pueblo of St. Augustine was burned, but the Spanish inhabitants were able to retreat to their fort.[43] There the Spaniards waited until dissensions among the colonists, sickness, and the threat of a Spanish relief expedition forced the seige to end. By August 1740, the Georgia—South Carolina expedition retreated northward and the campaign ended.

In Charles Town, a disappointed General Assembly learned of the progress of the expedition. The new Speaker of the Commons House, Dr. William Bull II, the son of the lieutenant governor, appointed a committee to consider the military correspondence from St. Augustine.[44] This committee then conferred with a similar body in the Upper House. Isaac Mazyck, a leader of the Commons from Charles Town, reported for this joint committee on July 19, 1740. The most important part of the committee's report was the statement that the St. Augustine expedition was a "lost cause" and that the Carolina troops should be returned to the province.[45] The committee stated that the danger to the weakened colony from its own slaves and from the French was greater than the Spanish threat. The committeemen remembered that a year before, in 1739, a bloody slave uprising had occurred in Stono in southern South Carolina, and there were rumors of other slave insurrections in the offing. The committee report closed with an appeal to the crown for funds to repay the South Carolinians for their losses and for the military expenditures of the Florida campaign.

Meanwhile other legislative committees were appointed as a result of the St. Augustine expedition. One of these committees was "to inquire into the Causes of the Disappointment of success in the Expedition against St. Augustine." A second committee was formed to petition George II for help. Speaker William Bull II selected some of the leading members in the assembly to serve on these committees. He also asked the Council to form a fifth joint committee to cooperate in the investigation of the failure of the St. Augustine campaign.

The fourteen members of the fifth joint committee were excused from other duties to work on this project.[46] Because they had to interview field

---

[43] Hewatt, "Account of South Carolina," pp. 326–27.
[44] *JCHA* (Easterby), 2:353.   [45] Ibid., p. 357.
[46] Ibid., pp. 364–67, 369, 381.

officers and peruse the written reports, the chairman of the joint committee had to ask for two extensions of time. The result of the committee's work was a report nearly 300 pages long.

The report opened with a history of the background of the 1740 campaign and the reasons for the assembly's support of the expedition. It included a discussion of earlier, more successful attacks on St. Augustine during the proprietary period. This part of the report closed with a discussion of the events in 1739 immediately preceding the expedition.

There followed a narrative of the St. Augustine expedition, nearly 150 pages in length. In this narration, the committeemen constructed a detailed yet somewhat biased account of the events in Florida. The authors relied primarily upon accounts written by participants, which they quoted extensively. These quotations were linked by narrative paragraphs which provided further explanation of the text of the letters.

In an interpretive summary, the committee criticized Oglethorpe for his treatment of the 1,000 Indian auxiliaries, his deployment of troops, and his failure to utilize the South Carolina volunteers effectively. The report concluded with 139 appendixes which included extracts from official military records, depositions from persons involved in the expedition, and copies of military correspondence.[47]

This report differed from other committee reports in its length and the thoroughness of research. It was printed by provincial printer Lewis Timothy. Copies were sent to the colonial agent in London to be used as justification for the South Carolinians' request for money from the crown. Colonial historians, such as Dr. Alexander Hewatt and more recent writers, have used the report as their primary source of information. Yet certain problems of interpretation arise from the report. The members of the committee who wrote the report overlooked the lack of surprise by the South Carolina troops and the poor timing of the campaign which was due partly to the slow pace of earlier legislative committees. The inadequacy of the military materials provided by the legislators to sustain a long seige was another result of committee activity.

Even though the legislative committee system during the St. Augustine expedition may be criticized, the colonists themselves had great faith in the use of assembly committees. South Carolinians believed that the advantages derived from careful study and discussion of bills and governmental expenditures were necessary for good government. They preferred the slow pace of legislation through several committees to the alternative of a faster, more autocratic government by royal officials. The use of committees in the years

[47] Ibid., 3:78–247.

1739 to 1742 thus exemplifies the importance of the South Carolina committee system in the government of the colony.[48]

The unsuccessful siege of St. Augustine did not mean the end of frontier war for South Carolina. The slow pace of Commons, Council, and joint committees concerned with military supplies, Indian affairs, and provincial defense, so evident in the St. Augustine expedition, continued until the end of King George's War in 1748. The committee activity of this period set an example which was followed during the French and Indian War (1756–1763) and later during the American Revolution.[49]

Between 1737 and 1748, the growth of the lower house's power to control taxes was of vital importance. Committees in this period were deeply involved in the struggle over taxes between the upper and lower houses. Under the leadership of Speaker Charles Pinckney and his successors, the Commons attempted to eliminate councilors from the five key joint committees that dealt with taxes and other monetary matters. The purge of Upper House members from all but one of these committees took years to accomplish. However, in the 1760s, when it was completed, the Council was virtually eliminated as a legislative force.[50]

To understand why commoners of the 1730s and the 1740s wanted to eliminate councilors from fiscal committees requires an understanding of the preliminary steps in the formation of tax bills. The first step in this process was an examination by the members of the committee on petitions and accounts, of claims against public funds for services and expenses of the previous year. During the debate over expenditures that followed, the Commons House would usually modify the committee's recommendations and then forward the amended report to a second committee. This second committee, the committee on the estimate, tabulated the sum of the claims and formulated an estimate of the taxes needed. Still another committee was concurrently auditing the treasurer's accounts to determine the amount of money left in the treasury, which was subtracted from the estimate. A fourth committee prepared a tax bill to raise the difference. A final committee was responsible for burning retired paper money, certificates of credit, and redeemed claim certificates after the creditors were paid by the provincial treasurer.[51]

---

[48] Ibid., p. 78 and fn.   [49] Ibid., 1:ix.

[50] See Chapters VI and VII below; also see *JCHA* (Jenkins), reel 17, unit 2, pp. 342, 360; John Drayton, *Memoirs of the American Revolution*, 1:66–70, 77, 152; William Roy Smith, *South Carolina as a Royal Province, 1719–1776*, p. 89; and see note 55, this chapter.

[51] *JCHA* (Easterby), 4:572.

From 1721 to 1736, all but the fourth of these committees were joint committees, so the councilors had a vital part in determining the final tax bill while it was being shaped in earlier committees. The commoners' first step in the exclusion of the Upper House from these committees came in 1737. The Speaker appointed the usual Commons financial committees and then intentionally "forgot" to invite the Upper House to participate. When the Council realized what was happening, it asked for a conference on the tax bill. The lower house replied that it was not "justified by the Usage of Parliament in appointing a committee of this House to confer with the Council on supplies [money] granted to His Majesty." Even though the Upper House protested, the lower house was adamant and the tax bill passed without members of the Upper House serving on the committee of the estimate. This action of 1737 was used by the Commons House as precedent for future exclusions of councilors from other committees.[52]

Although this early parliamentary battle had been won by the lower house, the war over control of taxes was far from ended. Clear evidence of this conflict was seen in 1739 when the Upper House requested a joint committee to review petitions and accounts according to the earlier procedure.[53] When the lower house refused, another hard struggle between the two houses occurred which resulted in failure to pass a tax bill during that session and a legislative deadlock. The Commons House in this and future conflicts fell back on its constitutional arguments of "rights and privileges" as Englishmen and the "sole [right of] modelling of all laws for imposing taxes."[54]

When the General Assembly reconvened after a short prorogation in May 1739, two factors further complicated the deadlock over taxes: the general anxiety felt by the entire colony over war and the increased determination of the Upper House to exert its influence upon the colony's government. Evidence of the councilors' attitude can be seen by their exclusion of the lieutenant governor, himself a councilor, from all legislative functions of that board when it was acting as an Upper House of the General Assembly.[55]

Through the spring of 1739 the controversy over tax committee member-

---

[52] Ibid., 1:245, 249–51.   [53] Ibid., pp. 622–24.

[54] Ibid., pp. 689, 695–704; and Greene, *Quest for Power*, pp. 53–61.

[55] M. Eugene Sirmans, "The South Carolina Royal Council, 1720–1763," *William and Mary Quarterly*, 3d ser., 38 (1961): 382, 384–85; Smith, *Royal Province*, pp. 312–21; and Governor James Glen to Board of Trade, 17 July 1750, PRO CO 5/406. These works describe the relationship between the governor and the Council.

ship continued. The Upper House's demand to be included was met by a greater determination by the lower house to prevent any councilors from sitting with them in committee meetings. Finally the Council accepted the fact that its members could not serve on the committee on petitions and accounts for that session, but declared it would not accept this decision as a precedent for future legislative sessions. The Council's declaration proved hollow, for Upper House members were permanently excluded from the committee from that time on.[56]

Added to this struggle over tax committee membership was another of equal magnitude which occurred almost simultaneously, namely, the right of the Council to amend money bills previously drafted by assembly committees and approved by the entire Commons House. The Commons wished to force the Council into a position in which the Upper House could accept or refuse money bills but not alter them.[57] The Council, of course, rejected this idea. The immediate result is illustrated by correspondence between the houses and references to heated debates in the journals of both houses. After several months of controversy, a conference committee established a "temporary" compromise that was to last nearly a decade.[58]

The compromise was that the Council could suggest amendments on money bills but these recommendations could be accepted or rejected at the discretion of the Commons. This agreement was followed until 1748, except during the St. Augustine expedition in 1740. In 1748, when both houses were extremely belligerent due to a controversy over control of the colonial agent, the Commons rejected ten of the Council's fourteen suggestions for amendments to a money bill. This rebuff was coupled with a committee resolution that in future the Commons would accept no more amendments.[59] This resolution was approved, and from 1749 to the end of the colonial period the commoners did refuse to accept amendments by the Council on monetary measures.[60] These developments indirectly gave the members of the Commons House power to control nearly every function of government through the management of money bills and tax measures.

[56] *JCHA* (Easterby), 1:706–7, 710–11, 713–14, 717–23; 2:41–42, 52, 57–58, 60–61, 135–36.

[57] This finally came about in the 1760s. Also see Smith, *Royal Province,* pp. 279–84, 289–329.

[58] *JCHA* (Easterby), 2:90–93, 97–98, 122, 131–43, 301–2.

[59] Ibid., 8:376–77, 390–91.

[60] Ibid., 2:331, 548–49; 3:453, 464; 5:168; 8:220; Sirmans, *Colonial South Carolina,* pp. 301–14.

CHAPTER VI

Committees and Legislative Supremacy in a Second Era of Frontier Conflict, 1749–1764

The government of South Carolina went through a process of gradual transformation in the period from 1749 to 1764. This was an era of intercolonial frontier war and peace and a host of internal political problems in South Carolina government.[1] A concurrent development was a gradual improvement in economic conditions which resulted in heightened prosperity for the planters and merchants, who increasingly cooperated in political affairs.[2] This period also was marked by the emergence of a new frontier area in the Appalachian valleys in western South Carolina. Indeed, as we have seen, by the middle of the eighteenth century an aristocratic planter-merchant oligarchy, which excluded the frontiersmen, emerged and firmly dominated the South Carolina legislature and its most important committees.[3]

This period in the colony's history has been called South Carolina's Golden Age. Yet an examination of the records of legislative committees indicates that such dilemmas of a frontier area as intercolonial war, Indian troubles, and political strife were continually recurring. The period was marked, for example, by an expansion of the prolonged power struggle between the Commons and the other branches of government, which, as we have seen, began in the mid-1720s. The numerous disputes of these years revolved around the relationship between the governor and the Commons House.[4] The governors (James Glen, 1743–1756; William Henry Lyttleton, 1756–1760; Thomas Boone, 1761–1764; and Lieutenant Governor William Bull II, 1760–1761 and 1764–1768) attempted to strengthen the executive authority at the expense of the Commons, but their approaches proved inadequate. Similarly the Upper House strove to resist encroachments upon its authority but failed.[5]

The Commons House committees, on the other hand, found excellent opportunities to expand their power and incidentally the authority of the entire legislature. Assembly committees, as will be seen, often made the executives pay the price of a loss of executive power before they would approve military appropriations for war.[6] Commons committees gained greater power over patronage, local administration, governmental finance, and the colonial agent. In its conflict with the Upper House, the assembly nearly destroyed the councilors' power to alter Commons House bills in conference committees.

At this time, the governors were well aware that by the use of quasi-executive standing committees, the commoners were usurping gubernatorial powers, but they could do little to stop the process. Governor James Glen indicated executive concern over these developments and complained that "The entire government was unhinged. . . ." Glen saw other instances of growing disrespect for the royal prerogative, such as the fact that in the Anglican churches, contrary to British tradition, Carolinians said no prayers for governors. Instead, South Carolina ministers prayed publicly for the Commons House members who, incidentally, controlled church finances through legislative committees.[7]

[1] James Glen, "A Description of South Carolina," in *Historical Collections of South Carolina,* ed. Bartholomew Rivers Carroll, 2:222–50; and William Watts Ball, *The State That Forgot: South Carolina's Surrender to Democracy,* p. 40.

[2] Jack Philip Greene, "The Role of the Lower Houses of Assembly in Eighteenth-Century Politics," *Journal of Southern History* 37 (1961): 460.

[3] David Ramsay, *Ramsay's History of South Carolina,* 2:252–55, 260–64, 266–67, 267–73; and Gugielma Melton Kaminer, "A Dictionary of South Carolina Biography during the Royal Period, 1719–1776" (Master's thesis, University of South Carolina, 1926), pp. 3–15, 23, 28–35, 44–46, 50–55, 64–66; Robert M. Weir, "The Harmony We Were Famous For: An Interpretation of Pre-Revolutionary South Carolina Politics," *William and Mary Quarterly,* 3d ser., 26, no. 4 (October 1969): 473–501.

[4] Mary Patterson Clarke, *Parliamentary Privilege in the American Colonies,* pp. 263–69; Jack Philip Greene, *The Quest for Power,* p. 9; also see *SCG,* reels 4, 5, 6 (1749–64) passim.

[5] See Abstracts of Correspondence between South Carolina Governors and the Board of Trade, PRO CO 5/406, and *Collections of the South Carolina Historical Society,* vols. 2–3 passim.

[6] *JCHA* (Jenkins), reels 15, 16, 17 (1755–1763), passim; and Oliver Morton Dickerson, *American Colonial Government, 1696–1765,* pp. 361–62.

[7] Greene, *Quest for Power,* pp. 221–22, 355–63, 362 fn. Glen to Board of Trade, 6 February 1744, PRO CO 5/406.

In addition to religious practices which favored the lower house, Governor Glen disliked the underrepresentation of the frontier in the Commons House of Assembly. The frontiersmen in the 1750s and 1760s, it will be recalled, found it difficult to vote or to meet the property qualifications for public office. Furthermore, the governor decried the use of the secret ballot by Commons House committeemen as a "vile Venetian juggle" which tended "to destroy the noble generous openness that is characteristic of Englishmen."[8] No doubt the real reason for Glen's criticism of the lower house was that he found the commoners virtually impossible to control.

Glen's comments about the assembly in the period from 1749 to 1756 could have been repeated in the years from 1757 to 1764. Particularly in the five years from 1757 to 1762, the trend toward greater Commons House power continued. As we will see, the two governors who followed Glen tried to reverse this trend.

To understand the governors' attitudes toward the political situation that developed gradually between 1749 and 1764, one must consider the relationship of mid-eighteenth-century colonial society to provincial politics. From the 1750s to the end of colonial rule, South Carolina's population expanded rapidly. This increase was most marked in the virtually unrepresented frontier regions, but it occurred throughout other parts of the province as well. The upsurge in total population was accompanied by increased numbers of wealthy planters and merchants who, as a whole, had ample time and money to enable them to perform public service as legislative committee members. During this fifteen-year period, a core of these planters and merchants served the twenty-two parishes in the Commons without pay. During a representative's three-year term, the frequent trips to Charles Town to attend committee meetings meant a considerable expenditure in time and money. However, most of those willing to serve under these circumstances looked upon the Commons as the protector of provincial liberties. Thus they considered their assembly committee service well worth the time and expense, and many ran and were elected to office year after year. Wealth, education, and repeated political success evidently gave many Commons House members a feeling of confidence.[9]

The extended service of many committeemen, besides developing increased confidence, created a sense of fellowship. Political power and legislative organization were a natural result. Thus, when members of the Com-

---

[8] Quoted in Herbert Levi Osgood, *The American Colonies in the Eighteenth Century,* 4:273; and Justin M. Winsor, ed., *Narrative and Critical History of America,* 5:333–35.

[9] Ramsay, *History,* 1:53.

mons House of Assembly came to Charles Town, they joined their colleagues on a host of committees with interlocking memberships. An examination of the *Journal of the Commons House of Assembly* in this period indicates that the Speaker made assignments to a variety of committees nearly every day the lower house was in session. Such intensity and diversity of activity and the existence of a core of experienced committee leaders created a base for political power.[10]

The stability of the developing power structure in the 1760s was enhanced by the fact that most of the key assignments were to standing committees. These normally became the most important committees because there was less and less check upon them by the other branches of government. The freedom of Commons standing committees in the 1760s was related to the decrease in the number of joint and conference committees with the Council.

A further factor encouraging the decline of joint committees was the superior speed and efficiency of the Commons legislative committee system. As committee procedure in the lower house improved through the use of subcommittees and more able members, legislative business proceeded more rapidly.

Thus, for a combination of reasons, power became centralized in standing committees composed of assemblymen skilled in committee procedure and dedicated to the principle of greater self-government. By the 1750s, legislative committee procedure had become refined and a definite routine had developed. After a subject was assigned to a committee, its members would investigate the subject and review relevant past Commons House procedures, resolutions, laws, or court cases. The chairman or another spokesman would present the committee's findings to the entire Commons in one of two ways. Often the chairman would give the committee's report to the clerk of the Commons House. The clerk would in turn refer the report to the Speaker for the first of three readings in the Commons. The second procedure was for the committee chairman to obtain the floor from the Speaker and read the report "from his seat" in the Commons chamber.[11]

Therefore the goals of greater legislative efficiency and self-government were served at the same time through a system in which important new ideas were developed. The crucial importance of legislative committees as a

[10] See *JCHA* (Jenkins), reels 15, 16, 17, passim; *JCHA* (Salley), 1765, passim; and Robert M. Weir, "The Harmony We Were Famous For: An Interpretation of Pre-Revolutionary South Carolina Politics," *William and Mary Quarterly*, 3d ser., 26, no. 4 (October 1969): 473–501.

[11] *JCHA* (Easterby), 9:321, 442.

factor in the growth of self-government should not overshadow the fascinating social and altruistic side of legislative committee work, however. Such work was most noticeable in the period after 1748, but there were examples of social and humanitarian work by committees as early as Governor Sir Francis Nicholson's administration in the 1720s.[12]

Sometimes legislative committee investigations resembled modern public health work. A topic which rarely failed to interest Commons committeemen was that of folk cures guaranteed to end the multitude of illnesses so prevalent in coastal South Carolina. Indeed, epidemics of all sorts virtually decimated the population throughout the colonial period. The old Charles Town saying that Carolina is a paradise in spring, a hell in summer, and a hospital in winter had a great deal of truth in it. In the 1750s and 1760s there was an annual exodus of many of the well-to-do to Newport, Rhode Island, or to England. Judging from the absenteeism due to sickness recorded in the legislative journals, even aristocratic Commons members were not immune to smallpox, "fevers," gout, flux, and a host of other maladies.[13]

An example of the exotic character of social and medical legislation as well as the often-overlooked altruistic side of Southern planter aristocrats is the case of two Negro slaves, Sampson and Caser [*sic*]. The two were reported to be able to cure snake bites. Two Speakers, Benjamin Smith and Andrew Rutledge, took an interest in the matter and appointed committees to investigate. According to the *Journal of the Commons House of Assembly:*

A committee be appointed to consider and report to the House the profit [*sic*] effectual way to procure a discovery of the cure for the Bite of Rattle Snakes from Sampson [also Caser] a Negro fellow belonging to Mr. Robert Hume, and a committee was appointed accordingly of the following gentlemen (that is to say) Mr. Thomas Wright, Mr. Mazyck, Mr. Pringle, Dr. Caw, and Mr. Guillard.

Several days later the chairman reported:

That having inquired into the reports about said Sampons [*sic*] curing several Negroes at different times, for many years found, they are fully satisfied that he has often been employed for that purpose, and that they understood he has always had good success in such cases, and have not heard he ever failed in such attempts.

[12] *JCHA* (Jenkins), reel 2, unit 3, p. 44; and *JCHA* (Salley), 1724/25–1725, p. 113; 1724, p. 19.
[13] For details see Carl Bridenbaugh, *Cities in the Wilderness,* pp. 339–400, 440–41; and idem, *Cities in Revolt,* pp. 128–31, 325–30.

The report went on to say:

Your Committee therefore beg leave to recommend to the House the usefulness of such a discovery, and are of the opinion it will be a General benefit to Mankind to be instructed to cure the Bites of such Dangerous Animals: and farther [*sic*] recommend that the said Negro may be freed at the public expense and have some allowance to support him during his natural life after he shall have discovered the Remedys proper for the Cure of such bites.[14]

Since this committee's task had low priority, it was several weeks before the chairman made his report. The committeemen had interviewed cured slaves and their masters and had acquired affidavits about the correct procedure for using the "snake oil," a mixture made of several South Carolina herbs and plants. This cure may have actually worked, because a majority of the seven-man committee that verified the effectiveness of the medicine were doctors. In 1749 they recommended that £300 be spent to free the two talented slaves, plus an additional small payment to be given to the Negroes for their discovery.[15]

Such conduct is in marked contrast to the traditionally repressive attitude shown by other legislative committees toward slaves in the period. Other committees continued to draft bills concerning slave discipline in the years from 1748 to 1764. The work of implementing Negro regulatory acts passed by the General Assembly devolved on various local enforcement committees of planters in charge of the parish slave patrols.[16] Members of the slave patrol committee were armed and had the responsibility for apprehending slaves suspected of criminal action. An example of the power of the local slave committee was noted by Massachusetts diarist and attorney, Josiah Quincy, Jr., in 1773. Quincy wrote that any three members of the slave patrol who were justices of the peace, as most successful planters were, could try a slave suspected of a crime on the spot. The slave enforcement committeemen even had the power to execute the Negro without any further recourse to justice.[17]

Another case in 1749 involving a Negro showed the altruistic side of South Carolina legislative committeemen. The Negro's name was Amory.

[14] *JCHA* (Jenkins), reel 15, unit 2, pp. 295–98; and *JCHA* (Easterby), 9:293–95, 300, 302–4, 316, 320, 412, 461, 478–80.

[15] *JCHA* (Jenkins), reel 15, unit 1, pp. 295–98.

[16] William A. Schaper, "Sectionalism and Representation in South Carolina," *Report of the American Historical Association, 1900,* 1:333.

[17] Josiah Quincy, Jr., "The Journal of Josiah Quincy, Jr., 1773," *Massachusetts Historical Society Proceedings* 49 (1915–1916): 446, 454–57.

He was a freeman awaiting passage to England, where he was to be educated. Prior to his passage, a rapacious slave dealer abducted Amory and sold him into bondage. The Speaker of the Commons House, upon learning of the injustice, appointed a committee to investigate. The committeemen verified the matter of the Negro's abduction and reported it to the Speaker and the assembly. The lower house promptly secured Amory's freedom and sent him to England.[18]

A contemporary but unrelated committee development which marked a step toward greater public involvement in government occurred in the mid-1750s. As a result of a fresh skirmish in the recurring conflict between upper and lower houses on the subject of taxes, a Council tax committee took the unprecedented step of publishing its report on the Commons' action in the *South Carolina Gazette.*[19] Once the precedent of public disclosure of governmental information was established, other committees of both houses and individual legislators, using pen names, began to break the older tradition of silence concerning parliamentary matters. During the last twenty years of colonial history, the two major Charles Town newspapers occasionally published accounts of provincial politics.[20]

By reason of all the developments just described, the political significance as well as the power of Commons committees steadily increased. The relative importance of an individual committee within the assembly's power structure was indicated by its size, activity, and membership. A relatively unimportant standing committee on religion might meet only three times a year and have only three members. By contrast, the powerful committee on Indian affairs was much larger and met frequently. An example of how committee size was related to the importance of the committee's task can be seen during the years 1754 and 1755, when a French-instituted Indian attack seemed imminent. At this time, the Speaker expanded the Indian affairs committee membership from its customary six to eleven. The members included the current Speaker, a future Speaker, several militia colonels, the wealthiest merchant in the colony, and several well-to-do planters.[21]

In the 1750s and early 1760s, a study of representative important Commons House committees not only indicates the growth of committee power, but provides an insight into the geographic and sectional basis of that power

[18] *JCHA* (Easterby), 9:293, 295, 300, 302–3, 326, 328.
[19] William Bull II was the chairman of the Council committee that ran this advertisement in the *South Carolina Gazette.*
[20] The *South Carolina Gazette and Country Journal* was the other paper.
[21] *JCHA* (Jenkins), reel 15, unit 2, p. 600.

within the lower house. An analysis of the committees of trade, Indian affairs, correspondence, and powder receiver/armory, reveals certain trends. As was the case in previous decades, assemblymen from midland and backcountry areas were not well represented on these committees. Chairmanships usually went to tidewater aristocrats. The few exceptions were frontier assemblymen who had unusual abilities or influence.[22]

One exception who proved this rule was Colonel George Gabriel Powell. Powell had long been associated with the Peedee upcountry section as a landowner. Like many successful planters, he resided part of the year in Charles Town. Powell was regularly elected to the Commons by his backcountry constituents and after a few sessions apparently won the confidence of the tidewater political leaders in Commons as well as the frontier farmers in his parish. The support of the farmers was evident because he was returned to office for over twenty years, from the 1750s to the 1770s. The backwoodsmen also elected him militia colonel year after year and rejoiced when he was appointed the first backcountry judge. The support of the political oligarchy can be seen in his assignment to some of the best committees and the fulfillment of his requests for frontier improvements, such as roads and churches. Indeed, by the 1760s Colonel Powell had become one of the most active participants in the Commons' twenty-two committees.

One of the legislative committees on which Powell sometimes served was the powder receiver/armory committee. This committee had the widest geographic spread of membership of those mentioned above. However, during peacetime, most of this committee's members were either relatively inexperienced or held few other important committee posts. Its chairman was normally the only member of real stature on the committee.

Although members of the powder receiver/armory committee were not often important leaders in the Commons House, the work they accomplished was essential, particularly during the French and Indian War. This committee had the important function of determining, through investigation and accounting procedures, whether provincial weapons and munitions were adequate to repulse an enemy attack. The decaying effect of the humid, subtropical climate made their job a troublesome one. After 1754, they had the added responsibility of working with the commissary general to provision South Carolina troops.[23]

Besides these jobs, the committee members were responsible for oversee-

---

[22] See Appendix II below; also see the list of Commons House leaders in Greene, *Quest for Power*, pp. 475–88.

[23] *JCHA* (Jenkins), reel 15, unit 1, pp. 41, 52; reel 16, unit 1, pp. 119–20.

ing collection of the powder duty from ship captains who docked in South Carolina ports. Employees of the armory committee were charged with acquiring the ships' surplus stone ballast, which was used in building new fortifications. Committee members audited the provincial powder receiver's accounts once a year, checking both the quality and quantity of arms in public armories and forts.[24]

Another committee which drew members from most sections of the province at this time was the committee on Indian affairs. The status of this committee fluctuated with different Speakers. Under some Speakers it was an ad hoc committee appointed each session. At other times it acted as a standing committee for an entire term of office. No matter how it was organized, its work was considered vital. Carolinians knew that they lived in an area only a few years removed from a frontier. They also were well aware that their lives and property depended, in large part, upon the natives who protected them from the French and from the French-oriented Indians to the west. This concern over Indian relations became crucial when the powerful Cherokee took to the warpath in 1760 to 1761.[25]

This concern over Indian relations was shared by the Council and governors of the period. In fact, South Carolina's Governor James Glen and Councilor Edmund Atkin took an active lead in developing Indian policy not only for South Carolina but for other colonies as well.[26]

Members of the joint Indian affairs committee in the 1750s and 1760s developed several methods of Indian diplomacy, for instance, giving friendly or neutral natives generous gifts and holding numerous conferences with their chiefs. Subject to legislative approval, they also had forts built in Indian territory to protect friendly natives from the French as well as to promote South Carolina's interests. Indian agents were sent out among the natives and purchased large land grants from the Indians rather than continuing the older pattern of small, unpaid, piecemeal occupation of Indian land by frontiersmen. The committee also urged British-oriented Indians to cooperate among themselves. During the latter part of Glen's administration, 1749 to 1756, Indian affairs were considered an integral part

[24] See *JCHA* (Easterby), 9:60, 66, 143–44, 153, 412, for samples of their work.
[25] Edmund Atkin, *Indians of the Southern Frontier*, pp. xxvii–xxviii, 4. Also see *JCHA* (Jenkins), reels 15, 16; Robert Lee Meriwether, *The Expansion of South Carolina, 1729–1765*, pp. 185–240; Chapman James Milling, *Red Carolinians*, pp. 266–306; John Richard Alden, *John Stuart and the Southern Colonial Frontier*, pp. 3–138; and James Adair, *History of the American Indians*, pp. 252–73.
[26] See note 27, this chapter; also see Mary F. Carter, "Governor James Glen" (Ph.D. dissertation, University of California, Los Angeles, 1951), pp. 14–15, 42–43, 48–57, 86–87, 93, 125–35, 158–59.

of the governor's plan to extend South Carolina's interest into the Ohio River Valley and to the Gulf Coast.[27]

As desirable as these programs appeared to the governors and Council, some Commons House committee members had doubts about them. Perhaps the reluctance of commoners to implement such programs as Governor Glen's plans to construct new Indian forts and to purchase vast new lands from the Cherokee was based upon an unwillingness to increase the colony's tax burden.[28] Since governmental money was involved in Indian affairs, these matters eventually were considered by committees of the lower house.[29]

By mid-century, members of the Commons legislative committees recognized the extent of the power they held in Indian affairs. This strength was illustrated in 1754 when commoners capitalized upon Governor James Glen's desire to build Fort Loudoun in what is now Tennessee. Assembly committeemen forced the governor to grant the Commons greater influence in return for their support of his fort. As political payment, Glen supported the lower house in certain struggles with the Upper House.[30]

The commoners on the Indian affairs committee in the 1750s began to demand control of the governor's duties regarding Indian gifts and diplomacy. Committee members also wanted to have a greater voice in Indian trade regulations. Assemblymen, as in earlier years, desired a tightening of the lax procedures for regulating Indian traders, because the brutal conduct of many traders continued to cause friction with the natives. By the end of Glen's administration in 1756, this so-called legislative committee was editing and writing drafts of the governor's speeches to Indian chiefs.[31] In 1751 William Bull II, a member of the joint committee, conducted six Catawba Indian chiefs to an Indian conference in Albany, New York and in

[27] Glen to Board of Trade, 4 April and 26 July 1748; 23 December 1749; 12 July and 2 October 1750; 5 July and December 1751; 23 December 1752; 5 June, 30 July, 25 October 1753; 26 August 1754; 29 May 1755; 14 April and 17 October 1756, all in PRO CO 5/406; Wilbur R. Jacobs, *Diplomacy and Indian Gifts,* pp. 5, 11–75; and Carter, "James Glen," pp. 34–35, 39–43, 57–66, 159, 161. Also see *The Colonial Records of South Carolina: Documents relating to Indian Affairs, May 21, 1750–August 7, 1754: The South Carolina Indian Books,* 2d ser., ed. William L. McDowell.

[28] Carter, "James Glen," passim.

[29] *JCHA* (Easterby), 9:509, 533–34, 536 (list of committee assignments and reports for the years 1748–1750).

[30] *JCHA* (Jenkins), reel 15, unit 1, pp. 19–20, 36, 71, 76–77, 280–85; unit 2, pp. 50–52, 286–90, 351–54, 395, 500, 537–38; reel 16, passim; and Meriwether, *Expansion of South Carolina,* pp. 194–210.

[31] *JCHA* (Jenkins), reel 15, unit 2, pp. 620–40, provides an example of the executive activity of the committee on Indian affairs.

1755 the joint committee demanded authority to select the annual presents sent to the Indians.

Even though the Indian affairs committee's activity may have detracted from Governor James Glen's power, its effectiveness was obvious. During Glen's administration there was no threat of major Indian conflict in South Carolina. When Glen's energetic successor, William Henry Lyttleton, arrived in 1756, he immediately reversed former practices and took personal control of Indian matters. Both Lyttleton and the next governor, Thomas Boone, tried to reduce the influence of the Indian affairs committee. The result was apparent in the colony's Indian policy. Some contemporary authorities consider the change to executive direction of Indian affairs a reason for the bloody Cherokee War.[32]

The representation of the committee on correspondence in the 1750s and 1760s was still centered in Charles Town, differing from the wider representation found in the Indian affairs committee.[33] The crucial issue involving this committee was the control of the colonial agent in London. By the late 1740s, the commoners claimed the power to dominate the committee on correspondence and to name the colonial agent. They based their claim on precedents established in the first three decades of the eighteenth century. However, the governors and Council in the 1740s and 1750s disagreed because they found nothing in the governors' instructions or other royal directives that justified the commoners' assertions.[34] The Commons House committeemen were determined to control the colonial agent, knowing that whoever dominated the agent indirectly influenced the attitude of the Board of Trade and other royal officials toward South Carolina.[35]

Commons House committees used various techniques to achieve domination of the agency. To increase the influence of the lower house members on the joint committee on correspondence, the Speaker "packed" more assemblymen on the committee. In addition, the power of financial committees

---

[32] Alexander Hewatt, "Historical Account of the Rise and Progress of the Colonies of South Carolina and Georgia," in *Historical Collections of South Carolina*, ed. Bartholomew Rivers Carroll, 1:444–45; Glen, "Description of South Carolina," pp. 215, 225; Edward McCrady, *The History of South Carolina under the Royal Government, 1719–1776*, pp. 325, 330–40; *SCG*, 30 May, 6 and 13 June 1761; Greene, *Quest for Power*, pp. 324, 327–38; William Gilmore Simms, *The History of South Carolina from its first European discovery to its erection into a Republic*, p. 62; Carter, "James Glen," p. 86; and Ramsay, *History*, 1:167, 173.

[33] See Appendix II below.

[34] Greene, *Quest for Power*, pp. 266–72, 262–68 fns.

[35] Peter Manigault (assemblyman and future Speaker of the Commons House) to Andrew Rutledge, 26 February 1764, Manigault Family Papers, #2733, South Caroliniana Library.

was used to influence the agents by threatening to withhold their expense account funds.[36]

One of the major political struggles of Governor Glen's administration grew out of a dispute between the governor, Council, and Commons over the choice of a colonial agent. As was often the case in colonial South Carolina, the members of the Commons House of Assembly used such a confrontation to further their own ends.

The specific problem started in 1749 when the long-standing colonial agent, Peregrine Furye, was dismissed from his job by the legislature.[37] Up to this time, the Commons committee on correspondence had maintained a reasonably harmonious working relationship with the Council's correspondence committee. In fact they often worked together as a joint committee to send letters to royal officials. In the past, they had even cooperated in the nomination of London agents.

The lower house in 1749 was determined to alter its earlier precedent and to select an agent of its own choice, James Crockatt, a South Carolinian living in England. The Council had another candidate for the post, Colonel Charles Pinckney. Governor James Glen, always eager to increase the power of the royal governor, wished to retain Peregrine Furye.[38]

A five-year power struggle ensued, ending in a Commons victory. The right to originate, or more precisely, not to originate, revenue bills was the device by which Commons committees wore down their opponents. Governor Glen, perhaps remembering that the Commons House committee on governmental claims had refused to pay his rent for the previous year, 1748, was the first to capitulate.[39] With Furye out of contention for the position, the commoners put pressure on the Upper House. In 1754, the councilors finally gave in when the commoners refused to allocate any money to the Upper House for printing or paper. The Upper House was forced to recognize Crockatt as the agent, giving a significant victory to the lower house. From this time on, selection of the colonial agent remained in the hands of the Commons House of Assembly and the commoners gained control of the joint committee on correspondence, as well.[40]

[36] *JCHA* (Easterby), 9:135–42, 161, 170, 183, 222–23, 274, 318–19; Sirmans, *Colonial South Carolina*, pp. 219, 276.

[37] *JCHA* (Easterby), 9:130, 134, 141–43.   [38] Ibid., pp. 219, 276.

[39] See note 34, this chapter; McCrady, *Royal Government*, pp. 281–82; and William Roy Smith, *South Carolina as a Royal Province, 1719–1776*, pp. 164–68.

[40] McCrady, *Royal Government*, pp. 281–92; Smith, *South Carolina as a Royal Province*, pp. 168–70; and *JCHA* (Jenkins), reels 15, 16, passim.

An indication of the operation of the committee on correspondence can be seen in the Charles Garth Letterbook. This manuscript collection is really misnamed, for it contains both the correspondence from the committee to Garth, who served as South Carolina's colonial agent for nearly thirteen years, and his replies to the committee on a host of subjects.[41]

Charles Garth was a member of the British House of Commons and was related to Governor Thomas Boone and a number of leading families in South Carolina. When Governor Boone suggested Garth as a possible agent to replace Thomas Middleton in 1762, the Commons House approved Boone's suggestion.[42] The new agent indicated a sound knowledge of the political situation on both sides of the Atlantic. He evidently knew enough about the Charles Town power structure to recognize the committee on correspondence members as the political leaders of the province. His loyalty to the Commons was clearly demonstrated. Garth even supported the assembly in the complaints to royal authorities in 1764 which caused Boone, his cousin, to be relieved of his gubernatorial office. (See pages 94–98 below.) Garth's support of South Carolina objectives was not overlooked by Carolinians; they retained him as their agent from 1764 to 1775. Indeed, Garth's loyalty to the committee on correspondence lasted until the American Revolution.[43]

In the 1750s and early 1760s, the committee on trade, like the committee on correspondence, was dominated by tidewater aristocrats. Often the chairman was a successful Huguenot merchant, well fitted for the job of developing new products and expanding South Carolina's trade.

Typical of the Commons leaders of this committee was Gabriel Manigault (1704–1781). Manigault was the son of Huguenot immigrants to the colony. By the late 1730s he was one of the most successful merchants in the colony and one of the few not engaged in slave trading. By the 1740s he was well known as one of the leading philanthropists in South Carolina. He was the president of the fire insurance company and the Charles Town Library Society, and active in a host of charitable activities. Due to his financial success he was often appointed to committees dealing with fiscal matters and served as provincial treasurer. Because of his business knowledge, his service on committees was certainly beneficial to the colony.

One of the committees on which Manigault sometimes served was the

[41] Charles Garth Letterbook, South Carolina Archives Department, Columbia.

[42] *JCHA* (Jenkins), reel 17, unit 2, pp. 14–23; and Greene, *Quest for Power,* pp. 271–77.

[43] Sir Louis Bernstein Namier, "Charles Garth and His Connexions," *English Historical Review* 54 (1939): 443–70, 632–52.

trade committee. We have previously seen the work of this committee in stimulating the colony's economy in 1748 by obtaining a royal bounty on indigo.[44] The trade committee did not stop its efforts after this success. Indeed, many of the successful planters and merchants on the committee continued to serve in the legislature in the 1750s. Some of them were appointed as a special committee "to encourage settlers in the back-country to plant Guatemala indigo . . ." in 1754. Although this special committee was unsuccessful in encouraging the frontier Scotch-Irish farmers to grow products which would fit into the mercantilistic system of the mother country, planting up-country indigo became a subject for a conference committee of both houses later in the 1750s.[45]

In 1754 a subcommittee of the committee on trade was appointed by the Speaker to look into the condition of the Charles Town waterfront. This subcommittee had a difficult task, since the dock facilities of the harbor had been nearly demolished by a hurricane two years before. In its report, the subcommittee recommended a plan to repair shipping facilities. There must have been conflicts within this legislative committee because the Speaker replaced three of the original members prior to the final report.[46]

These lower house committees of the 1750s were representative of the Commons' work. From 1748 to 1764, the assembly and its committees continued to grow in efficiency and power. The tax committees, exemplifying this increased competence, developed new methods, such as issuance of claim certificates, to expedite their tasks. This improvement in legislative operation was due to the development of a group of experienced legislative leaders who gave continuity to committee work and to the efficient direction of the Speakers in these years.[47]

A major test of the General Assembly and its committees came during the Cherokee War, the greatest threat to the province since the Yamassee conflict of 1716 to 1717. Probable causes of the Cherokee conflict were the aggressive actions of the governors, the accumulation of native grievances over the loss of their lands, cheating by Indian traders, and the inconsistencies in colonial Indian policy.[48]

In a matter of weeks after the start of the war in 1759, the newly constructed Fort Loudoun and many frontier settlements were destroyed by the Cherokee. The only remaining major backcountry strong points, Fort

[44] *JCHA* (Easterby), 8:193–96.   [45] *JCHA* (Jenkins), reel 15, unit 2, p. 51.
[46] Ibid., p. 80.

[47] Ibid., reels 15, 16, passim; see also Appendix II below.

[48] See note 32, this chapter; *JCHA* (Easterby), 8:96–196 passim; Sirmans, *Colonial South Carolina*, pp. 324–33.

Prince George and Ninety-six, were endangered by the Cherokee in 1760. Many problems faced the committee members who met in Charles Town: military defeats, a smallpox epidemic which killed many Carolina soldiers sent to fight on the frontier, and rumors of a slave insurrection which caused lowcountry planters to withhold some of their militia from backcountry duty. South Carolina committeemen became even more disturbed when they learned that the Creek Indian nation on their southwest frontier was considering going on the warpath against them. In the midst of these crises, there was a change in governors when William Henry Lyttleton was promoted by the British Board of Trade to be governor of Jamaica.[49]

During this tense period, Commons committees worked almost day and night, at a faster pace than they had during the St. Augustine expedition twenty years earlier. Often one committee would be assigned to consider a governor's message, to send a reply to the governor, and to draft a bill related to the subject of the governor's message.[50] For example, when Lieutenant Governor William Bull II requested funds to send rangers to patrol the frontier in 1760, committeemen, many of them serving on several related committees, considered his written request, drafted their affirmative reply, and wrote the bill funding the expenses for the ranger troop.

Committee members also worked diligently in 1760 to 1761 to consider citizens' claims for damages caused by Indians. The committee on petitions and accounts promptly recommended payments to cover the claimants' losses, subject to the approval of the lower house. Assemblymen were equally industrious in raising money for the newly activated militia regiment's salary and in taking other steps to improve the situation on the frontier after they realized the magnitude of the war damage. At Lieutenant Governor Bull's request, commoners raised money to sustain the backwoods population who had lost virtually everything.[51] A committee of the General Assembly even took the lead in requesting that Bull prevent a contingent of British regulars from leaving the uneasy frontier in 1760. As was the case in the 1740 St. Augustine expedition, a Commons committee found fault with the handling of the military situation. This time it was Lieutenant Governor

---

[49] Meriwether, *Expansion of South Carolina*, pp. 218–40; Howard H. Peckham, *The Colonial Wars, 1689–1762*, pp. 201–4; David Duncan Wallace, *The Life of Henry Laurens and a Sketch of the Life of Lieutenant-Colonel John Laurens*, pp. 98–108; *SCG*, 22 September 1759, 17 April, 17 and 26 July 1760, 1 and 8 October 1761; and *JCHA* (Jenkins), reel 16, unit 3, and reel 17, unit 1 passim.

[50] *JCHA* (Jenkins), reel 18, unit 3, pp. 32–51.

[51] Ibid., reel 16, unit 3 (20–21 January 1761); also reel 17 passim; and Richard Maxwell Brown, *The South Carolina Regulators*, pp. 10–13.

William Bull II who was criticized, perhaps unjustly, for acting too slowly in this crisis.[52] The actions of the assembly committeemen in the Cherokee War indicated the flexibility and responsiveness of the South Carolina legislative committee system in a period of great danger.

A different test of the legislative committee system closely followed the Cherokee War. This event was the Christopher Gadsden election controversy of 1762 to 1764. The primary participants in the controversy were Governor Thomas Boone and the Commons House of Assembly. Boone's policies reflected the new philosophy of British imperial administration in the years after the conclusion of the French and Indian War. The governor's legislative program emphasized central political authority from London at the expense of local autonomy. These ideas were unpopular in Charles Town; legislative committeemen were understandably reluctant to give up their power after nearly four decades of increasing self-rule.[53]

One of Governor Boone's first efforts to increase royal authority in South Carolina, it will be recalled, was to control Indian policy by reducing the power of the joint committee on Indian affairs. After this success, Boone attempted to control the assembly's internal operation, but he did not have the same success. Boone tried to alter the Election Act of 1721, the act which established the minimum number of legislative meetings each year and which set quorum limits. The commoners stoutly opposed executive attempts to amend the law and were dismissed by the governor in 1762.[54]

This was the year of the triennial election, an opportunity for Boone to assert his power. In this election Assemblyman Christopher Gadsden, a merchant, planter, and militia captain, was elected from St. Paul's parish. One of the church wardens of the vestry committee in charge of the voting failed to swear a required oath to authenticate the election properly. Previously in such cases, the Speaker had called the committee on privileges and elections to investigate technicalities which might invalidate an election. Usually the report of the committee satisfied the entire assembly. Other governors had then routinely administered the oath of office to the newly elected assemblyman. In fact only once before, under Sir Francis Nicholson

[52] *JCHA* (Jenkins), reel 16, unit 3, pp. 8–9.

[53] Jack Philip Greene, "The Gadsden Election Controversy and the Revolutionary Movement in South Carolina," *MVHR* 46 (1959): 469–92.

[54] Ramsay, *History*, 2:253–55; McCrady, *Royal Government*, pp. 354–66; David Duncan Wallace, *A Constitutional History of South Carolina, 1725–1775*, p. 56; and idem, *Henry Laurens*, pp. 109–15; Greene, *Quest for Power*, pp. 323–24; and *JCHA* (Jenkins), reel 17, unit 2 passim.

in the 1720s, had a governor ever refused to administer an oath, and Nicholson relented upon learning of a precedent of a similar case in the British House of Commons.[55]

However in 1762, when Christopher Gadsden and the two-man committee who escorted him to the governor's chamber returned to the Commons House, they reported that Boone had refused to administer the oath of office to Gadsden. When the Commons House protested Governor Boone's action, he again dissolved it.

Boone made an unfortunate decision in excluding Gadsden, who was already an accepted member of the assembly's leadership clique. He was among the most active members of the lower house committee system, and a talented political writer who, a decade later, was to become one of the first revolutionary leaders in South Carolina. Gadsden immediately became the center of a storm which was to cost Governor Thomas Boone his job.[56]

When the lower house reconvened later that year, an ad hoc committee to consider the "rights and liberties" of the Commons and to determine the validity of Gadsden's election was formed by Speaker Benjamin Smith. This committee was also authorized to investigate the validity of the governor's dissolution of the previous assembly. The committee was filled with able commoners, largely hand-picked by Smith to support the position of home rule and Gadsden's right to be a member of the lower house.[57] The committee report, although written thirteen years before the American Revolution, touched upon many of the key ideological issues of that conflict. In affirming Gadsden's right to serve, the commoners employed such arguments as traditional rights of Englishmen, natural rights, and rights of the electorate. All of these principles were buttressed by appropriate precedents in British law.[58]

When he received the committee report Governor Boone refused to alter his position. As a result of Boone's refusal to apologize to the lower house, Speaker Smith called the standing committee on privileges and elections for further investigations. This committee supported the position that Christo-

[55] Clarke, *Parliamentary Privilege,* pp. 146–47; Greene, *Quest for Power,* p. 192; Smith, *Royal Province,* pp. 98–104; and *JCHA* (Arch.), 7:176–77, 180–81, 200.

[56] See Chapter VIII below and Gadsden's committee assignments in Appendix II below.

[57] *JCHA* (Jenkins), reel 17, unit 2, pp. 20–29; Greene, "Gadsden Election," p. 476; and McCrady, *Royal Government,* pp. 355–66.

[58] *JCHA* (Jenkins), reel 17, unit 2, pp. 29–30.

pher Gadsden's election was indeed valid. The committeemen then reaffirmed all the previous rights of the Commons House which they claimed had been jeopardized by Boone's actions. When this committee's report was debated, a large majority of the lower house resolved to "do no further business" until the executive apologized to them. The Speaker was also directed to instruct the committee on correspondence to inform Colonial Agent Charles Garth of the Commons' position.[59]

At this point in the controversy, government practically stopped in South Carolina. Commoners refused to originate money bills and they did not pay the governor's salary for two years. Assemblymen began to use the technique of non-attendance to keep the legislative session alive but below the quorum limit, thus prolonging the stalemate. Boone, in retaliation, employed his parliamentary weapons and repeatedly prorogued or dissolved the assembly. Boone even refused to call the Commons House often enough to meet the minimum requirement of two meetings a year set by the election act of 1721.[60]

The commoners, including Gadsden, who was later formally elected by St. Paul's parish, replied by attacking Governor Boone publicly in the *South Carolina Gazette*. A legislative committee approved the printing of a pamphlet at public expense which recapitulated the arguments of the previously mentioned committees, such as political rights of Englishmen, natural rights, and precedents from the British House of Commons and the South Carolina Commons House of Assembly. Copies of the committee report were published and sent to England and to other colonies. After several months of deadlock, the uproar of the unpaid public creditors reached a peak. Garth's influence in England caused key royal officials to support the colonists. Finally, the chief British colonial official, the Earl of Halifax, recalled Governor Boone. Halifax's action left Lieutenant Governor William Bull II to administer the colony.

The Gadsden election crisis had a great impact on South Carolina. Combined with two other crises, the Cherokee War, which preceded the 1762 election, and the Stamp Act which immediately followed it, this test of legislative power prepared home-rule forces for greater struggles in the future. Both the experience of victory in an extended two-year struggle with the representatives of royal authority and the constitutional arguments raised

[59] Ibid., p. 49; and *SCG*, 5 February 1763.

[60] *JCHA* (Jenkins), reel 17, unit 3 passim. From 24 June to 17 September 1763, there was so little legislative activity that the Commons Journals during this period consist of only thirty-two handwritten pages. During a normal four-week session, the journals had several hundred manuscript pages.

by commoners on legislative committees were to affect the attitudes of the colonists in future. This altercation over the seating of Christopher Gadsden was of great significance in explaining the political and psychological climate of events in the final decade of South Carolina colonial history.[61]

[61] Greene, "Gadsden Election," pp. 490–92.

CHAPTER VII

Legislative Committees and the Road to Revolution, 1764–1774

The last years of colonial South Carolina, 1765 to 1774, were filled with events which involved committee activity. These events were the result of a number of crises, the first of which was the Stamp Act of 1765. As a consequence of this and other difficulties, such as the John Wilkes case and the intercolonial commercial boycotts of British products after 1769, the colony's government was in almost constant turmoil. Most of the controversy of this decade involved either legislative committees or extralegal committees. The problems which a number of committees attempted to solve were often quite different from those of the earlier provincial political struggles. After 1765, South Carolinians began to react against British imperial officials in controversies related to problems in other colonies.[1]

In addition, the decade differed from the first forty years of the royal era in that many of the most important issues were not considered by the General Assembly. Nongovernmental bodies began to influence the political affairs of the colony in many key respects.[2] Some of these extralegal bodies were voluntary associations organized for the purpose of anti-British activity, unofficial committees of correspondence to write to colonists in other provinces, and a Charles Town General Committee which coordinated anti-British activities.

The major reason for the inability of the regular constitutional structure to solve key problems was the conflict between the legislative and executive branches of government described in the last chapter. This conflict became so pronounced that the Commons House of Assembly refused to function actively after 1769. The members of the Commons simply met in insufficient numbers to establish a quorum and thereby were unable to pass any legislation, with the exception of six bills, in six years. The assemblymen preferred inaction to compromising their political principles.[3] The last two British governors, Lord Charles Greville Montagu and Lord William Campbell, were similarly unwilling to compromise their positions as defenders of the royal prerogative. This deadlock created a governmental vacuum which members of radical extralegal committees used to their own advantage.

However, the lower house's accomplishments of the previous forty years were not forgotten during this stalemate. When the assemblymen occasionally did act upon legislative problems, they formed committees which acted speedily and effectively.[4] These same assemblymen carried their knowledge of committees into the operation of the new extralegal organizations to which nearly all of them belonged.

This shift in political power from the legislature to extralegal organizations was accompanied by an unrelated though equally significant economic prosperity. Governmental turmoils failed to affect the economy of the colony.[5] Except for a small minority of governmental creditors who at one time had to wait seven years for Commons committees to pay them, a majority of the population appears to have supported the legislature.

An investigation of social and political causation is more revealing. Although the colony had only existed for some eighty years, social classes were starting to develop.[6] Judging from the records of parish vestry commit-

[1] Laurence Henry Gipson, *The British Empire before the American Revolution*, 12:218.

[2] Edward McCrady, *The History of South Carolina under the Royal Government, 1719–1776*, pp. 560–622, 659–723.

[3] See *JCHA* (Jenkins), reels 18, 19, passim; and Jack Philip Greene, *The Quest for Power*, p. 415.

[4] *JCHA* (Jenkins), reel 19, unit 3 passim.

[5] *South Carolina Gazette and Country Journal*, 6 June 1775; and Bull to Lord Hillsborough, in *Extracts from the Journals of the Provincial Congresses of South Carolina, 1775–1776*, ed. William E. Hemphill and Wylma A. Wates, p. xv; Jackson T. Main, *The Social Structure of Revolutionary America*, pp. 44–114. See Herbert Aptheker, *The Colonial Era*, pp. 22–59, 72–91, 129–41, for a different (Marxian) interpretation which emphasizes class struggle and economic causation.

[6] Alexander Hewatt, "Historical Account of the Rise and Progress of the Colonies of South Carolina and Georgia," in *Historical Collections of South Carolina*, ed. Bartholomew Rivers Carroll, 1:501–20; see population estimates in David Duncan Wallace, *South Carolina: A Short History, 1520–1948*, pp. 709–10; *SCG*, 17 September 1737, and 19 January 1740; Marcus Wilson Jernegan, *The American Colonies, 1492–1759*, pp. 289–90, 313, 324, 357–58; Curtis Putnam Nettles, *The Roots of American Civilization*, pp. 537–38; William A. Schaper, "Sectionalism and

tees, there were always a few poor whites in every part of the colony, but their number was small in the tidewater. According to the contemporary historian Dr. Alexander Hewatt, the largest social group was the colonial equivalent of a middle class: yeomen farmers, clerks, small planters, successful artisans. At the apex of South Carolina society was the aristocracy who, through service on legislative committees, continued to dominate the province. The base of the society was provided by the Negro slaves who made up the largest part of the total population. The slave-owning aristocrats who controlled legislative committees were gradually growing in number. The South Carolina legislators were determined to continue their role as leaders of the colony in an age of reemerging royal power.[7]

Accompanying these social trends after 1764 was a change in the patronage system. Legislative committees were faced with political problems connected with the growing power of non-South Carolinian royal officials from Britain, often called "placemen." The British placemen were particularly unpopular because many of them were appointed to positions of trust and responsibility that had been previously held by colonists. A result of this royal policy was that most South Carolinians were limited to membership in the Commons House of Assembly.[8]

The assembly's attitude toward frontiersmen in this period was quite different. Among the colony's leaders there was no dislike of the colonists of the "meaner sort." Normally the aristocratic attitude toward them ranged from paternalism to indifference or condescension. In times of emergency, Commons committee members would come to their aid.[9] By the 1760s low-country assemblymen did not even oppose greater representation of frontiersmen in the Commons House as they had in earlier decades. Moreover, Commons leaders occasionally passed laws for the creation of new

Representation in South Carolina," *American Historical Association Annual Report,* 1900, 1:247–73; Daniel Boorstin, *The Americans: The Colonial Experience,* pp. 100, 103, 312; Clarence Ver Steeg, *The Formative Years, 1607–1763,* pp. 265–66; Carl Bridenbaugh, *Cities in the Wilderness,* pp. 417–18; Harriet Horry Ravenal, *Eliza Pinckney,* pp. 5, 18; and Thomas Jefferson Wertenbaker, *The Old South,* pp. 19–21, 345–46.

[7] Hewatt, "Account of South Carolina," pp. 504–5.

[8] Carl Bridenbaugh, *Myths and Realities: Societies of the Colonial South,* pp. 6–10.

[9] See note 6 above. *JCHA* (Jenkins), reel 17, unit 1, pp. 138, 147; and *JCHA* (Easterby), 2:404–16, are two of many examples. Also see the vestry journals of St. Philip's Church, Charleston, and St. Helena's Church, Beaufort, S.C., available in the South Carolina Historical Society and South Carolina Archives; Frederick Dalcho, *An Historical Account of the Protestant Episcopal Church in South Carolina,* passim; and Richard Maxwell Brown, *The South Carolina Regulators,* pp. 10–11.

parishes as long as the tidewater region did not lose its position of power.[10] Yet since 1748 other matters had often diverted the concern of low-country committeemen from the problem of adequate backcountry representation.

This lack of attention produced hard feelings, particularly among upcountry settlers. Frontiersmen blamed the assembly and its committees for their lack of courts and the absence of schools, sheriffs, roads, and churches. Frontier dissatisfaction was at first expressed in petitions to the members of Commons and Council committees asking for redress of grievances.[11] Later, the frontiersmen began to act directly to solve their problems.

An example of their direct action occurred in 1768 when a group of frontiersmen who called themselves Regulators banded together to try to resolve their problems rather than passively depend upon legislative committee action. These Regulators used vigilante action as one solution and exerted pressure upon the provincial government for redress of their grievances.

A major problem of the backcountry after the conclusion of the Cherokee War in 1761 was a lack of justice.[12] The reasons for the frontiersmen's concern were real. After the defeat of the Indians, Cherokee land was ceded to the South Carolinians. This available land caused a widespread southward movement of new settlers from as far north as Pennsylvania to the South Carolina upcountry. Many of these new citizens were hard-working Scotch-Irish farmers. Unfortunately a troublesome minority of drifters, lazy Indian traders, criminals, half-breeds, and escaped bond servants accompanied them. A small faction of the militia who fought in the Cherokee conflict remained in the backcountry after 1761 to loot the abandoned farmhouses and steal governmental provisions intended for the impoverished frontiersmen. Bands of these criminals terrorized the countryside, and there were virtually no courts or sheriffs to take action against the lawbreakers.[13]

Because previous petitions for assistance to Charles Town legislative com-

---

[10] Schaper, "Sectionalism," pp. 329–50; Greene, *Quest for Power*, pp. 173–74, citing Thomas Cooper and David J. McCord, *South Carolina Statutes*, 2:683–91; 3:50–55, 135–40; and McCrady, *Royal Government*, pp. 437–39.

[11] Brown, *South Carolina Regulators*, pp. 1–37 and passim.

[12] Frederick Jackson Turner, *The Frontier in American History*, pp. 87–88, 105, 108, 116–17; Charles Woodmason, *The South Carolina Backcountry on the Eve of the Revolution*, pp. 244, 250–56 (Regulator Remonstrance); Schaper, "Sectionalism," pp. 346–60; and Brown, *South Carolina Regulators*, pp. vii, 41–48, 60.

[13] McCrady, *Royal Government*, pp. 623, 635–42; Hewatt, "Account of South Carolina," pp. 488–90; *JCHA* (Jenkins), reels 18, 19, passim; John Belton O'Neal Landrum, *Colonial and Revolutionary History of Upper South Carolina*, pp. 21, 35–50; and Brown, *South Carolina Regulators*, pp. 18–47.

mittees had been ignored, the respectable frontiersmen took the law into their own hands. Offenders, drifters, and questionable characters were whipped or punished in more severe ways. Coupled with this was a lengthy remonstrance of their problems sent to the General Assembly.

This petition, evidently drafted by Reverend Charles Woodmason, a circuit-riding Anglican minister who served the upcountry, was signed by more than one thousand backwoodsmen. When this document, along with rumors of a march to Charles Town by armed Regulators, came before the assemblymen, there was a flurry of legislative committee activity. Word of the growth of an anti-Regulator movement arrived later in Charles Town. This new development, threatening even more widespread violence and the possibility of retribution against the lowcountry, increased the governmental concern.[14]

In this tense atmosphere, the Commons began to act. As was often the case in such emergencies, leading backcountrymen were called to the capital to testify before Commons House committees on government and legal affairs. Backcountry assemblymen such as Tacitus Gaillard suddenly became very active in the legislative committees considering frontier problems.[15]

The result of these deliberations was to be the Circuit Court Act of 1768. Previous committee meetings on the subject of backcountry courts could be traced to the 1720s, but no legislation had resulted. The most recent committee to have studied the problem of frontier justice met in March and October, 1765, and again in 1766.[16] The members of Commons House committees had then suggested that four circuit courts be established in the upcountry. The Council took no action on these recommendations, thereby frustrating further judicial reform. The reason for the upper chamber's inaction was the fact that commoners wanted to control the selection of judges. Royal authorities also objected to the provision supported by the Commons that the justices' length of service be determined by their good conduct rather than the King's pleasure. This provision was viewed as a threat to crown control of judicial matters and therefore was opposed by the King's representatives.[17]

---

[14] Woodmason, *South Carolina Backcountry*, pp. 171–80; and *JCHA* (Jenkins), reels 18, 19, passim.

[15] See the list of backcountry leaders in the Commons House of Assembly in Greene, *Quest for Power*, pp. 479, 481, 488. These included Tacitus Gaillard, George Gabriel Powell, and Joseph Kershaw.

[16] *JCHA* (Jenkins), reel 18, 27 February 1766; and *JCHA* (Salley), 1765, pp. 9, 38, 43–44, 70, 107–8, 110, 116, 137, 152, 156 contain references to courts.

[17] McCrady, *Royal Government*, pp. 626–30; David Duncan Wallace, *A Constitutional History of South Carolina, 1725–1775*, p. 27; *JCHA* (Salley), 1765, pp.

The importance of victory in this issue seemed to outweigh the original reason for the measure. Better courts for the frontier were temporarily forgotten by lower house committees. The responsibility for acquiring judicial tenure for good behavior was assigned to the members of the committee on correspondence and their colonial agent, Charles Garth. Throughout the remainder of 1766 and 1767, Garth negotiated with the British authorities who were blocking any changes in the South Carolina judicial system. As this bargaining in England was taking place, backcountry unrest persisted.[18]

When the Regulator remonstrance was forwarded to the legislators by Governor Montagu in November, 1767, Speaker Peter Manigault decided that decisive action was needed. Manigault promptly referred the backcountry petition to the Commons' most prestigious committee, the committee on the state of the province. The next day the chairman, William Wragg, read the committee report which favored the establishment of both a circuit and a county court system. That same day, another committee, chaired by Regulator leader Tacitus Gaillard, was ordered to transform Wragg's committee recommendation into a bill. As was often the case, Gaillard's committee was nearly identical to the previous committee, and the bill was reported to the Commons chamber two days later.[19] By the time this measure had been debated by the Council and amended in a conference committee, the county court section was deleted. Yet the bill establishing circuit courts was a great improvement in upcountry justice.[20]

The committee on correspondence then was assigned the responsibility for seeing that the law was not disallowed in England. The committee wrote its agent, Charles Garth, to do anything possible to see that the measure was passed. Garth's efforts were insufficient, for the act was not approved by the Privy Council. When news of the disallowance reached Charles Town, another Commons committee was appointed, led by a middle-country legis-

---

107–8, 110; Brown, *South Carolina Regulators*, p. 65; William Roy Smith, *South Carolina as a Royal Province, 1719–1776*, pp. 133–41; and Bull to Board of Trade, 15 March 1765, cited in Greene, *Quest for Power*, p. 400.

[18] Garth to Earl of Shelburne, 22 July 1767, *Collections of the South Carolina Historical Society*, 2:191; and Garth to South Carolina Joint Committee on Correspondence, 16 June, 14 August 1768, in "Charles Garth Correspondence," *South Carolina Historical and Genealogical Magazine* 28 (1927): 228–29; 29 (1928): 120.

[19] *JCHA* (Jenkins), reel 18, 10 and 13 November 1767.

[20] Ibid., 19, 20, 28, and 30 January 1768; and reel 19 passim; David Duncan Wallace, *The Life of Henry Laurens*, pp. 127–30 (Laurens was a member of the legislative committee); Brown, *South Carolina Regulators*, pp. 74–76; and David Ramsay, *History of South Carolina*, 1:121–23.

lator, Colonel George Gabriel Powell. This committee, which included most of the backcountry legislators, wrote a new bill which promptly passed both houses and was signed by Governor Montagu. The assembly voted £70,000 to finance the building of courthouses and jails in key backcountry hamlets. By 1772 the courts were completed, and the new judges were appointed by Lieutenant Governor Bull.

In that same year, 1772, the second Circuit Act was disallowed in Great Britain. This royal action was simply ignored by the South Carolina General Assembly, which continued to maintain the Circuit Court system. The other grievances of the backcountry never could be resolved by the colony's legislative committee system because of the deadlock of constitutional government in the 1770s and the outbreak of the American Revolution.[21]

This matter of adequate frontier justice was typical of the problems the backcountry farmers faced in presenting their case before the General Assembly. A major concern of westerners was the absence of representatives who were frontiersmen themselves. In the 1760s, only one man in the Commons was in a position to speak for the backcountry. That man was Colonel George Gabriel Powell, mentioned earlier. Powell was sympathetic to frontier problems, but by the 1760s he himself was a kind of absentee frontier landowner. It was not until 1769, after the Regulator uprising, that a Scotch-Irish frontiersman was to sit in the Commons House in Charles Town.

That man was Captain Patrick Calhoun, the father of John C. Calhoun, later vice-president of the United States and nineteenth-century Southern political spokesman. In the eighteenth century, Patrick Calhoun was well known in the backcountry. Typical of many Carolina frontiersmen, he came south from Virginia in 1756 to the Long Canes region. Due to his ability he rapidly distinguished himself on the frontier; he became a deputy surveyor and one of the most prosperous farmers in the area. Just as Calhoun and other frontiersmen began to prosper in 1761, the Cherokee War reduced them to poverty. Calhoun became a ranger captain and helped defeat the

---

[21] *SCG,* 6 April 1769; Earl of Hillsborough to George III (recommendation for disallowal of the Circuit Court Act), *Collections of the South Carolina Historical Society,* 2:191–92; *JCHA* (Jenkins), reel 19, unit 1, pp. 28–34; Brown, *South Carolina Regulators,* pp. 77–81, 96, 104–5, 108–9, 138; Greene, *Quest for Power,* pp. 401–2 fns.; and idem, "Bridge to Revolution: The Wilkes Fund Controversy in South Carolina, 1769–1775," *Journal of Southern History* 39 (1963): 19–52; and Marvin Ralph Zahniser, "The Public Career of Charles Cotesworth Pinckney" (Ph.D. dissertation, University of California, Santa Barbara, 1963), pp. 22–26. Also see notes 12–18, this chapter.

Indians. When the war was over, Captain Calhoun became the first western justice of the peace. With this political background he was elected to the Commons. Once he arrived in Charles Town he experienced the same inactivity as previous frontiersmen and served on few committees. His presence, however, did bring some help to the frontier.

In contrast to the frontiersmen who brought their grievances to the Commons House of Assembly and gained at least some of their objectives, particularly judicial reform, was another dissatisfied class of South Carolinians, the urban artisans. Instead of directing political action toward Commons committees, the urban workers' anger was directed toward Britain. The artisans disliked the unfavorable economic position in which they were placed by British mercantile regulations. The dissatisfaction of the artisans became apparent when the workmen joined extralegal committees and organizations such as the Sons of Liberty that had an important role after 1765.[22]

Thus it can be seen that the change in the nature of committee activity in the 1760s was accompanied by a number of concomitant though essentially unrelated changes in the economic and social structure of the colony. The lowcountry South Carolina aristocrats used a number of methods in an attempt to maintain their legislative power against the challenge of British placemen, frontiersmen, and artisans. A favorite method was persuasion achieved through personal and social contact. Since virtually all important provincial business, justice, and social events occurred in Charles Town, the aristocratic committee leaders in the city had ample opportunity to use intimacy and charm to win others to their point of view. In particular, the few assemblymen whose constituencies were in remote frontier areas frequently accepted not only the hospitality but some of the political views of the tidewater majority in the Commons House when visiting the capital. The comparatively small population of ruling whites, 80,000, was interconnected through business and interrelated through marriage, and tended to become increasingly a closed society into which only certain fortunate assemblymen from outlying districts were taken. This exclusiveness was reflected in legislative committees where the best assignments went to members of this inner group.[23] The backcountry assemblymen who were not accepted by the Charles Town establishment naturally had few committee posts.

[22] Richard Walsh, *Charleston's Sons of Liberty*, pp. 38, 58, 71–73, 141.
[23] Frederick P. Bowes, *The Culture of Early Charleston*, pp. 115–30; Woodmason, *South Carolina Backcountry*, pp. 221–23, 239–40, 244, 255; Hennig Cohen, ed.,

Although social factors were an important consideration in committee assignments, it was the opinion of the Speaker of the Commons House that counted most, since he made all committee assignments. An example of the Speakers' power in selecting committee members can be seen in the six years ending with 1764. In this period more than seventy representatives were elected to the Commons House, but only fifty-two of them had an important role in legislative committees. Eighteen representatives had few or no committee assignments.

Of these fifty-two fortunate members, a core of thirty-one dominated the most important committees. Ninety percent of the thirty-one first-ranking committeemen were representatives of St. Philip's, St. Michael's (Charles Town) or nearby low-country parishes. The assignment of the remaining top committee positions indicates no general sectional pattern except in second-echelon committees, where there was a slightly greater percentage of legislators from southern parishes than from northern and eastern areas.[24] Care must be taken in interpreting raw committee data on the assignments of assemblymen from various parishes, since some members of the lower house represented two or more parishes at different times in the six-year period ending in 1764.

In addition to the social and geographical factors just mentioned, two key qualifications influenced committee assignments, specifically, longevity and special abilities.[25] For example, Commons members who were physicians or attorneys usually had particularly active committee roles. This tradition appears to explain, in part, the efficiency of operation in the lower house. Important committeemen often served on the same standing committee or similar ad hoc committees for years and were thus experts in certain legislative fields. The fact that governors and the twelve-man Council were often less well versed in these fields was one of the reasons for the frequent Com-

---

The South Carolina Gazette, 1732–1775, pp. 17–24; also see the numerous genealogical articles in the *South Carolina Historical and Genealogical Magazine* and the *South Carolina Historical Magazine.* (See Mary B. Prior, *et al., Consolidated Index, I–XL, 1900–1939, to the South Carolina Historical Magazine with Subject Index, I–LXI, 1900–1960;* Barnwell family, pp. 29–36, Bull family, pp. 80–83, Manigault family, pp. 400–401, Pinckney family, pp. 484–87, and the general listing of genealogies, p. 703.)

[24] See the committee assignment charts in the appendixes of this book; Greene, *Quest for Power,* pp. 206–7, and assembly leader tables, pp. 475–86; and *JCHA* (Jenkins), reels 16–18 passim.

[25] See my appendixes, below, and Greene's assembly leader tables for an indication of the longevity of legislative committee experience by members of the lower house. Several assemblymen served in the Commons for over twenty years.

mons legislative victories in contests with the other branches of govern-ment.[26]

Many of the active committeemen were leaders in the political friction between the mother country and South Carolina in the period from 1765 to 1774. To understand the political deadlock that developed between pro-British conservatives and anti-imperialist radicals in legislative committees and extralegal committees, we must go back to 1765, two years before the Regulator problems became acute. The significance of the friction in South Carolina during this period was that local provincial struggles began to be associated with the larger American struggle for self-rule. The success of colonials in Charles Town was partly a reflection of the organization and political experience accumulated since the colony's first revolution of 1719.[27]

The hard feelings which began accumulating with the Stamp Act of 1765 led gradually but surely to the legislative deadlock of 1769 and thereafter. Committee activity had two forms during 1765 and 1766, the first two years of this period of developing strain. Traditional legislative committees func-tioned in the critical Stamp Act issue by petitioning the crown and voting funds to send a committee of three (Thomas Lynch, Christopher Gadsden, and John Rutledge) to the Stamp Act Congress in New York. Another manifestation of Commons interest was the examination of official corre-spondence from other colonial legislatures relative to the injustices, as the colonists saw them, of the Stamp Act.[28] When the Act was rescinded in March, 1766, South Carolina assemblymen voted to erect a statue costing £1,000 (currency) of William Pitt, the British parliamentary leader respon-sible for the rescission.[29]

During the Stamp Act controversy, extralegal committees operated in a number of different ways. Some tried to frustrate the activities of stamp collectors. Others started riots to indicate their displeasure with the new tax. Some moderates, such as the merchants, petitioned the crown for removal of

[26] Herbert Levi Osgood, *The American Colonies in the Eighteenth Century,* 4:142–43.

[27] John Drayton, *Memoirs of the American Revolution,* 1:36, 49–57; and McCrady, *Royal Government,* pp. 576, 584–85. McCrady mentions that two of the three committees of the Stamp Act Congress in New York were chaired by South Carolinians. Hewatt, "Account of South Carolina," pp. 517, 521–22; Bull to Board of Trade, PRO, records relating to South Carolina, South Carolina Archives, 32:56–57, quoted in Walsh, *Sons of Liberty,* p. 46; and Ver Steeg, *Formative Years,* p. 278.

[28] *JCHA* (Salley), 1765, pp. 141–42, 162.

[29] Woodmason, *South Carolina Backcountry,* pp. 204–11.

the Stamp Tax. Another larger body was the "Association." The "Association" idea spread southward from New England to South Carolina. It was basically a vigilante organization that asked citizens to sign a pledge not to buy imported British goods. Royal sympathizers who refused to sign often lived in danger of retribution by an extralegal enforcement committee. Other groups who took an active part in searching for stamped goods were committees of the Sons of Liberty, local fire companies, and artisan groups. The center of extralegal activity was Charles Town's St. Michael's parish in the workmen's part of town.[30]

Of the extralegal groups in 1765, the Sons of Liberty, largely comprised of mechanics, was the most active and radical. Its leaders were two men who had served in the Commons and brought knowledge of committee organization to their cause. One was Peter Timothy, the radical editor of the *South Carolina Gazette* and a former assemblyman, and the other was Christopher Gadsden, an aristocratic, libertarian planter-merchant. Gadsden took the lead in calling the attention of lower classes of Carolina society to the problems of natural and constitutional rights, and the British violations of their liberties. Sometimes Gadsden's and Timothy's exhortations caused rowdy behavior, as was illustrated by a nine-day period of rioting in the capital. Men carrying Union Jacks with the word "Liberty" inscribed upon them roamed the city. One extralegal committee from St. Michael's parish even captured the official stamp collectors who were staying at the fort on Johnson's Island in Charles Town Harbor and brought them into town as prisoners. Other extralegal committees searched the homes of non-associators and conservative governmental leaders for revenue stamps until the Stamp Act was rescinded.[31]

The protests against the growing power of royal rule took a different form after the rescinding of the Stamp Act. Insight into the new trend can be gained by looking at the letters of Colonel Henry Laurens. Laurens was a successful Huguenot merchant-planter, Cherokee War veteran, and loyal British subject. He was, in 1765 and 1766, a moderately conservative Commons representative and active legislative committee member from Charles

[30] Hewatt, "Account of South Carolina," pp. 526–28, 530; McCrady, *Royal Government*, pp. 576–77; Bowes, *Early Charleston*, p. 127; Walsh, *Sons of Liberty*, pp. 30, 38; *SCG*, 3 August 1769; William M. Dabney and Marvin Dargan, *William Henry Drayton and the American Revolution*, pp. 30–33; and Woodmason, *South Carolina Backcountry*, pp. xvii–xviii, 86, 295–96.

[31] Drayton, *Memoirs*, 1:36–59; McCrady, *Royal Government*, pp. 565–70; Wallace, *Henry Laurens*, p. 120; *SCG*, 6 October 1765; and Christopher Gadsden, *The Writings of Christopher Gadsden, 1746–1805*, passim.

Town. He viewed the violence of the radical mobs during the Stamp Act with disgust. However, in the late 1760s and 1770s he was also troubled by the unconstitutionality of the Stamp Act and other attempts by royal officials to promote the imperial supremacy of the British parliament. Colonel Laurens's attitudes, according to South Carolina's contemporary historian, Dr. Alexander Hewatt, were typical of the majority of the forty-eight members of the Commons during the time of the Stamp Act.[32]

Colonel Laurens and the majority of the commoners disliked the venal placemen who flocked to the province from the British Isles to take the most valuable offices. After the 1760s, South Carolina, as has been mentioned, became one of the chief dumping grounds for British spoilsmen. By the 1770s, this trend had grown so pronounced that only three of the twelve members of the Council were native South Carolinians. One of the nine British councilors, Sir Egerton Leigh, a particularly rapacious and obnoxious individual, exemplified the reason Laurens and other commoners gradually changed their allegiance to the cause of independence by the end of this decade.[33] Leigh used his position as Justice of the Vice Admiralty Court to seize two of Laurens's ships on false charges that the Navigation Acts had been violated. Leigh then sold the ships for his own profit, thereby angering the thrifty Huguenot. Another act that enraged Laurens was Leigh's rape of Laurens's eighteen-year-old niece who happened also to be Leigh's sister-in-law. Furthermore, Leigh threatened in 1768 to hinder legislation drafted by Commons committees to help the frontiersmen unless his judicial fees were increased. Actions such as Leigh's were some of the reasons for Carolinians' loathing of placemen.[34]

In the years after 1765, the effects of British mercantilistic regulations also concerned Laurens and his contemporaries on legislative committees. A

[32] Hewatt, "Account of South Carolina," pp. 510, 517–18; Wallace, *Henry Laurens,* pp. 116–23; also see the Henry Laurens Letterbooks, South Carolina Historical Society, and "Correspondence of Henry Laurens," *South Carolina Historical and Genealogical Magazine* 28–31 (1927–1930), passim.

[33] Josiah Quincy, Jr., "Journal of Josiah Quincy, Jr., 1773," *Massachusetts Historical Society Proceedings* 49 (1915–1916): 448–49; Wallace, *Henry Laurens,* pp. 89, 103; Dabney and Dargan, *William Henry Drayton,* pp. 11–12, 47–50; Robert M. Calhoon and Robert M. Weir, "The Scandalous History of Sir Egerton Leigh," *William and Mary Quarterly,* 3d ser., 26, no. 1 (1969): 31–46.

[34] Drayton, *Memoirs,* 1:64; Smith, *Royal Province,* p. 140; and Henry Laurens Letterbooks, South Carolina Historical Society. Laurens wrote numerous letters to his son and to his business acquaintances in England, New York, Philadelphia, Georgia, and East Florida about Leigh's actions. He even published a pamphlet describing Leigh's misdeeds which he circulated to all the colonies and Great Britain. Also see Edmund S. Morgan, "The Puritan Ethic and the American Revolution," *William*

reaction against British mercantilism came in 1769 when South Carolinians joined in sympathy with New England colonies and Virginia in a second Association against the Townshend Acts. By the 1770s, many of the South Carolina commoners, like Laurens, had a number of business and personal acquaintances in several provinces. It was little wonder Carolinians felt concern for events in other colonies. A series of royal disallowances of important acts passed in the late 1760s must have disturbed the assemblymen, who had spent many hours in committee meetings drafting the vetoed bills. Some cases in point were the previously mentioned Circuit Court Acts, laws to form new backwoods parishes, and an act to end the importation of new Negro slaves. Laurens and other Commons committee leaders wrote many of these laws, which were drafted either as matters of principle or in response to provincial need.[35]

Thus a governmental deadlock occurred in the late 1760s and 1770s when committee members of the Commons House were faced with an imperial problem much more formidable than their earlier disputes with the local Council and provincial governors. An example of this struggle between Britain and South Carolina was the Wilkes incident. The background of this controversy, which virtually halted government in Charles Town for six years, was unrelated to Carolina problems. John Wilkes was a vituperative British editor who published articles highly critical of King George III in England during the 1760s. Wilkes espoused some of the governmental principles revered by South Carolinians. Articles published by Wilkes in 1763 brought him both notoriety and royal displeasure. He was elected to a number of offices, including membership in the British House of Commons and the post of Lord Mayor of London. However, royal authorities barred him from holding these positions.[36]

Wilkes' cause appealed to people throughout the British Empire, who formed organizations to raise money for his legal defense. In Charles Town, the radicals formed Wilkes clubs, and other citizens formed the Society for the Defense of British and American Liberties. In December, 1769, a majority of elected representatives in Charles Town supported Wilkes' cause by

and Mary Quarterly, 3d ser., 24 (1967): 28–29; Ramsay, *History,* 2:484–86; Wallace, *Henry Laurens,* pp. 137–50; and Calhoon and Weir, "Scandalous History," pp. 31–46.
[35] *Collections of the South Carolina Historical Society,* 2:191–93; JCHA (Jenkins), reel 19, units 1–3 passim; and McCrady, *Royal Government,* pp. 596–622, 644–83.
[36] Greene, *Quest for Power,* pp. 403–14; and McCrady, *Royal Government,* pp. 683–92.

voting £10,000 (currency) for the defense of British and American liberties. This action marked a turning point in colonial legislative history. Indeed, the relatively harmonious relationship between Great Britain and South Carolina was never restored after 1769.[37]

Legislative committees played a vital part in this affair, and the man who appointed these committees was Speaker Peter Manigault, son of Gabriel Manigault, the wealthiest merchant in South Carolina and perhaps in all the Southern colonies. The grandson of a Huguenot immigrant, Peter was reared in a home where the precepts of service to the colony were of first importance. Besides the advantages of wealth and a father who was active in provincial politics, Peter Manigault had the additional benefits of an English education, an advantage greatly admired in the frontier province. He was a graduate of the Inner Temple in London and this legal training enabled him to advance rapidly in South Carolina politics. Indeed, in a matter of a few years he was selected to be Speaker of the Commons House while still in his thirties. He demonstrated his political abilities in this period.

In 1769, Speaker Manigault, a moderate who favored the cause of home rule within the empire, carefully selected a committee of radical and moderate assemblymen to meet on the busy last day of the legislative session. The purpose of this committee was to indicate Commons support of Wilkes. Since the Commons controlled the Provincial Treasurer, it was an easy matter to order the expenditure of funds for any purpose. Without the Council to check their actions, commoners freely voted funds for causes they felt were just. Assemblymen also withheld support from those persons or acts they disliked. In this same era, besides the appropriation for Wilkes, commoners spent £1,000 for the statue of William Pitt, but unpopular Governor Boone had to wait years before he received his salary from the lower house.[38]

Former Commons Speaker William Bull II was then serving one of his five short terms as executive. After he recognized the intent of the December, 1769, Wilkes expenditure, Bull tactfully reported the matter to his superiors in London. The British officials, understandably unhappy, ordered a survey of the activities of the South Carolina Commons House of Assembly by Lieutenant Governor Bull and the British Attorney General. The Board of Trade, after reading the two reports, ordered new measures to prevent any

---

[37] *JCHA* (Jenkins), reel 19, unit 1, p. 215.
[38] Hewatt, "Account of South Carolina," p. 532; Boone to George III, 24 June 1766, *Collections of the South Carolina Historical Society,* 2:195; and Woodmason, *South Carolina Backcountry,* pp. 199, 204, 211.

future recurrence of the Commons' independent actions. Additional royal instructions were sent to place the Provincial Treasurer under control of royal officials and to restore the Council's role in shaping monetary legislation and expenditures.[39]

The remaining six years of colonial history are a study in legislative futility. There was virtually no legislative committee activity, as indicated by the almost total lack of legislation. In fact, from March, 1771, to March, 1775, no laws were passed, and the record in the last two years before the war improved very slightly, with only two laws being passed.[40]

In this troubled period, standing committees were formed at the start of each three-year term or whenever a new house was elected after a dissolution by the governor. The committee members' activities reflected the determination of Speakers Peter Manigault and Rawlins Lowndes to insist upon their "constitution rights." Commons committees also wished to retain the legislative role they had won in previous decades. The busiest legislators served on ad hoc committees that considered and answered governors' messages. Other active committees were those on grievances and correspondence, but there was a notable absence of the five committees dealing with tax matters. Although the committees continued to investigate petitions and public accounts, since the Commons House refused to do any real business, taxes were not passed and creditors were not paid. In fact, seven years passed without the passage of a tax bill.[41]

Only the able Lieutenant Governor William Bull II, even though a staunch loyalist, could persuade commoners to take any constructive action. In 1774, at Bull's urging, the Commons again showed signs of positive action. Members of its committees on governmental finance attacked the problem of seven years of public debts. A large number of assemblymen on the committee on petitions and accounts worked diligently to bring their accounts up to date.[42] Their reports were debated and creditors were granted certificates which they were to keep until the next tax bill passed. The assembly then established a procedure by which a subcommittee of any five of the twenty members on the standing committee of petitions and accounts, together with the Commons clerk, were to act as agents to issue such certificates. This

---

[39] Bull to Hillsborough, 12 and 16 December 1769, PRO records relating to South Carolina, South Carolina Archives, 32:132–36, cited in Greene, *Quest for Power,* pp. 404–6; and *Collections of the South Carolina Historical Society,* 2:195.

[40] *JCHA* (Jenkins), reel 19, units 1–3 passim.

[41] Ibid. The years were 1768–1775.

[42] Ibid., unit 3, pp. 6, 8, 12–13, 15, 37–38, 115, 129–40, 160, 162–63, 184.

granting of certificates was in reality a subterfuge developed by a legislative committee to circumvent the royal prohibition on the use of provincial currency. By an unwritten agreement, these certificates were accepted as money within the province by everyone except the Lieutenant Governor. This practice must have proved embarrassing for the placemen councilors, who were charged to oppose such activities. However, since the political appointees' salaries had not been paid in several years, their empty pocketbooks overcame their duty to the crown.[43]

With one other exception in 1774, the *Journals of the Commons House of Assembly* related the following legislative spectacle.[44] Throughout the 1770s, the normal pattern of behavior at the beginning of a legislative session was for a bare house to form and go through the opening rituals, appoint standing committees, and then receive the governor's opening address. The committee members who were assigned by the Speaker to reply to the message studied the address and then drafted a response to the executive. In the case of Governors Lord Montagu and Lord Campbell, the replies were often less than cordial. Most of the legislative business, which was slight, consisted of committees examining petitions for frontier and internal improvements.[45] Commoners often used the technique of assembling less than the quorum but more than the minimum of seven, thus keeping the house alive but unproductive. In this situation, it will be recalled, the lower chamber would form itself into a committee of the whole house and select a chairman who would replace the Speaker. When such a procedure was used, discussion was not recorded in the *Journal* and consequently the governor and the Council were unable to know what occurred. At such times, the chairman of the committee of the whole house could, if he wished, meet for only a few minutes and then adjourn the grand committee for the remainder of the day.[46]

Occasionally in the 1770s, the Commons House showed signs of its former vigor. One such example was in 1772 when the Commons was ordered to meet at Beaufort, a remote village sixty miles south of the provincial capital, by order of Governor Lord Montagu. On previous occasions the General Assembly had met at Ashley's Corners or Dorchester due to epidemics in Charles Town. Montagu's decision was motivated by a desire

---

[43] Ibid., pp. 163–65; and McCrady, *Royal Government*, p. 728.

[44] *SCG*, 6 September 1773, and 24 October 1774; and *JCHA* (Jenkins), reel 19, units 1–3 passim.

[45] *JCHA* (Jenkins), reel 19, unit 3, pp. 6, 36, 42, 47, 52, 69, 160–65, 181–82, 184, 188–89, 230, 236, 245–49, 286, 291.

[46] Ibid., units 1–3 passim.

to show the assembly the power of royal prerogative and thus put members in "their place." Undoubtedly, the governor felt that moving the commoners from the seedbed of radicalism in Charles Town would make them more cooperative.[47]

The result of this executive maneuver was a surprising show of enthusiasm by the representatives. In fact, when the Commons was convened in Beaufort the largest number of members in years attended. Assemblymen were present during the first few days instead of gradually drifting into the capital as was their usual pattern. After the appointment of standing committees, the first ad hoc committee turned the normally routine task of answering the governor's opening message into a defiant indication of their opinion. The committee members roundly criticized Lord Montagu for calling them to Beaufort. They also took him to task for his activities during the previous session. The commoners then went so far as to ask his reasons for calling the meeting at Beaufort. The relocation of the capital was soon referred for action to members of the committees on privileges and elections and on correspondence. Needless to say, the executive, sensing the futility of this attempt to gain legislative cooperation, quickly terminated the lower house session and called the next meeting for Charles Town.[48]

Governors Montagu, Bull, and Campbell were well aware of the obstructionistic activities of the determined lower chamber. They countered this obstructionism by a series of prorogations or dissolutions. In the 1770s, it was common for a session to last only a few days before the governor would prorogue the meeting, calling for another session to meet a month or so later.[49]

The only legislative continuity came from legislative extrasessionary committees, particularly the committee on correspondence, which met year around. Its previously mentioned duties of corresponding with official agencies and promoting the colony's well-being through its colonial agent, Charles Garth, continued. A new responsibility for the committee began to grow in the last decade of provincial history. This new responsibility was to serve as a channel of communication with other colonies. The Virginia Resolves, Massachusetts Circular Letter, and countless other media of corre-

---

[47] Ibid., unit 2, pp. 4–8 (Montagu to the Commons House of Assembly, 8 October 1772); and see Walsh, *Sons of Liberty*, pp. 30–58, for a discussion of the Mechanics party, the center of the radical party in Charles Town. Also see Carl Bridenbaugh, *Cities in Revolt*, pp. 223–24, 284, 334, 350–52, 418–19, 425.

[48] *JCHA* (Jenkins), reel 19, unit 2, pp. 1–29; *SCG*, 12 November 1772, 14 January, 22 February 1773; and McCrady, *Royal Government*, pp. 693–704.

[49] *JCHA* (Jenkins), reel 19, units 1–3 passim.

spondence describing restriction of home rule, were received by the committee, saved, and later reported to the entire Commons House of Assembly when it met.[50]

As it became more active, the committee on correspondence increased its membership. This gradual enlargement had an important effect on South Carolina politics. This committee's actions in the Gadsden election case (1762 to 1764), the Stamp Act, and the Intolerable Acts, all indicate its power. Since the last three Speakers were all moderate politicians who favored greater self-government within the British Empire, most of their appointments to the committee on correspondence went to fellow low-country assemblymen with similar opinions.[51] During the period from 1765 to 1774, the members of the committee began to oppose crown policies which emphasized greater centralization of royal authority. As time passed, grievances against the British accumulated and many assemblymen on this committee gradually moved to a position of support for radical objectives. It was understandable that the leadership clique of the South Carolina revolutionary movement of 1775 to 1776 should come from this committee's membership.[52]

Because of all these cumulative influences, many South Carolina legislative committeemen gradually began to shift their political position from conservative supporters of the crown to moderate or even radical advocates of greater self-rule. The assemblymen's anti-British sentiment resulted from the growing power of royal authority and the venal and corrupt actions of British placemen who represented the crown in South Carolina. Royal disallowances of the work of South Carolina legislative committees, such as the Circuit Court and Negro Tariff Acts, further incensed the committee members who drafted the legislation to solve important provincial problems.[53] The colony was on the high road to revolution.

[50] Ibid., unit 3, pp. 7, 25, 112, 162, 168, 187–88.
[51] See Appendix II.
[52] *JCHA* (Jenkins), reel 19, unit 3, p. 7; and Hemphill and Wates, *Journals of the Provincial Congresses*, pp. 3–8, 71–73.
[53] Charles Garth Letterbook, South Carolina Archives Department, pp. 50–199.

CHAPTER VIII

Revolutionary Committee Activity, 1774–1776

Revolutionary developments in South Carolina from 1774 to 1776 were closely related to the growth in power of extralegal political organizations. These bodies became powerful largely as a result of the troubled character of the decade. In South Carolina a major cause for political unrest was the John Wilkes impasse, mentioned previously, which had nearly stopped constitutional government within the colony since 1769.[1] With the exception of hastily arranged demonstrations, most of this political activity was organized by nonlegislative leadership committees in Charles Town.

Leaders of these extralegal protest groups were usually members of the Commons House of Assembly who used their governmental experience to give direction to the provincial revolutionary movement.[2] As imperial British leaders began to take a harsher line in coping with disturbances elsewhere in North America, particularly in New England, many respectable South Carolinians became more critical of British policies.[3]

In December, 1773, South Carolinians' concern over British policy shifted from New England to Charles Town Harbor. The problem was the arrival of the ship *London* carrying a load of East Indian tea. The tea ship docked at Charles Town at a time when South Carolinians and their fellow colonists were protesting against the Tea Act taxes.[4] The radicals in South Carolina politics, led by Christopher Gadsden, took advantage of the hostile climate of public opinion toward royal officials. Four days after the *London* arrived, the South Carolina radical leaders called a general meeting of all citizens at the Great Hall of the Exchange Building to discuss the constitutional issues at stake.[5] The number and enthusiasm of the listeners was so great that the supporting timbers of the building began to crack. The principal result of this meeting was the appointment of an extralegal executive committee to secure signatures on a petition to boycott British tea. The second task of the executive committee was to plan for another general meeting in January, 1774, if the crisis had not been resolved.[6] The members of the extralegal executive committee were largely those radicals who were opposed to the present actions of the British government. Some of the men even wished complete independence.[7]

This committee of activists was not the only one at work during the holiday season. Lieutenant Governor Bull called his Board of Councilors to meet and help plan strategy to prevent a Southern version of the Boston Tea Party. The merchants of the Charles Town Chamber of Commerce organized themselves into groups to prevent a general boycott that would harm their businesses.[8] Although these two bodies supported the royal position on taxation, the organization and enthusiasm of the radicals helped the extralegal body to gain its objectives.

The extralegal executive committee appointed by the first protest meeting continued to be very active. It called a second general meeting in Charles Town on December 17, 1773.[9] The committee was able to control this meeting, selecting Christopher Gadsden as the major speaker. Gadsden, who, it will be recalled, was the major figure in a governmental struggle of the 1760s, had become a leader in the radical organizing committee and was an outspoken foe of British parliamentary supremacy and a champion of the

[1] Jack Philip Greene, "Bridge to Revolution: The John Wilkes Fund Controversy in South Carolina, 1769–1775," *Journal of Southern History* 39 (1962): 19–52.

[2] Edward McCrady, *The History of South Carolina under the Royal Government, 1719–1776*, pp. 723, 736–42; also see David Duncan Wallace, *A Chapter of South Carolina History*, pp. 3, 4, 8.

[3] See the microfilm copies of the South Carolina colonial newspapers of the Charleston Library collection, including the *South Carolina Gazette, South Carolina Gazette and Country Journal*, and *South Carolina and American General Gazette*, from 1773 to 1776.

[4] Bull to Earl of Dartmouth, 24 December 1773, quoted in Lawrence Henry Gipson, *The British Empire before the American Revolution*, 12:86; and *SCG*, 6 December 1773.

[5] Agnes Hunt, *The Provincial Committees of Safety and the American Revolution*, p. 130; and *SCG*, 6 December 1773.

[6] Gipson, *British Empire*, 12:218–19.

[7] Hunt, *Provincial Committees of Safety*, p. 130.

[8] *Extracts from the Journals of the Provincial Congresses of South Carolina, 1775–1776*, ed. Hemphill and Wates, pp. xvi–xvii.

[9] *SCG*, 20 December 1773.

cause of greater home rule.[10] At the conclusion of this five-hour meeting, it was resolved that no tea be landed, but no specific steps to enforce this resolution were proposed. The extralegal executive committee was again charged with drawing up an agenda of business to be considered at a third general meeting.[11]

While this series of general meetings was being held, Lieutenant Governor Bull, in the last of his five terms, and his Council tried to seek a compromise solution to the problem of the tea. The councilors knew that, according to British marine law, they must unload the *London* within twenty days. When nineteen days had passed and the possibility of civil strife by armed radicals continued, it was obvious to Bull that the extralegal committee had rallied enough public support to cause a great deal of trouble if the tea was landed and the hated taxes collected. On December 22, 1773, Bull prudently ordered Captain Alexander Curling of the *London* to unload his cargo without paying the tea duty. The extralegal committee had no time to raise objections. Royal customs officials immediately impounded the tea shipment for nonpayment of taxes, storing it in government warehouses until July, 1776.[12] After the cargo was stored, the tea crisis ended in Charles Town.

The effectiveness of the extralegal committee in opposing the Tea Act marked the beginning of increased influence on public affairs by such committees. During January and February, 1774, public interest in the growing strength of the protest committee rose, partly because of news of the Boston Tea Party and the subsequent reaction of the British parliament and George III.[13] Moderate politicians and respectable planters, who previously had viewed the radical leaders of the extralegal committees and general meetings with disdain, now began to join the cause.

Another well-attended general meeting in Charles Town on January 20, 1774, expanded the original extralegal committee to a membership of ninety-nine. Many of these new committee members were well-known country gentlemen and participants in the Commons House of Assembly. The duties of this enlarged group, known as the General Committee, were to recommend to a subsequent general meeting every means necessary "to assert, preserve, and secure the natural and constitutional Rights and Privi-

[10] Richard Walsh, *Charleston's Sons of Liberty,* pp. 26, 31–36, 40, 47–49, 52–53, 62–67.

[11] *SCG,* 20 December 1773.

[12] McCrady, *Royal Government,* pp. 724–27; and William M. Dabney and Marvin Dargan, *William Henry Drayton and the American Revolution,* p. 21.

[13] *SCG,* 24 January 1774; and Gipson, *British Empire,* 12:222.

leges of Britain [*sic*] American Freemen against arbitrary and illegal encroachments."[14]

During the activity of the extralegal committee, the only business of the Commons House, then prorogued until March, 1774, was that conducted by the committee of correspondence.[15] Many of its members, including Speaker Rawlins Lowndes, were either sympathetic or actively supporting the actions of the extralegal General Committee. It was little wonder they did, for the news of British parliament sent by their London agent, Charles Garth, was hardly promising to the cause of greater self-government.[16] The letters received from the other ten provincial committees of correspondence were also filled with criticisms of the new colonial policy of George III.[17]

There were probably several effects of this interlocking membership of key Commons committees and extralegal organizations. One of these was that inside information became available to anti-governmental leadership. In addition, the support given by assembly members provided a stamp of approval to what might otherwise have seemed a rabble-rousing minority effort.

The March, 1774, session of the Commons House of Assembly illustrates the role of Commons members in the opposition to recent royal actions.[18] On March 16, Speaker Lowndes introduced letters collected by the committee on correspondence from other provincial legislatures. This correspondence was filled with the fear of losing colonial constitutional liberties and with criticism of the actions of British authorities. The South Carolina Commons House resolved to have its committee of correspondence send letters to the other colonies supporting American liberties. Concern over problems of taxation, struggles with the Council, and an executive prorogation prevented further action in this session.

This cessation of the Commons in March and a later series of repeated prorogations until August, 1774, deprived South Carolinians of their legal method of expressing their grievances.[19] The attention of the public turned more and more to the nonlegislative General Committee. This committee, although without official sanction, was beginning to act as the colony's de

[14] John Drayton, *Memoirs of the American Revolution*, 1:131–32; Gipson, *British Empire*, 12:218–19; and *SCG*, 24 January, 14 and 21 February, and 7 March 1774.
[15] See the Charles Garth Letterbook, 2 July 1766–27 March 1775, South Carolina Archives, pp. 180–98.
[16] Ibid., pp. 166–92.
[17] *JCHA* (Jenkins), reel 19, unit 3, p. 112.
[18] Ibid., pp. 99–165.
[19] Ibid., pp. 112, 115–78.

facto spokesman for matters concerning provincial-imperial relations. The members of the committee held regular meetings at the Liberty Tree on Isaac Mazyck's estate. Finally, on March 16, the General Committee was given greater authority by a vote of the citizens at a General Meeting; they now could call future meetings and enforce the resolutions made at these meetings.[20] This important step toward vesting executive power in the extralegal committee was based only on the then questionable authority of the will of the people.

News of the British Coercive Acts, Quebec Act, and other anti-colonial developments in London, which reached South Carolinians in June, 1774,[21] resulted in more vigorous activity by extralegal committees. The General Committee called a meeting on July 6, 1774, of 104 elected representatives from all parts of the colony, even including the heretofore overlooked backcountry, to discuss the Boston Port Act. This gathering was chaired by Speaker Rawlins Lowndes and Colonel George Gabriel Powell, a middle-country planter and assemblyman. Forty-two of the forty-eight members of the Commons House were present at this vital gathering.[22] Radical newspaper editor Peter Timothy said, "It was such an example of pure democracy as has rarely been seen since the days of the Ancient city republics."[23]

It must have been quite a meeting, lasting from mid-morning to midnight for three days. Some of the accomplishments of this committee were the proposal of a bill of rights similar to the principles raised earlier in the Gadsden Affair and Stamp Act crisis, and the selection of five delegates to go to the First Continental Congress in Philadelphia in September, 1774. A new General Committee, theoretically representing all geographic sections,[24] was appointed to give direction to the home-rule faction in the colony. It was given practically unlimited power and was to act as the province's unofficial committee of correspondence.[25]

The importance of this committee was particularly great between June, 1774, and July, 1775, when it functioned as a de facto government. In this

[20] *SCG*, 21 March 1774; and Hemphill and Wates, *Journals of the Provincial Congresses*, pp. xiv–xvii.

[21] Drayton, *Memoirs*, 1:126; see South Carolina newspapers for this period, particularly *SCG*, reel 7; and Charles Garth Letterbook, South Carolina Archives, pp. 162–77.

[22] Drayton, *Memoirs*, 1:126; Walsh, *Sons of Liberty*, p. 105; Gipson, *British Empire*, 12:220–22; and McCrady, *Royal Government*, pp. 742–43.

[23] *SCG*, 11 July 1774.

[24] William A. Schaper, "Sectionalism and Representation in South Carolina," *American Historical Association Annual Report*, 1900, 1:357–59.

[25] Drayton, *Memoirs*, 1:125–35.

period the General Committee acted as the center of all activity of those moderates who opposed new British policy and the radicals who desired independence. The new General Committee's first meeting was on June 9, 1774, when they chose Charles Town Assemblyman Charles Pinckney as their president. The committee continued to meet every two weeks thereafter until March, 1776, when royal rule ended.[26]

The election of the General Committee and the First Continental Congress delegates, as well as the passage of resolutions, was an important move toward independence. These actions, lacking official sanction or funds from the constitutionally authorized assembly, were of questionable validity. The assemblymen who served in both the Commons House and General Committee took steps to make both the July resolution and Philadelphia delegation appear less irregular.

By private agreement prior to a routine convening of the Commons House in August, 1774, the representatives assembled much earlier than their regular hour of 9:00 A.M.[27] A message committee of two performed the traditional task of informing the governor that the house was formed. The early-rising Commoners found the elderly chief executive, William Bull II, asleep. They delivered the message that the Commons had assembled "agreeable to His Honour the Lt. Governor's Prorogation" to a prone executive and quickly returned to the lower chamber.

Colonel George Gabriel Powell, the chairman of the General Meeting, reported the work of that gathering to the lower house, particularly the appointment of delegates to the First Continental Congress. Powell then proposed that the Commons House "do resolve to recognize, ratify, and confirm the said appointments . . . and that this House do also resolve a sum not exceeding £1,500 (sterling) to defray the expenses which the said Deputies will be at in said Service." Members immediately resolved to advance the money and approve the work of the July General Meeting. After this rapid but monumental vote, the Commoners were starting to consider the menace of the Creek Indians when Bull, now fully awake, called the lower house to the Council chamber and ended the session by proroguing the Commons until September.[28]

[26] Wallace, *Chapter of South Carolina History*, pp. 6, 7 fn., 8, citing Public Records of South Carolina, 34:177, 188; and *South Carolina and American Gazette*, 1 and 8 July 1774.

[27] Hemphill and Wates, *Journals of the Provincial Congresses*, pp. xvi–xix, xxi–xxiii.

[28] *JCHA* (Jenkins), reel 19, unit 3, pp. 172–73; and Gipson, *British Empire*, 12:222, 223, 224, quoting Bull to Earl of Dartmouth, 3 August 1774.

The actions of the commoners enabled South Carolina delegates to go to the First Continental Congress, where they played a leading part. Their legislative training in the South Carolina committee system had prepared them well. Christopher Gadsden was recognized as one of the leaders in the militant anti-British faction in Philadelphia. Carolinians' skill in committee negotiation was brought to bear in the committees of the First Continental Congress that determined which colonial articles would not be exported to Great Britain. The final report of the members of the committee indicated that South Carolina rice was one of the few American products not banned by the Continental Associations.[29]

While the delegates were meeting in Philadelphia, the stature of the extralegal General Committee continued to grow in Charles Town. On November 9, 1774, the General Committee called for the formation of a new larger organization, the General Provincial Committee, to better represent all parts of the province.[30] This new extralegal body, which first met on January 11, 1775, was later known as the First Provincial Congress.

At this eight-day January meeting of the Provincial Congress, a number of important events occurred. The thorny matter of representation of all sections was improved by enlarging the size of the legislature to 184 and increasing the number of frontier representatives by creating new electoral districts in the backcountry. Delegates were elected to the Second Continental Congress and members of a new General Committee were selected. The Provincial Congress also resolved that it "establish such future Regulations as shall be thought proper."[31]

Between meetings of the first and second South Carolina Provincial Congresses, the ninety-nine-man General Committee continued to guide the cause of home rule in South Carolina. As these developments occurred in Charles Town, a network of extralegal committees was formed in villages, parishes, and hamlets across the province. There were local committees on correspondence, on observation and inspection, on enforcement, and on safety to implement the resolutions of the Continental and Provincial Congresses. Members of these extralegal bodies circulated the Continental Association petitions. Petitioners pledged not to use or import British prod-

[29] Francis W. Ryan, Jr., "The Role of South Carolina in the First Continental Congress," *South Carolina Historical Magazine* 60 (1959): 151–52.

[30] *SCG*, 21 November 1774.

[31] Hemphill and Wates, *Journals of the Provincial Congresses*, pp. xviii–xix, 1–40; Edward McCrady, *The History of South Carolina in the Revolution*, pp. 38–41; and Hunt, *Provincial Committees of Safety*, pp. 131–32.

ucts and promised to support the Provincial Congress. Loyalists who refused to sign were either reported to the General Committee or disciplined by local committees.[32]

As the power of revolutionary committees grew, royal officials tried unsuccessfully to halt this rebellious activity. Lieutenant Governor William Bull II was well aware of the growing spirit of revolution. As early as August, 1774, he wrote the Earl of Dartmouth that the colony's resident leaders were conducting with "perseverance, secrecy, and unanimity" designs that were at cross purposes "with royal rule."[33] Bull could do little to win the support of the legislature to halt the course of anti-governmental activity. His position was weakened by the fact that he was a "lame-duck" executive, waiting to be replaced by Lord William Campbell. The undermanned Upper House was so discredited that it could not provide an acceptable solution to the problem of disloyalty.[34] Members of the lower house, although courteous in deference to Bull's past services, opposed his actions to negate the power of the Provincial Congress. Their action was natural, because all but four of the commoners were leaders in the extralegal legislature.[35]

An example of the problems Bull faced occurred in April, 1775. South Carolinians learned from their colonial agent that large numbers of British troops were being dispatched to America.[36] The General Committee and the Provincial Congress authorized a five-man secret committee of those bodies to seize governmental arms from provincial armories and the State House. On the night of April 21, an undisguised "secret" group, led by Lieutenant Governor Bull's nephew, William Henry Drayton, and many assemblymen,

[32] Drayton, *Memoirs,* 1:162, 182–87, 221, 231; Bull to Earl of Dartmouth, 3 August 1774, and 19 December 1774, PRO records relating to South Carolina, South Carolina Archives, 34:188–89, quoted in Hemphill and Wates, *Journals of the Provincial Congresses,* pp. xv, xviii–xix; Walsh, *Sons of Liberty,* pp. 65–75; Dabney and Dargan, *William Henry Drayton,* pp. 66–77; and Lelia Sellers, *Charleston Business on the Eve of the American Revolution,* pp. 212, 228.

[33] 3 August and 19 December 1774 (see note 32 above); Drayton, *Memoirs,* 1:176–80; and McCrady, *Royal Government,* pp. 772–73.

[34] William Henry Drayton, "A Letter of a Freeman of South Carolina to the Deputies of North America Assembled in the High Court of Congress at Philadelphia," p. 18, quoted in Dabney and Dargan, *William Henry Drayton,* pp. 4, 37–49.

[35] McCrady, *Royal Government,* pp. 771–73; and Hemphill and Wates, *Journals of the Provincial Congresses,* pp. xxii–xxiii.

[36] Charles Garth Letterbook, South Carolina Archives Department, 27 January, 7 and 18 February 1775, pp. 184–92.

took 800 guns, 200 cutlasses, 1,600 pounds of powder, and some minor stores.[37]

When the Lieutenant Governor learned of the raid, he interrogated State House employees, but they refused to testify against the commoners who paid their salaries. On April 25, Bull reported the theft of munitions to the lower house and asked it to investigate. Speaker Rawlins Lowndes referred Bull's request to the Commons "committee to view the public arms," directing the committee members to report their findings the next day.[38]

The following morning the committee, which included some of the armory raiders, solemnly reported:

That with all the enquiry your Committee have made, they are not able to obtain any certain Intelligence relative to the removal of the public arms and Government powder as mentioned in His Honour's Message, but thinks there is reason to suppose that some of the Inhabitants of this colony may have been induced to take so extraordinary and uncommon a step in consequence of the late alarming accounts from Great Britain.

After receiving this message, Bull again prorogued the Commons House until June, 1775.[39]

On learning in May of the battles of Lexington and Concord, the nonlegislative General Committee, acting in its executive capacity, called the first Provincial Congress for a June meeting. At this gathering, a new and more aggressive revolutionary policy was developed which included the creation of a new provincial army. The Provincial Congress recognized that the ninety-nine-man General Committee was too large to act as an effective executive for the home-rule cause. A new executive committee, the thirteen-man Council of Safety, was then created to make day-to-day decisions and to control the armed forces. The General Committee was retained to make important decisions between sessions of the Provincial Congress.[40]

Although the exact division of responsibility between the General Committee and Council of Safety was unclear, this system of wartime executive committee leadership worked reasonably well. The members of the Council of Safety worked particularly hard. Judging from the memoirs of William

[37] Drayton, *Memoirs,* 1:221–25; and Dabney and Dargan, *William Henry Drayton,* pp. 72–74.

[38] *JCHA* (Jenkins), reel 19, unit 3, pp. 272–73.

[39] Ibid., pp. 279, 288.

[40] "Papers of the First Council of Safety," ed. Alexander Samuel Salley, *South Carolina Historical and Genealogical Magazine* 1 (1900): 41–42.

Henry Drayton, one of its active members, and from correspondence written by its president, Henry Laurens, they sometimes toiled for fourteen or even eighteen hours a day.[41] Subcommittees of this group even authenticated all the new provincial currency.[42] The Council of Safety was deeply concerned with problems of frontier defense and Indian diplomacy, fearing that Indians might be loyal to the British. Members personally investigated the training and deployment of their newly recruited troops. Others on the Council of Safety struggled with the problems of military personnel and logistics, as well as raising volunteers to their cause in the upcountry.[43]

As is sometimes the case in committees, a split developed in the Council of Safety over the result of its efforts. Particularly in the first Council (June–November, 1775), there was a sizeable faction of moderates headed by Charles Pinckney. These men favored bold steps that would cause the mother country to allow South Carolina to achieve greater self-rule within the British Empire. The more radical group, headed by Drayton, favored a complete separation. As a result, the actions of the first Council of Safety were more tentative than were those of the second council. This latter group, formed in November, 1775, acted with the determination to defend the colony against external British invasion and to smother loyalist sympathy within.[44]

In the months between November, 1775, and March 10, 1776, the Second Provincial Congress was the ultimate authority in the province. In fact, after Governor Lord Campbell dissolved the last Commons House of Assembly in August, 1775, there was no other form of representative government.[45] The Provincial Congress grew so bold that it physically took over the colony's State House.[46] The governor and other royal officials were

[41] Drayton, *Memoirs*, 1:200–213; "Journal of the Council of Safety," *Collections of the South Carolina Historical Society*, 2:22–65; Dabney and Dargan, *William Henry Drayton*, pp. 76–79; David Duncan Wallace, *The Life of Henry Laurens*, pp. 204–31; "Papers of the [First and Second] Councils of Safety," *South Carolina Historical and Genealogical Magazine* 1 (1900): 290–93; 2 (1901): 101.

[42] South Carolina Provincial Currency and Script, South Caroliniana Library, #1723.

[43] "Journal of the Council of Safety," *Collections of the South Carolina Historical Society*, 2:23, 26, 30, 37–39, 52; also see James H. O'Donnel, "A Loyalist View of the Drayton-Tennent-Hart Mission to the Upcountry," *South Carolina Historical Magazine* 67 (1966): 15–29.

[44] Hunt, *Committees of Safety*, pp. 153–54.

[45] *JCHA* (Jenkins), reel 19, unit 3, p. 314; and Hemphill and Wates, *Journals of the Provincial Congresses*, pp. vii, xix–xx.

[46] Hemphill and Wates, *Journals of the Provincial Congresses*, p. 34.

virtually prisoners, since they were observed around the clock. Even their mail was read by extralegal committees.[47]

The internal proceedings of both of the Provincial Congresses were printed by newspaper publisher Peter Timothy, a former assemblyman serving as the province's congressional secretary. According to his *Journals,* the methods of committee procedure of the older Commons House of Assembly were used.[48] Although the increased size of the new legislature caused committees to be larger, an examination of assignments shows that the old pattern of frontier discrimination and dominance of important committees by tidewater aristocrats remained. The concentration of committee assignments can be seen in the fact that, of the 269 delegates who served in both Provincial Congresses, only 127 occupied the 487 positions on recorded committees.

This evidence suggests that, as in the case of most assemblies, a comparatively small nucleus of active participants was responsible for the legislature's actions. Of the 127 congressional leaders, 60 percent had served as members of either the Council or the lower house. The value of their previous parliamentary training in committees of the General Assembly is clear.[49]

The legislative committees appointed by the Provincial Congresses were chiefly ad hoc committees devoted to provincial defense. There were over seventy-five different committees at work in the two congresses. Many of them were carryovers from the Commons, such as those on public accounts or the state of the province. Others, such as committees on the revolutionary militia and secret committees, reflected the different character of the revolutionary society in which they worked.[50]

The greatest testimonial to the competency of these legislative committees is the fact that they realized their objectives. In these months, the province withstood loyalist attacks on the frontier and a British invasion menace on the coast. Although faced with these problems of survival, committees charged with drafting a new constitution modified the older British form of

---

[47] "Papers of the First Council of Safety," *South Carolina Historical and Genealogical Magazine* 1 (1900): 63–65, 292–93, 299–300; Dabney and Dargan, *William Henry Drayton,* pp. 78–79, 83–84, 86–88, 107, 109–10, and Committee of Intelligence to John Stuart, 21 June 1775, PRO CO 5/76, cited on p. 121; Walsh, *Sons of Liberty,* pp. 70–72.

[48] Hemphill and Wates, *Journals of the Provincial Congresses,* pp. xxvi–xxvii, xxix–xxx.

[49] Ibid., pp. xxi–xxiii.

[50] Ibid., passim.

government into a new framework.[51] The Provincial Congress adopted the new South Carolina state constitution on March 26, 1776, marking the fulfillment of the ideal of self-government which had been growing ever since South Carolina's first revolution of 1719.[52]

The contributions of the South Carolina committee system to America's historical development are important. The most obvious of these were the men trained in the Commons House of Assembly who became national political leaders. One such leader was Henry Laurens, presiding officer of the wartime Continental Congress and a commissioner at the Peace of Paris in 1783.[53] South Carolina's delegation to the Constitutional Convention, including Charles Pinckney, Charles Cotesworth Pinckney, and John Rutledge, played an important part in the Convention's committee deliberations in Philadelphia. In fact, Charles Pinckney's preliminary draft of a constitution anticipated thirty-one of the final provisions of the federal Constitution of 1787. During the Federalist period General Charles Cotesworth Pinckney became well known as a diplomat and later candidate for President of the United States. John Rutledge used his training in the legislative committees of the Commons House in federal posts, serving as a leader of the United States House of Representatives and as a Supreme Court Justice.[54]

Perhaps an overlooked contribution of the South Carolina colonial committee system was the example it gave the new nation. South Carolina politicians, along with leaders from Virginia and Pennsylvania, brought their knowledge of the use of standing committees to the nation's capital. Partly as a result of their work, by the 1820s this institution had become a regular part of the legislative practice of the House of Representatives. New generations of pioneers from South Carolina and other Eastern states spread the concept of legislative committees to Western states and territories. One

[51] Hunt, *Provincial Committees of Safety,* pp. 151–52, 156–57, 168–71.

[52] Reverend Oliver Hart Diary, South Caroliniana Library, p. 135; and Hemphill and Wates, *Journals of the Provincial Congresses,* p. xviii.

[53] See Wallace, *Henry Laurens,* for the only major biography of Laurens.

[54] David Duncan Wallace, *South Carolina: A Short History, 1520–1948,* pp. 252, 272–74, 338–39, 338 fn., cites C. G. Singer, *South Carolina in the Confederation* (Philadelphia, 1941), pp. 162–63, 166–67; Clinton Rossiter, *1789: The Grand Convention,* pp. 132, 161–62, 171, 187–89, 200–227, 249–50, 253; Richard Barry, *Mr. Rutledge of South Carolina,* passim; Forest McDonald, *E Pluribus Unum: The Formation of the American Republic, 1776–1796,* pp. 119, 129, 155, 159, 161, 164–65, 172–73, 176–78, 180–81, 184, 232; and Marvin Ralph Zahniser, "The Public Career of Charles Cotesworth Pinckney" (Ph.D. dissertation, University of California, Santa Barbara, 1963), passim.

hundred years after the close of the Revolutionary War, legislative commit-tees were used from the Atlantic to Pacific Oceans and remain important instruments of federal, state, and local governments today.[55]

[55] George Galloway, *History of the House of Representatives,* pp. 1–2, 8–9, 11–13, 40–41, 51, 55, 58–62, 75–86, 94–96, 109, 115–16, 128, 130–31, 191, 208–21; Lord James Bryce, *The American Commonwealth* 1:154–63; Charles L. Clapp, *The Congressman: His Work as He Sees It,* pp. 183–279; Woodrow Wilson, *Congressional Government: A Study in American Politics,* passim. Also see the following works devoted to the role of modern legislative committees: Gladys Marie Kammerer, *The Staffing of the Committees of Congress;* William E. Rhode, *Committee Clearance of Administrative Decisions;* Clinton Ivan Winslow, *State Legislative Committees: A Study in Procedure;* and William F. Buckley, Jr., *The Committee and Its Critics: A Calm Review of the House Committee on Un-Ameri-can Activities.*

Committee Assignments and Memberships in the South Carolina Commons House of Assembly under the Revolutionary Government, 1720–1721

Governor: James Moore, Jr.

Tables 1 and 2 illustrate the chief interests, activities, and leadership of the South Carolina Commons House of Assembly during the revolutionary period. The data are drawn from the microfilm of "Records of the States of the United States, South Carolina Records, Journal of the Commons House of Assembly," William Sumner Jenkins, editor. The only copy available is the "foul copy," that is, the rough draft made by the clerk of the Commons House. The record is thus fragmentary and difficult to read. The committees listed here probably represent a significant amount of the committee activity. Other committees may have met but are not mentioned in the records.

Most of the committees were special ad hoc bodies. A large number of joint committees with the Council also met in these months. There was only one standing committee. Since the assemblymen were elected at Charles Town from the city as a whole, not as representatives of election precincts, it is impossible to determine the parish of residence.

In these tables and those of Appendixes II and III, no mention is made of committee chairmanships. Incomplete data and inconsistent methods of recording committee information often make it difficult to know who the chairmen were. Often the first assemblyman listed among the committee's membership was the chairman and usually the chairman presented the report to the legislature. Unfortunately in many cases the first man listed did not give the report and in such cases it is impossible to determine accurately who the chairman was.

The following symbols apply throughout appendixes: [1] Died during the session. [2] Standing or sessionary committee. [3] Parish of residence uncertain or cannot be determined. * Dates following the names indicate term of office. † Numbers in parentheses indicate number of times a member served on that committee, if more than one.

TABLE I

Committee Assignments of the South Carolina Commons House of Assembly, 1720–1721

MEMBER[3]	ASSIGNMENTS	TOTAL MEMBERSHIPS (*in brackets*)

Allen, Andrew [5]
 Tax bill; answer governor's message; conference with governor and Council; examine bank commissioners' accounts; grand jury selection.

Cattell, William[1] [0]

Drake, Jonathan [7]
 Joint conference on settling poor immigrants; petitions and accounts; state of Indian trading store; examine bank commissioners' accounts; revise laws expired or near expiring; powder receiver's accounts; fortify Charles Town by taxing owners of male Negro slaves.

Dry, William [7]
 Conference with governor and Council; grand jury selection; revise laws expired or near expiring; joint committee to plan for Governor Nicholson's arrival; petitions and accounts (2nd committee); on Col. Rhett's allegations; joint committee to petition the king and Lord Carteret.

Elliott, William [0]

Emms, Ralph [0]

Fenwick, John [11]
 Committee of the whole house; example pilots' petition; courts of justice; joint conference on settling poor immigrants; petitions and accounts; to regulate taverns and public places; conference with governor and Council; state of Indian trading store; on Col. Rhett's allegations; petitions and accounts (2nd committee); fortify Charles Town by taxing owners of male Negro slaves.

Gendron, William [3]
 Conference with governor and Council; grand jury selection; revise laws expired or near expiring.

Hall, Arthur [4]
 Joint conference for settling poor immigrants; to regulate taverns and public places; conference with governor and Council; fortify Charles Town by taxing owners of male Negro slaves.

Hamilton, Paul [1]
 Tax bill.

Harris, Richard [1]
 Conference with governor and Council.

Hepworth, Thomas [2]
 Speaker. Examine bank commissioners' accounts; grand jury selection.

Hext, Hugh [o]

Huger, Daniel [4]
    Conference with governor and Council; examine bank commissioners' accounts; revise laws expired or near expiring; petitions and accounts (2nd committee).

Izard, Walter, Sr. [6]
    To regulate taverns and public places; conference with governor and Council; examine bank commissioners' accounts; ways and means for fortification and watch in Charles Town; powder receiver's accounts; view the public arms.

Johnson, Peter [o]

Jones, Samuel [1]
    Tax bill.

Logan, George [10]
    Draft a schedule; courts of justice; joint conference on settling poor immigrants; petitions and accounts; to regulate taverns and public places; conference with governor and Council; ways and means for fortification and watch in Charles Town; joint conference to plan for Governor Nicholson's arrival; fortify Charles Town by taxing owners of male Negro slaves; joint committee to petition the king and Lord Carteret.

Lynch, Thomas, Sr. [5]
    To regulate taverns and public places; conference with governor and Council; state of Indian trading store; examine bank commissioners' accounts; accounts of commissioners of rice trade.

Middleton, Arthur [10]
    Courts of justice; answer governor's message; joint conference on settling poor immigrants; to regulate taverns and other public places; conference with governor and Council; ways and means for fortification and watch in Charles Town; joint committee to plan for Governor Nicholson's arrival; on Col. Rhett's allegations; fortify Charles Town by taxing owners of male Negro slaves; joint committee to petition the king and Lord Carteret.

Moore, Roger [5]
    Address His Majesty on Chief Justice Trott; conference with governor and Council; revise laws expired or near expiring; powder receiver's accounts; on Col. Rhett's allegations.

Ouldfield, John [2]
    Tax bill; accounts of commissioners of rice trade.

Raven, John [1]
    Accounts of commissioners of rice trade.

Seabrook, Joseph [o]

Skene, Alexander [12]
    Answer governor's message; joint conference on settling poor immigrants; petitions and accounts; to regulate taverns and public places; conference with governor and Council; ways and means for fortification and watch in Charles Town; powder receiver's accounts; joint committee to plan for Governor Nicholson's arrival; on Col. Rhett's allegations; view the public

arms; fortify Charles Town by taxing owners of male Negro slaves; joint committee to petition the king and Lord Carteret.

Smith, George [4]

Examine commissioners of Fort Johnson; revise laws expired or near expiring; view the public arms; petitions and accounts (2nd committee).

Smith, Richard [1]

Conference with governor and Council.

Stanyarne, John [0]

Waring, Benjamin, Jr. [2]

Tax bill; accounts of commissioners of rice trade.

Wilkinson, William [1]

Conference with governor and Council.

Wilkinson, Christopher [4]

Joint conference on settling poor immigrants; petitions and accounts; examine bank commissioners' accounts; fortify Charles Town by taxing owners of male Negro slaves.

TABLE 2

Committee Memberships of the South Carolina Commons House of Assembly, 1720–1721

Draft a Schedule
George Logan
Examine Pilots' Petition
John Fenwick
Address His Majesty on Chief Justice Trott
Roger Moore
Courts of Justice
John Fenwick, George Logan, Arthur Middleton
Tax Bill
Andrew Allen, Paul Hamilton, Samuel Jones, John Ouldfield, Benjamin Waring
Answer Governor's Message
Andrew Allen, Arthur Middleton, Alexander Skene
Joint Conference on Settling Poor Immigrants
Jonathan Drake, John Fenwick, Arthur Hall, George Logan, Arthur Middleton, Alexander Skene, Christopher Wilkinson
Petitions and Accounts (First Committee)
Jonathan Drake, John Fenwick, George Logan, Alexander Skene, Christopher Wilkinson
Draft a Bill to Regulate Taverns and Public Places
John Fenwick, Arthur Hall, Walter Izard, George Logan, Thomas Lynch, Arthur Middleton, Alexander Skene

Appendix I

Examine Commissioners of Fort Johnson
George Smith
Grand Jury Selection
Andrew Allen, William Dry, William Gendron, Thomas Hepworth
Conference Committees with Governor and Council (no subject mentioned)
Andrew Allen, William Dry, John Fenwick, William Gendron, Arthur Hall, Richard Harris, Daniel Huger, Walter Izard, George Logan, Thomas Lynch, Arthur Middleton, Roger Moore, Alexander Skene, Richard Smith, William Wilkinson
State of the Indian Trading Store
Jonathan Drake, John Fenwick, Thomas Lynch
Examine Bank Commissioners' Accounts
Andrew Allen, Jonathan Drake, Thomas Hepworth, Daniel Huger, Walter Izard, Thomas Lynch, Christopher Wilkinson
Revise Laws Expired or Near Expiring
Jonathan Drake, William Dry, William Gendron, Daniel Huger, Roger Moore, George Smith
Ways and Means for Fortification and Watch in Charles Town
Walter Izard, George Logan, Arthur Middleton, Alexander Skene
Powder Receiver's Accounts
Jonathan Drake, Walter Izard, Roger Moore, Alexander Skene
Accounts of the Commissioners of the Rice Trade
Thomas Lynch, John Ouldfield, John Raven, Benjamin Waring
Joint Committee to Plan for Governor Nicholson's Arrival
William Dry, George Logan, Arthur Middleton, Alexander Skene
On Colonel Rhett's Allegations
William Dry, John Fenwick, Arthur Middleton, Roger Moore, Alexander Skene
View the Public Arms
Walter Izard, Alexander Skene, George Smith
Petitions and Accounts (Second Committee)
William Dry, John Fenwick, Daniel Huger, George Smith
Fortify Charles Town by Taxing the Owners of Male Negro Slaves
Jonathan Drake, John Fenwick, Arthur Hall, George Logan, Arthur Middleton, Alexander Skene, Christopher Wilkinson
Joint Committee to Petition the King and Lord Carteret
William Dry, George Logan, Arthur Middleton, Alexander Skene

Committee Assignments and Memberships in the South Carolina Commons House of Assembly during Selected Segments of the Royal Period, 1721–1776

The following tables illustrate several aspects of committee activity in the South Carolina Commons House during the royal period. Detailed study of the membership of the various committees shows who occupied positions of leadership on important committees and the geographical distribution of political power. For example, Colonel Charles Pinckney was a representative of Charles Town's St. Philip's and nearby Christ Church parishes for nearly a decade. Over the years he gave Charlestonians and inhabitants of the tidewater more than adequate representation on committees dealing with financial matters, military policy, and other legislation. In certain standing committees dealing with financial matters there is clear evidence of tidewater dominance. However, the fact that by 1770 both eastern and western parishes were represented on standing committees, such as those on petitions and accounts, the armory, and Indian affairs, shows that sectional rivalry was in some cases placated.

I selected these four segments of the royal period to present a representative sample of the types of legislative committees employed by the Commons House. They include periods of peace and war, of prosperity and economic depression (1721–1725), of relative political tranquility and political turmoil (1765 and 1772–1775). Committee assignments are presented for every decade of the royal period, except the 1730s, which are presented in Appendix III.

Because so many ad hoc committees functioned in the legislature during this period, they are grouped into general classifications, such as internal improvements, Charles Town, and others.

My sources of information were several editions of the *Journals of the Commons House of Assembly*. For the 1720s, I used the manuscript volumes in the South Carolina Archives Department; the microfilm edition, edited by William Sumner Jenkins, in Records of the States of the United States, South Carolina Records; and the edition published by the South Carolina Historical Commission and edited by Alexander S. Salley. For 1749–1750, my source was the edition published by the South Carolina Archives and edited by James Harrold Easterby and others. In the 1765 committee chart, I used the Salley edition. The final segment, 1772–1775, is based on the Jenkins edition. For further information, see my bibliography.

TABLE 3

Legislative Committee Assignments, by Parish,
of the South Carolina Commons House of Assembly, 1721–1725
Governor: Sir Francis Nicholson

TOTAL
MEMBERSHIPS
(*in brackets*)

Christ Church Parish

Bond, Jacob, 1725*   [3]
 Petitions and accounts; privileges and elections; provincial poor and immigration.
Fenwick, Robert,[3] 1721–1724   [18]
 1721: Joint conference committee (3)†; to draft bills; special standing; wills, courts, and justice; militia and town watch. *1722:* Joint conference; miscellaneous ad hoc (3). *1723:* Paper currency and legal tender; miscellaneous ad hoc (2). *1724:* Reply to governor and Council; wills, courts, and justice (2); miscellaneous ad hoc.
Lynch, Thomas, Sr.,[3] 1721–1724   [35]
 1721: Joint conference (3); reply to governor and Council; treasurer's accounts; militia and town watch; Indian trade; miscellaneous ad hoc. *1722:* Joint conference (2); to draft bills (2); reply to governor and Council; petitions and accounts; armory/fortifications; address the king or important royal officials; investigations; paper currency and legal tender; churches and religious matters; miscellaneous ad hoc (6). *1723:* On the estimate; petitions and accounts; address the king or important royal officials; trade, agriculture, and industry; miscellaneous ad hoc (3). *1724:* Paper currency and legal tender; to draft bills; miscellaneous ad hoc.

Prince George Winyaw Parish

Mairant, James Nicholas,[3] 1721–1724   [0]
Wilkinson, Christopher,[3] 1721–1724   [2]
 1722: Miscellaneous ad hoc. *1724:* Miscellaneous ad hoc.
Woodward, John,[3] 1721–1725   [16]
 1721: Special standing; miscellaneous ad hoc. *1722:* Indian affairs; armory/fortifications (2); churches and religious matters. *1723:* Indian affairs; powder receiver's accounts; armory/fortifications; paper currency and legal

tender. *1724:* Miscellaneous ad hoc (4). *1725:* Indian affairs; militia and town watch.

St. Andrew's Parish

Bellinger, Edmund,[3] 1721–1724 [8]
    1721: Powder receiver's accounts; internal improvements; miscellaneous ad hoc. *1722:* Petitions and accounts. *1723:* On the estimate; petitions and accounts. *1724:* Powder receiver's accounts; investigations.
Cattell, William Peter, 1721–1725 [8]
    1722: Provincial poor and immigration; internal improvements. *1724:* Indian affairs. *1725:* Indian affairs; churches, religious matters (2); paper currency and legal tender; on Charles Town.
Smith, George, 1721–1725 [38]
    1721: Joint conference (2); to draft bills (3); petitions and accounts; internal improvements; miscellaneous ad hoc (2). *1722:* Correspondence; joint conference (4); treasurer's accounts (2); petitions and accounts; address the king or important royal officials; provincial poor and immigration (2); paper currency and legal tender (2); churches, religious matters; miscellaneous ad hoc. *1723:* Indian affairs; joint conference; treasurer's accounts; powder receiver's accounts; acts expired or near expiring; Indian trade; miscellaneous ad hoc. *1724:* Indian affairs (2); joint conference; to draft bills; petitions and accounts; paper currency and legal tender; internal improvements.

St. Bartholomew's Parish

Bayly, Peter, 1725 [1]
    Indian affairs.
Blakeway, William,[1,3] 1721–1722 [26]
    1721: Joint conference (3); reply to governor and Council (2); petitions and accounts; special standing; address the king and important royal officials; wills, courts, and justice (2); militia and town watch; Indian trade; miscellaneous ad hoc (3). *1722:* Correspondence; joint conference; reply to governor and Council; petitions and accounts; address the king or important royal officials; internal improvements; churches, religious matters; tax bill (2); miscellaneous ad hoc (2).
Hall, Arthur,[3] 1725. (St. Paul's 1721–1724[3]) [11]
    1722: On Charles Town. *1723:* Miscellaneous ad hoc (2). *1724:* Indian affairs; investigations; internal improvements; miscellaneous ad hoc. *1725:* Joint conference (3); powder receiver's accounts.
Johnson, John, 1721–1723 [0]
Nichols, Henry, 1721–1725 [9]
    1722: To draft bills. *1723:* Miscellaneous ad hoc. *1724:* Indian affairs; reply to governor and Council. *1725:* Joint conference (2); armory/fortifications; privileges and elections; Charles Town (Charles City).

Sanders, William, 1724–1725 [2]
    1725: Indian affairs; on Charles Town.
Seabrook, Joseph, 1722–1725 [1]
    1723: Miscellaneous ad hoc.
Tradd, Robert,[3] 1722–1724 [1]
    1722: Treasurer's accounts.

St. George Parish, Dorchester

Izard, Walter, Sr., 1721–1725 [33]
    1721: Petitions and accounts; miscellaneous ad hoc (2). *1722:* Indian affairs; joint conference (3); to draft bills (2); petitions and accounts; armory/fortifications; address the king or important royal officials; churches, religious matters (3); miscellaneous ad hoc (3). *1723:* Treasurer's accounts; on the estimate; wills, courts, and justice; paper currency and legal tender; Indian trade; miscellaneous ad hoc (2). *1724:* wills, courts, and justice; paper currency and legal tender; churches, religious matters; miscellaneous ad hoc. *1725:* Indian affairs (2); wills, courts, and justice; churches, religious matters.
Smith, Richard,[3] 1721–1724, 1725 [13]
    1721: Churches, religious matters; on Charles Town; miscellaneous ad hoc. *1722:* To draft bills (2); reply to governor and Council; armory/fortifications; provincial poor and immigration (2); miscellaneous ad hoc. *1723:* Trade, agriculture, and industry; miscellaneous ad hoc. *1725:* Indian affairs.
Waring, Benjamin, Jr., 1721–1724 [23]
    1721: Special standing; internal improvements; militia and town watch. *1722:* Joint conference; to draft bills; armory/fortifications; provincial poor and immigration; wills, courts, and justice; internal improvements (3); churches, religious matters; miscellaneous ad hoc (3). *1723:* Joint conference; armory/fortifications; wills, courts, and justice; paper currency and legal tender; miscellaneous ad hoc (3). *1724:* Indian affairs; wills, courts, and justice.
Waring, Thomas, 1725 [1]
    Indian affairs.

St. Helena's Parish

Barnwell, John,[3] 1721–1724 [43]
    1722: Committee of the whole house (2); Indian affairs; correspondence (3); joint conference; to draft bills; reply to governor and Council (2); armory/fortifications; address the king or important royal officials; investigations; paper currency and legal tender (4); churches, religious matters; on Charles Town; miscellaneous ad hoc (8). *1723:* Indian affairs (2); reply to governor and Council; on the estimate; address the king or important royal officials; paper currency and legal tender (2); on Charles Town; tax bill; miscellaneous ad hoc (2). *1724:* Indian affairs; joint conference; to draft bills; paper currency and legal tender; miscellaneous ad hoc.

Greene, Daniel, 1725 [0]

Hepworth, Thomas,[3] 1721–1725. (Represented St. Paul's Parish, 1721– 1724.) [27]

> *1721:* Petitions and accounts; special standing; wills, courts, and justice (2). *1722:* To draft bills (3); reply to governor and Council; treasurer's accounts; petitions and accounts (2); privileges and elections; wills, courts, and justice; paper currency and legal tender; churches, religious matters. *1723:* Indian affairs (2); correspondence; joint conference; treasurer's accounts; miscellaneous ad hoc. *1724:* Speaker. *1725:* Indian affairs; petitions and accounts; privileges and elections; wills, courts, and justice; on the state of the province; miscellaneous ad hoc.

Heyward, Thomas, 1725 [2]

> Armory/fortifications; militia and town watch.

Whitaker, Benjamin, 1722–1725 [42]

> *1722:* Reply to governor and Council (3); investigations; paper currency and legal tender; miscellaneous ad hoc (2). *1723:* Correspondence; joint conference; reply to governor and Council (3); on the estimate; investigations; paper currency and legal tender (2); acts expired or near expiring; miscellaneous ad hoc (3). *1724:* Indian affairs; to draft bills (2); reply to governor and Council (4); wills, courts, and justice (2); miscellaneous ad hoc (3). *1725:* Indian affairs (2); reply to governor and Council (2); privileges and elections; investigations; wills, courts, and justice; paper currency and legal tender; on the state of the province; acts expired or near expiring.

St. James' Parish, Goose Creek

Adams, William, 1724–1725 [1]

> *1724:* Indian affairs.

Chicken, George, 1721–1725 [30]

> *1721:* Petitions and accounts; militia and town watch; miscellaneous ad hoc (2). *1722:* Indian affairs (2); correspondence; treasurer's accounts; petitions and accounts; armory/fortifications; address the king or important royal officials; miscellaneous ad hoc (4). *1723:* Indian affairs; on the estimate; petitions and accounts; armory/fortifications; address the king or important royal officials; wills, courts, and justice; miscellaneous ad hoc (3). *1724:* Miscellaneous ad hoc. *1725:* Indian affairs (3); to draft bills; petitions and accounts.

Dry, William, 1725 [9]

> Indian affairs (2); correspondence; joint conference; petitions and accounts; wills, courts, and justice; paper currency and legal tender; on the state of the province; on Charles Town.

Fitch, Tobias, 1725 [1]

> Powder receiver's accounts.

Herbert, John, 1725 [4]

> Indian affairs; churches, religious matters; on Charles Town; miscellaneous ad hoc.

Moore, James, Jr., 1721–1724   [1]
     1721–1724: Speaker. *1724:* Indian affairs.
Moore, Roger,[3] 1721–1724 (Represented St. James' Parish, Santee, 1725.)   [11]
     1721: Petitions and accounts; militia and town watch. *1722:* Reply to
     governor and Council; armory/fortifications; privileges and elections; paper
     currency and legal tender. *1723:* Miscellaneous ad hoc (2). *1724:* Indian
     affairs; internal improvements; paper currency and legal tender.
Smith, Thomas, 1721–1724   [32]
     1721: Correspondence; treasurer's accounts; on Charles Town; Indian trade;
     miscellaneous ad hoc (3). *1722:* Joint conference; to draft bills (2);
     armory/fortifications (2); paper currency and legal tender; churches, re-
     ligious matters. *1723:* Indian affairs; joint conference; on the estimate;
     paper currency and legal tender; Indian trade; miscellaneous ad hoc (7).
     1724: Indian affairs; to draft bills; powder receiver's accounts; internal im-
     provements; churches, religious matters; miscellaneous ad hoc.

St. James' Parish, Santee

Broughton, Nathaniel, 1725   [1]
     Petitions and accounts.

St. John's Parish, Berkeley

Butler, Hugh, 1725   [0]
Drake, Jonathan, 1724   [7]
     Joint conference; powder receiver's accounts; privileges and elections; in-
     vestigations; internal improvements; miscellaneous ad hoc (2).
Pawley, Percival,[3] 1721–1723   [33]
     1721: Internal improvements; militia and town watch; miscellaneous ad
     hoc. *1722:* Indian affairs (2); correspondence; joint conference (2); to
     draft bills; armory/fortifications; address the king or important royal offi-
     cials (2); provincial poor and immigrants; paper currency and legal
     tender (3); internal improvements; churches, religious matters (2); acts
     expired or near expiring; on Charles Town; miscellaneous ad hoc (7).
     1723: Indian affairs; joint conference; address the king or important royal
     officials; miscellaneous ad hoc (2).
Waties, William,[3] 1721–1724   [9]
     1721: Internal improvements; miscellaneous ad hoc. *1723:* Indian affairs
     (2); joint conference; paper currency and legal tender; on Charles Town.
     1724: Wills, courts, and justice; miscellaneous ad hoc.

St. John's Parish, Colleton

Beresford, Richard,[3] 1721–1722   [14]
     1721: Correspondence; joint conference (2); to draft bills; reply to gover-
     nor and Council; petitions and accounts; wills, courts, and justice. *1722:*

Indian affairs; treasurer's accounts; armory/fortifications; provincial poor and immigration; internal improvements; miscellaneous ad hoc (2).

Borton, Thomas,[3] 1725   [0]

Wilkinson, William,[3] 1721–1724   [7]
1721: Joint conference. *1723:* Indian affairs; joint conference; paper currency and legal tender; acts expired or near expiring; miscellaneous ad hoc. *1724:* Petitions and accounts.

St. Paul's Parish

Chamberlain, Job, 1725   [0]

Eve, Abraham,[3] 1721–1723   [3]
1721: Miscellaneous ad hoc. *1722:* Armory/fortifications; privileges and elections.

Fenwick, John, 1721–1725   [60]
1721: Correspondence joint conference; reply to governor and Council (2); special standing; tax bill; militia and town watch; Indian trade; miscellaneous ad hoc (4). *1722:* Indian affairs; joint conference (3); to draft bills (3); petitions and accounts; armory/fortifications; investigations; provincial poor and immigration (2); paper currency and legal tender (4); churches, religious matters (3); miscellaneous ad hoc (5). *1723:* Indian affairs (3); joint conference (2); to draft bills; address the king or important royal officials; miscellaneous ad hoc (3). *1724:* Joint conference. *1725:* Indian affairs (2); correspondence; joint conference (2); petitions and accounts; investigations; provincial poor and immigration; on the state of the province; paper currency and legal tender (3); miscellaneous ad hoc (2).

Raven, John, 1721–1725   [4]
1721: Miscellaneous ad hoc. *1722:* Miscellaneous ad hoc. *1724:* Indian affairs. *1725:* Powder receiver's accounts.

St. Philip's Parish, Charles Town

Allein, Richard,[3] 1721–1724   [30]
1721: Joint conference (3); reply to governor and Council; treasurer's accounts; address the king or important royal officials (2); wills, courts, and justice (2); tax bill; militia and town watch; miscellaneous ad hoc. *1722:* Joint conference (2); to draft bills (2); reply to governor and Council; address the king or important royal officials; internal improvements; miscellaneous ad hoc. *1723:* To draft bills; reply to governor and Council; treasurer's accounts; on the estimate; miscellaneous ad hoc. *1724:* Reply to governor and Council (2); paper currency and legal tender (2); internal improvements.

Allen, Eleazer, 1725   [9]
Correspondence; reply to governor and Council (2); wills, courts and justice; provincial poor and immigration; paper currency and legal tender; on the state of the province; miscellaneous ad hoc (2).

Allen, Samuel, 1725 [o]
Ashby, John,[3] 1724–1725 [o]
Eveleigh, Samuel, Sr., 1725 [3]
   Paper currency and legal tender (2); miscellaneous ad hoc.
Hill, Charles,[3] 1721–1724 [33]
   1721: To draft bills; treasurer's accounts; miscellaneous ad hoc (2). *1722:*
   Joint conference; to draft bills (3); reply to governor and Council; petitions and accounts; internal improvements; churches, and religious matters
   (2); acts expired or near expiring; miscellaneous ad hoc (2). *1723:* Indian affairs; correspondence; joint conference (2); to draft bills; treasurer's
   accounts; on the estimate; armory/fortifications; miscellaneous ad hoc (3).
   1724: Reply to governor and Council; churches and religious matters; on
   Charles Town; miscellaneous ad hoc (3).
Huger, Daniel,[3] 1721–1724 [13]
   1721: Powder receiver's accounts. *1722:* Petitions and accounts; armory/
   fortifications; churches, religious matters. *1723:* On the estimate; miscellaneous ad hoc. *1724:* Indian affairs; joint conference; paper currency
   and legal tender; internal improvements (2); miscellaneous ad hoc (2).
Hume, Robert, 1725 [6]
   Indian affairs; powder receiver's accounts; armory/fortifications; churches,
   religious matters; acts expired or near expiring; on Charles Town.
Lloyd, John, I, 1721–1725 [44]
   1721: Correspondence; joint conference (5); to draft bills (2); reply to
   governor and Council (3); special standing; address the king or important
   royal officials; wills, courts, and justice (2); tax bill; miscellaneous ad hoc.
   1722: Miscellaneous ad hoc (3). *1723:* Indian affairs (2); correspondence
   (3); joint conference; petitions and accounts; armory/fortifications; wills,
   courts, and justice; trade, agriculture, and industry; miscellaneous ad hoc
   (2). *1724:* Reply to governor and Council (2); committee of the whole
   house; wills, courts, and justice (2); paper currency and legal tender;
   on Charles Town. *1725:* Investigations (2); paper currency and legal tender
   (2); miscellaneous ad hoc.
Parker, John,[3] 1723–1725 [4]
   1723: Acts expired or near expiring. *1724:* Petitions and accounts. *1725:*
   Armory/fortifications; on Charles Town.
Rhett, William, Jr., 1725 [6]
   Indian affairs; joint conference; petitions and accounts; paper currency and
   legal tender (2); miscellaneous ad hoc.
Wragg, Joseph, 1722–1724 [20]
   1722: To draft bills; treasurer's accounts; petitions and accounts (2). *1723:*
   Correspondence; treasurer's accounts (2); on the estimate; petitions and
   accounts; miscellaneous ad hoc (3). *1724:* Reply to governor and Council
   (2); treasurer's accounts; Charles Town (Charles City); paper currency
   and legal tender; miscellaneous ad hoc (3).
Yeomans, William, 1724 [1]
   Miscellaneous ad hoc.

St. Thomas and St. Dennis Parish

Atkin, James, 1725 [o]

Broughton, Thomas, 1725 [1]
    Speaker. (Also a member of the Council.) Paper currency and legal tender.

Darby, Michael, 1721–1723 [6]
    1722: Petitions and accounts; armory/fortifications; miscellaneous ad hoc.
    1723: Powder receiver's accounts; Petitions and accounts; acts expired or
    near expiring.

Simmons, Peter, 1722–1724 [11]
    1722: Paper currency and legal tender; miscellaneous ad hoc (3). *1723:*
    Powder receiver's accounts; acts expired or near expiring; Indian trade;
    miscellaneous ad hoc. *1724:* Reply to governor and Council; miscellaneous
    ad hoc (2).

No parish affiliation could be found for the following members of the Commons House who were elected in 1721 before the use of the parish system:

Allen, Andrew,[3] 1721–1724 [22]
    1721: Treasurer's accounts; miscellaneous ad hoc. *1722:* To draft bills (2);
    armory/fortifications; petitions and accounts; paper currency and legal
    tender; internal improvements (2); churches, religious matters; mis-
    cellaneous ad hoc (2). *1723:* Indian affairs (2); on the estimate (2); peti-
    tions and accounts; paper currency and legal tender; miscellaneous ad hoc
    (2). *1724:* Internal improvements; miscellaneous ad hoc.

Bull, John,[3] 1721–1724 [o]

Capers, Richard,[3] 1721–1724 [o]

Eveleigh, Charles, 1722 [1]
    1722: Petitions and accounts.

Jackson, John,[3] 1721–1724 [2]
    1722: Indian affairs; miscellaneous ad hoc.

Wilkins, John,[3] 1721–1724 [1]
    1724: Miscellaneous ad hoc.

TABLE 4

Legislative Committee Memberships
of the South Carolina Commons House of Assembly, 1721–1725
Governor: Sir Francis Nicholson

Indian Affairs[2]
    1722: John Woodward, John Jackson, Walter Izard, John Barnwell, George
    Chicken, Percival Pawley, Richard Beresford, John Fenwick.
    1723: John Woodward, Andrew Allen, George Smith, John Barnwell,

Thomas Hepworth, George Chicken, William Waties, Percival Pawley, William Wilkinson, John Fenwick, Charles Hill, John Lloyd, Thomas Smith.

1724: William Peter Cattell, George Smith, Arthur Hall, Henry Nichols, Benjamin Waring, Jr., John Barnwell, Benjamin Whitaker, William Adams, James Moore, Jr., Roger Moore, Thomas Smith, John Raven, Daniel Huger.

1725: John Woodward, William Peter Cattell, Peter Bayly, William Sanders, Walter Izard, Richard Smith, Thomas Waring, Thomas Hepworth, Benjamin Whitaker, George Chicken, William Dry, John Herbert, John Fenwick, Robert Hume, William Rhett, Jr.

Correspondence[2]

1721: Thomas Smith, Richard Beresford, John Fenwick, John Lloyd.

1722: George Smith, William Blakeway, John Barnwell, George Chicken, Percival Pawley.

1723: Thomas Hepworth, Benjamin Whitaker, Charles Hill, John Lloyd, Joseph Wragg.

1725: William Dry, John Fenwick, Eleazer Allen.

Joint Conference Committees with the Council

1721: Robert Fenwick, Thomas Lynch, Sr., George Smith, William Blakeway, Richard Beresford, William Wilkinson, John Fenwick, Richard Allein, John Lloyd.

1722: Robert Fenwick, Thomas Lynch, Sr., George Smith, William Blakeway, Walter Izard, Benjamin Waring, Jr., John Barnwell, Thomas Smith, Percival Pawley, John Fenwick, Richard Allein, Charles Hill.

1723: George Smith, Benjamin Waring, Jr., Thomas Hepworth, Benjamin Whitaker, William Waties, Thomas Smith, Percival Pawley, William Wilkinson, John Fenwick, John Lloyd, Charles Hill.

1724: George Smith, John Barnwell, Jonathan Drake, John Fenwick, Daniel Huger.

1725: Arthur Hall, Henry Nichols, William Dry, John Fenwick, William Rhett, Jr.

To Draft Bills (various committees)

1721: Robert Fenwick, Richard Beresford, Charles Hill, John Lloyd, George Smith.

1722: Thomas Lynch, Sr., Henry Nichols, Walter Izard, Richard Smith, Benjamin Waring, Jr., Thomas Hepworth, John Barnwell, Thomas Smith, Percival Pawley, John Fenwick, Richard Allein, Charles Hill, Joseph Wragg, Andrew Allen.

1723: John Fenwick, Richard Allein, Charles Hill.

1724: Thomas Lynch, Sr., John Barnwell, Benjamin Whitaker, Thomas Smith, George Smith.

1725: George Chicken.

Reply to or Consider a Message from the Governor or the Council.

1721: John Lloyd, John Fenwick, Richard Allein, Richard Beresford, William Blakeway, Thomas Lynch, Sr.

1722: Charles Hill, Roger Moore, John Barnwell, Benjamin Whitaker, Richard Smith, William Blakeway, Thomas Lynch, Sr., Thomas Hepworth, Richard Allein.

1723: Richard Allein, John Barnwell, Benjamin Whitaker.

1724: Peter Simmons, Charles Hill, Joseph Wragg, John Lloyd, Richard Allein, Benjamin Whitaker, Henry Nichols, Robert Fenwick.

1725: Eleazer Allen, Benjamin Whitaker.

Treasurer's Accounts[2]

1721: Andrew Allen, Charles Hill, Richard Allein, Thomas Smith, Thomas Lynch, Sr.

1722: Joseph Wragg, Richard Beresford, George Chicken, Thomas Hepworth, Robert Tradd, George Smith.

1723: Charles Hill, Joseph Wragg, Richard Allein, Thomas Hepworth, Walter Izard, George Smith.

1724: Joseph Wragg.

Powder Receiver's Accounts[2]

1721: Daniel Huger, Edmund Bellinger.

1723: Michael Darby, Peter Simmons, George Smith, John Woodward.

1724: Jonathan Drake, Thomas Smith, Edmund Bellinger.

1725: Robert Hume, John Raven, Tobias Fitch, Arthur Hall.

On the Estimate (of governmental expenses)[2]

1723: Andrew Allen, Charles Hill, Daniel Huger, Joseph Wragg, Richard Allein, Thomas Smith, John Barnwell, Benjamin Whitaker, George Chicken, Walter Izard, Edmund Bellinger, Thomas Lynch, Sr.

On the Armory and To View Fortifications[2] (sometimes separate committees)

1722: Andrew Allen, Thomas Lynch, Sr., John Woodward, Walter Izard, Richard Smith, Benjamin Waring, Jr., George Chicken, John Barnwell, Roger Moore, Thomas Smith, Percival Pawley, Richard Beresford, Abraham Eve, John Fenwick, Daniel Huger, Michael Darby.

1723: John Woodward, Benjamin Waring, Jr., George Chicken, Charles Hill, John Lloyd.

1725: Henry Nichols, Thomas Heyward, Robert Hume, John Parker.

Special Standing Committee[2]

1721: Robert Fenwick, John Woodward, William Blakeway, Benjamin Waring, Jr., Thomas Hepworth, John Fenwick, John Lloyd.

Petitions and Accounts[2]

1721: George Smith, William Blakeway, Walter Izard, Thomas Hepworth, William Dry, Roger Moore, Richard Beresford, George Chicken.

1722: Thomas Lynch, Sr., Edmund Bellinger, George Smith, William Blakeway, Walter Izard, Thomas Hepworth, William Dry, John Fenwick, Charles Eveleigh, Daniel Huger, Joseph Wragg, Michael Darby, Andrew Allen, George Chicken, Charles Hill.

1723: Thomas Lynch, Sr., Edmund Bellinger, John Lloyd, Joseph Wragg, Michael Darby, Andrew Allen, George Chicken.

1724: George Smith, William Wilkinson, John Parker.

1725: Jacob Bond, Thomas Hepworth, William Dry, Nathaniel Broughton, John Fenwick, William Rhett, Jr., William Dry, George Chicken.

Address His Royal Majesty, Former Proprietors, or Important Royal Officials
1721: William Blakeway, Richard Allein, John Lloyd.
1722: Thomas Lynch, Sr., George Smith, William Blakeway, John Barnwell, Percival Pawley, Richard Allein, George Chicken, Walter Izard.
1723: Thomas Lynch, Sr., John Barnwell, Percival Pawley, John Fenwick, George Chicken.

Investigations
1722: Thomas Lynch, Sr., John Barnwell, Benjamin Whitaker, John Fenwick.
1723: Benjamin Whitaker.
1724: Edmund Bellinger, Arthur Hall, Thomas Hepworth, Jonathan Drake.
1725: Benjamin Whitaker, John Fenwick, John Lloyd.

Privileges and Elections[2]
1722: Abraham Eve, Roger Moore, Thomas Hepworth.
1724: Jonathan Drake.
1725: Thomas Hepworth, Benjamin Whitaker, Henry Nichols, Jacob Bond.

Wills, Courts, and Justice (various committees)
1721: John Lloyd, Richard Allein, Richard Beresford, Thomas Hepworth, William Blakeway, Robert Fenwick.
1722: Thomas Hepworth, Benjamin Waring, Jr.
1723: John Lloyd, George Chicken, Walter Izard, Benjamin Waring.
1724: John Lloyd, William Waties, Benjamin Whitaker, Walter Izard, Benjamin Waring, Jr., Robert Fenwick.
1725: Eleazer Allen, Thomas Hepworth, Benjamin Whitaker, William Dry, Walter Izard.

Provincial Poor and Immigration (various committees)
1722: John Fenwick, Percival Pawley, Richard Beresford, Richard Smith, Benjamin Waring, Jr., William Peter Cattell, George Smith.
1725: John Fenwick, Eleazer Allen, Jacob Bond.

Trade, Agriculture, and Industry (various committees)
1723: Thomas Lynch, Sr., Richard Smith, John Lloyd.

Paper Currency and Legal Tender (various committees)
1722: Thomas Lynch, Sr., George Smith, John Barnwell, Thomas Hepworth, Benjamin Whitaker, Roger Moore, Thomas Smith, Percival Pawley, John Fenwick, Peter Simmons, Andrew Allen.
1723: Robert Fenwick, Christopher Wilkinson, Walter Izard, Benjamin Waring, Jr., John Barnwell, Benjamin Whitaker, Thomas Smith, William Waties, William Wilkinson, John Woodward, Andrew Allen.
1724: Thomas Lynch, Sr., George Smith, Walter Izard, John Barnwell, Roger Moore, Richard Allein, Daniel Huger, John Lloyd, Joseph Wragg.
1725: William Peter Cattell, Benjamin Whitaker, William Dry, John Fenwick, Eleazer Allen, Samuel Eveleigh, Sr., John Lloyd, William Rhett, Jr., Thomas Broughton.

Internal Improvements (various committees)
> *1721:* Percival Pawley, William Waties, Benjamin Waring, Jr., Edmund Bellinger, George Smith.
> *1722:* Charles Hill, Richard Allein, Percival Pawley, Richard Beresford, Benjamin Waring, Jr., William Peter Cattell, William Blakeway, Andrew Allen.
> *1724:* Daniel Huger, Richard Allein, Jonathan Drake, Roger Moore, Thomas Smith, George Smith, Arthur Hall, Andrew Allen.

On the State of the Province
> *1725:* William Dry, Benjamin Whitaker, Thomas Hepworth, John Fenwick, Eleazer Allen.

Churches and Religious Matters (various committees, some ad hoc, others standing)
> *1721:* Richard Smith.
> *1722:* Thomas Lynch, Sr., George Smith, William Blakeway, Walter Izard, Benjamin Waring, Jr., John Barnwell, Thomas Hepworth, Thomas Smith, Percival Pawley, John Fenwick, Charles Hill, Daniel Huger, John Woodward, Andrew Allen.
> *1724:* Walter Izard, Thomas Smith, Charles Hill.
> *1725:* William Peter Cattell, Walter Izard, John Herbert, Robert Hume.

Indian Trade
> *1721:* Thomas Lynch, Sr., William Blakeway, Thomas Smith, John Fenwick.
> *1723:* George Smith, Walter Izard, Thomas Smith, Peter Simmons.

On Acts Expired or Near Expiring[2]
> *1722:* Charles Hill, Percival Pawley.
> *1723:* Michael Darby, John Parker, William Wilkinson, Benjamin Whitaker, George Smith, Peter Simmons.
> *1725:* Robert Hume, Benjamin Whitaker.

On Charles Town (various committees, including those on Charles City)
> *1721:* Thomas Smith, Richard Smith.
> *1722:* Percival Pawley, Arthur Hall, John Barnwell.
> *1723:* John Barnwell, William Waties.
> *1724:* Charles Hall, John Lloyd, Joseph Wragg.
> *1725:* Robert Hume, John Parker, John Herbert, William Sanders, William Dry, William Peter Cattell, Henry Nichols.

Militia/Town Watch (various committees)
> *1721:* Percival Pawley, Roger Moore, Robert Fenwick, Thomas Lynch, Sr., William Blakeway, Benjamin Waring, Jr., George Chicken, John Fenwick, Richard Allein.
> *1725:* John Woodward, Thomas Heyward.

Miscellaneous Ad Hoc Committees
> *1721:* Richard Smith, William Blakeway, Charles Hill, John Lloyd, Abraham Eve, John Fenwick, John Raven, Richard Allein, Percival Pawley, Thomas Smith, William Waties, George Chicken, Walter Izard, Ed-

mund Bellinger, George Smith, Thomas Lynch, Sr., John Woodward, Andrew Allen.

1722: Richard Smith, Michael Darby, Charles Hill, John Lloyd, John Fenwick, John Raven, Richard Allein, Percival Pawley, Richard Beresford, John Barnwell, Benjamin Whitaker, George Chicken, Walter Izard, Benjamin Waring, Jr., George Smith, William Blakeway, Robert Fenwick, Thomas Lynch, Sr., Christopher Wilkinson, Peter Simmons, Andrew Allen, John Jackson.

1723: Richard Smith, Charles Hill, Daniel Huger, John Lloyd, Joseph Wragg, John Fenwick, Richard Allein, Percival Pawley, William Wilkinson, Roger Moore, Thomas Smith, John Barnwell, Benjamin Whitaker, George Chicken, Henry Nichols, Joseph Seabrook, Walter Izard, Benjamin Waring, Jr., George Smith, Arthur Hall, Robert Finwick, Thomas Lynch, Sr., Thomas Hepworth, Peter Simmons, Andrew Allen.

1724: Andrew Allen, John Wilkins, William Yoemans, Charles Hill, David Huger, Joseph Wragg, Thomas Smith, John Barnwell, Benjamin Whitaker, George Chicken, Walter Izard, Arthur Hall, Robert Fenwick, Thomas Lynch, Sr., Christopher Wilkinson, John Woodward, Jonathan Drake, William Waties, Peter Simmons.

1725: Samuel Eveleigh, Sr., William Rhett, Jr., John Fenwick, Eleazer Allen, John Herbert, Thomas Hepworth, John Lloyd.

On the Tax Bill

1721: John Lloyd, John Fenwick, Richard Allein.

1722: William Blakeway.

1723: John Barnwell.

TABLE 5

Legislative Committee Assignments, by Parish,
of the South Carolina Commons House of Assembly,
1749–1750
Governor: James Glen

	TOTAL MEMBERSHIPS (*in brackets*)

Christ Church Parish

Rutledge, Andrew, 1749–1750*   [11]
   1749: Speaker; Indian affairs; correspondence; joint conference; to draft bills (3)†; reply/consider governor/Council messages (2); Indian presents; address the king or important royal officials; Negro and slave matters.
   1750: Speaker.

Rutledge, John, 1749–1750 [29]
 1749: Indian affairs; to draft bills (3); reply/consider governor/Council messages (5); Indian presents; provincial poor and immigration; paper currency and legal tender; on trade; on Charles Town; Negro and slave matters (2); commissary's accounts; miscellaneous ad hoc (2). *1750:* Joint conference; to draft bills; reply/consider governor/Council messages (3); provincial poor and immigration; townships; internal improvements; on Charles Town; miscellaneous ad hoc.

Prince Frederick Parish

Mazyck, Isaac, 1749–1750 [26]
 1749: Correspondence; joint conference; reply/consider governor/Council messages (2); provincial poor and immigration (2); paper currency and legal tender; on religion; miscellaneous ad hoc (3). *1750:* To draft bills (4); petitions and accounts; courts of justice; on Charles Town (3); miscellaneous ad hoc (6).

Prince George Winyaw Parish

Foissin, Elias, 1750 [o]
Ouldfield, John, 1749–1750 [15]
 1749: Indian affairs; to draft bills; reply/consider governor/Council messages; Indian presents; appointments of local/provincial officials; provincial poor and immigration (2); public accounts; burning old bills of credit. *1750:* To draft bills (2); treasurer's accounts; petitions and accounts; miscellaneous ad hoc (2).

Prince William Parish

Bull, William, II, 1749 [o]
 Speaker.

St. Andrew's Parish

Bellinger, George, 1749–1750 [7]
 1749: Powder receiver's accounts; public accounts. *1750:* Petitions and accounts; internal improvements (2); on religion; miscellaneous ad hoc.
Cattell, Charles, 1749–1750 [8]
 1749: To draft bills; privileges and elections; tax bill; laws expired or near expiring; commissary's accounts. *1750:* Internal improvements; on religion; miscellaneous ad hoc.
Drayton, Thomas, 1749–1750 [9]
 1749: Reply/consider governor/Council messages; miscellaneous ad hoc. *1750:* Reply/consider governor/Council messages (2); provincial poor and immigration; internal improvements (2); on religion; miscellaneous ad hoc.

St. Bartholomew's Parish

Austin, George, 1749–1750 [38]
    1749: Indian affairs; correspondence; joint conference (2); to draft bills (4); reply/consider governor/Council messages (4); on the estimate; Indian presents; address the king or important royal officials; provincial poor and immigration (2); paper currency and legal tender; on trade; on Charles Town; Indian trade; Negro and slave matters (2); miscellaneous ad hoc (3). *1750:* To draft bills (2); reply/consider governor/Council messages; courts of justice; townships; on Charles Town (2); miscellaneous ad hoc (5).

Bond, Jacob, 1749–1750 [0]

Brisbane, William, 1749–1750 [8]
    1749: On Charles Town; Negro and slave matters; burning old bills of credit. *1750:* To draft bills (2); powder receiver's accounts; internal improvements; miscellaneous ad hoc.

Godin, Isaac, 1750 [0]

St. George Parish, Dorchester

Graeme, James, 1749–1750 [29]
    1749: Indian affairs; correspondence; joint conference; to draft bills (8); reply/consider governor/Council messages (4); address the king or important royal officials; courts of justice; provincial poor and immigration (2); paper currency and legal tender; internal improvements; on Charles Town(2); Indian trade. *1750:* Reply/consider governor/Council messages (4); on Charles Town.

Smith, Benjamin, 1749–1750 [29]
    1749: To draft bills (5); reply/consider governor/Council messages (4); treasurer's accounts; powder receiver's accounts; Indian presents; provincial poor and immigration (2); paper currency and legal tender; internal improvements (2); on religion; on Charles Town (2). *1750:* To draft bills; reply/consider governor/Council messages (5); on religion (2); on Charles Town.

St. Helena's Parish

Glen, Thomas, 1749–1750 [12]
    1749: Committee of the whole house; armory/fortifications; Negro and slave matters. *1750:* To draft bills (2); reply/consider governor/Council message; petitions and accounts; provincial poor and immigration; townships; internal improvements; tax bill; miscellaneous ad hoc.

Irving, James, 1749–1750 [26]
    1749: Indian affairs; correspondence; to draft bills (2); reply/consider governor/Council messages (2); on the estimate; tax bill; Indian presents; address the king or important royal officials; Negro and slave matters; miscellaneous ad hoc (2). *1750:* To draft bills (4); reply/consider governor/

Council messages; townships; internal improvements; on Charles Town (3); commissary's accounts; miscellaneous ad hoc (2).

Lloyd, John, 1749–1750 [9]
>*1749:* Reply/consider governor/Council messages; privileges and elections; provincial poor and immigration; tax bill; miscellaneous ad hoc. *1750:* To draft bills; treasurer's accounts; on Charles Town; miscellaneous ad hoc.

St. James' Parish, Goose Creek

Allen, William, 1749 [7]
>*1749:* To draft bills; powder receiver's accounts; appointments of local/ provincial officials; privileges and elections; on Charles Town; miscellaneous ad hoc (2).

Gough, Richard, 1750 [0]

Singleton, Richard, 1749–1750 [21]
>*1749:* To draft bills; reply/consider governor/Council messages (5); on the estimate; petitions and accounts; grievances; on religion. *1750:* To draft bills (6); joint conference; reply/consider governor/Council messages (2); petitions and accounts; miscellaneous ad hoc.

Taylor, Peter, 1749–1750 [21]
>*1749:* Indian affairs; reply/consider governor/Council messages; armory/ fortifications; Indian presents; address the king or important royal officials; appointments of local/provincial officials; privileges and elections; provincial poor and immigration; townships; laws expired or near expiring; Negro and slave matters; miscellaneous ad hoc (3). *1750:* Courts of justice; internal improvements; on Charles Town; miscellaneous ad hoc (4).

Villepontoux, Zacharias, 1749–1750 [3]
>*1749:* Provincial poor and immigration; on religion; Negro and slave matters.

St. James' Parish, Santee

Gaillard, Tacitus, 1749–1750 [2]
>*1749:* Internal improvements; funds in the treasury.

Mayrant, John, 1749–1750 [4]
>*1749:* Internal improvements; funds in the treasury; miscellaneous ad hoc. *1750:* Petitions and accounts.

St. John's Parish, Berkeley

Cordes, John, 1749–1750 [3]
>*1749:* Courts of justice; public accounts. *1750:* Petitions and accounts.

Maxwell, James, 1749–1750 [4]
>*1749:* Indian affairs; Indian presents; on trade. *1750:* Miscellaneous ad hoc.

Ward, John, 1749–1750 [0]

St. John's Parish, Colleton

Boone, William, Sr., 1749–1750   [9]
  1749: To draft bills; reply/consider governor/Council messages; on the estimate; armory/fortifications; courts of justice; Negro and slave matters; miscellaneous ad hoc. *1750:* Miscellaneous ad hoc. (2).

Lloyd, Thomas, 1749–1750   [4]
  1749: Treasurer's accounts; armory/fortifications; privileges and elections; burning of old bills of credit.

Mathews, Anthony, 1749–1750   [16]
  1749: Indian affairs; to draft bills (2); reply/consider governor/Council messages (2); treasurer's accounts; armory/fortifications; Indian presents; Negro and slave matters; miscellaneous ad hoc (2). *1750:* To draft bills; internal improvements; miscellaneous ad hoc (3).

St. Paul's Parish

Crawford, David, 1749–1750   [2]
  1749: Petitions and accounts. *1750:* Petitions and accounts.

Lowndes, Rawlins, 1749–1750   [0]

Sacheverell, Thomas, 1749–1750   [8]
  1749: Joint conference (2); to draft bills; reply/consider governor/Council messages; treasurer's accounts; courts of justice; commissary's accounts; miscellaneous ad hoc.

St. Peter's Parish

Dale, Thomas, 1749–1750   [24]
  1749: Indian affairs; joint conference; to draft bills (2); reply/consider governor/Council messages; powder receiver's accounts; address the king or important royal officials; courts of justice; provincial poor and immigration; laws expired or near expiring; on Charles Town; Negro and slave matters (2); miscellaneous ad hoc (4). *1750:* To draft bills (3); on Charles Town; miscellaneous ad hoc (3).

St. Philip's Parish, Charles Town

Dart, John, 1749–1750   [28]
  1749: Indian affairs; correspondence; to draft bills (4); reply/consider governor/Council messages (2); on the estimate; grievances; Indian presents; address the king or important royal officials; paper currency and legal tender; on trade; tax bill; on Charles Town (2); Indian trade; Negro and slave matters; miscellaneous ad hoc (7). *1750:* To draft bills; on Charles Town.

Deas, David, 1749–1750   [14]
  1749: Indian affairs; correspondence; reply/consider governor/Council messages; Indian presents; provincial poor and immigration; paper currency and legal tender; miscellaneous ad hoc. *1750:* To draft bills; treasurer's accounts; petitions and accounts; on trade; on Charles Town; miscellaneous ad hoc (2).

Hext, David, 1749–1750 [27]
    1749: to draft bills (3); joint conference; grievances; on religion; on Charles Town (2); Indian trade; miscellaneous ad hoc (5). *1750:* To draft bills (3); provincial poor and immigration; tax bill; on Charles Town (2); miscellaneous ad hoc (6).

Prioleau, Samuel, 1749–1750 [10]
    1749: To draft bills; provincial poor and immigration; laws expired or near expiring; on Charles Town. *1750:* To draft bills; treasurer's accounts; internal improvements (3); miscellaneous ad hoc.

Roche, Jordan, 1749–1750 [23]
    1749: Indian affairs; correspondence; to draft bills (2); reply/consider governor/Council messages (2); on the estimate; Indian presents; privileges and elections; provincial poor and immigration (2); paper currency and legal tender; on Charles Town; Indian trade; miscellaneous ad hoc (4). *1750:* To draft bills (2); on Charles Town (2); miscellaneous ad hoc.

St. Thomas and St. Dennis Parish

Beresford, Richard, 1749–1750 [4]
    1749: Laws expired or near expiring; burning old bills of credit. *1750:* Petitions and accounts; miscellaneous ad hoc.

Gray, Henry, 1749–1750 [3]
    1749: Reply/consider governor/Council messages; commissary's accounts; miscellaneous ad hoc.

Miller, Stephen, Jr., 1749–1750 [3]
    1749: Powder receiver's accounts; tax bill; miscellaneous ad hoc.

TABLE 6

Legislative Committee Memberships of the South Carolina
Commons House of Assembly,
1749–1750
Governor: James Glen

Indian Presents
    1749: John Dart, David Deas, Jordan Roche, James Maxwell, Anthony Mathews, James Irving, Peter Taylor, George Austin, Benjamin Smith, Andrew Rutledge, John Rutledge, John Ouldfield.

Indian Affairs[2]
    1749: Thomas Dale, John Dart, David Deas, Jordan Roche, James Maxwell, Anthony Mathews, James Irving, Peter Taylor, George Austin, James Graeme, Andrew Rutledge, John Rutledge, John Ouldfield.

Address the King or Important Royal Officials
    1749: Thomas Dale, John Dart, James Irving, Peter Taylor, George Austin, James Graeme, Andrew Rutledge.

Joint Conference Committees with the Council
   1749: Thomas Dale, David Hext, George Austin, James Graeme, Andrew Rutledge, Isaac Mazyck, Thomas Sacheverell.
   1750: Richard Singleton, John Rutledge.
On Trade[2]
   1749: John Dart, James Maxwell, George Austin, John Rutledge.
   1750: David Deas.
Paper Currency and Legal Tender (various committees)
   1749: John Rutledge, Isaac Mazyck, George Austin, James Graeme, Benjamin Smith, John Dart, David Deas, Jordan Roche.
Internal Improvements (various committees)
   1749: Tacitus Gaillard, John Mayrant, James Graeme, Benjamin Smith.
   1750: Samuel Prioleau, Anthony Mathews, Thomas Glen, James Irving, Peter Taylor, George Bellinger, George Cattell, Thomas Drayton, William Brisbane, John Rutledge.
Townships
   1749: Peter Taylor.
   1750: John Rutledge, George Austin, Thomas Glen, James Irving.
Public Accounts[2]
   1749: John Ouldfield, George Bellinger, John Cordes.
On Charles Town (various committees)
   1749: Thomas Dale, John Dart, David Hext, Samuel Prioleau, Jordan Roche, William Allen, George Austin, William Brisbane, James Graeme, Benjamin Smith, John Rutledge.
   1750: Thomas Dale, John Dart, David Deas, David Hext, Jordan Roche, James Irving, John Lloyd, Peter Taylor, George Austin, James Graeme, Benjamin Smith, Isaac Mazyck, John Rutledge.
Indian Trade[2]
   1749: George Austin, James Graeme, John Dart, David Hext, Jordan Roche.
Laws Expired or Near Expiring[2]
   1749: Thomas Dale, Samuel Prioleau, Richard Beresford, Peter Taylor, George Cattell.
Tax Bill[2]
   1749: James Irving, David Hext, John Lloyd, John Dart, Stephen Miller, Jr.
   1750: George Cattell, James Irving, John Lloyd, John Dart, Stephen Miller, Jr., Thomas Glen, David Hext.
Courts of Justice
   1749: Thomas Dale, John Cordes, William Boone, Thomas Sacheverell, James Graeme.
   1750: Peter Taylor, George Austin, Isaac Mazyck.
Privileges and Elections[2]
   1749: George Cattell, Thomas Lloyd, John Lloyd, William Allen, Peter Taylor, Jordan Roche.
Provincial Poor and Immigration (various committees)
   1749: Thomas Dale, David Deas, Samuel Prioleau, Jordan Roche, John

Lloyd, Peter Taylor, Zacharias Villepontoux, George Austin, James Graeme, Benjamin Smith, John Rutledge, Isaac Mazyck, John Ouldfield.

1750: David Hext, Thomas Glen, George Austin, Thomas Drayton, John Rutledge.

Local and Provincial Appointments of Various Officials
  1749: John Ouldfield, William Allen, Peter Taylor.

Treasurer's Accounts[2]
  1749: Benjamin Smith, Thomas Lloyd, Anthony Mathews, Thomas Sacheverell.

  1750: John Ouldfield, John Lloyd, David Deas, Samuel Prioleau.

To Draft Bills (various committees)
  1749: Andrew Rutledge, John Rutledge, John Ouldfield, Charles Cattell, George Austin, James Graeme, Benjamin Smith, James Irving, William Allen, Richard Singleton, William Boone, Anthony Mathews, Thomas Sacheverell, Thomas Dale, John Dart, David Hext, Samuel Prioleau, Jordan Roche.

  1750: John Rutledge, Isaac Mazyck, John Ouldfield, George Austin, William Brisbane, Benjamin Smith, Thomas Glen, James Irving, John Lloyd, Richard Singleton, Anthony Mathews, Thomas Dale, John Dart, David Deas, David Hext, Samuel Prioleau, Jordan Roche.

On the Estimate (of governmental expenses)[2]
  1749: George Austin, James Irving, Richard Singleton, William Boone, John Dart, Jordan Roche.

Powder Receiver's Accounts[2]
  1749: George Bellinger, Benjamin Smith, William Allen, Stephen Miller, Jr., Thomas Dale.

  1750: William Brisbane.

Grievances[2]
  1749: John Dart, David Hext, Richard Singleton.

Armory[2] *and Fortifications* (various committees, form varied from year to year)
  1749: Thomas Glen, Peter Taylor, William Boone, Thomas Lloyd, Anthony Mathews.

Reply to or Consider Messages from the Governor or Council (various committees)
  1749: Andrew Rutledge, John Rutledge, Isaac Mazyck, John Ouldfield, Thomas Drayton, George Austin, James Graeme, Benjamin Smith, James Irving, John Lloyd, Richard Singleton, Peter Taylor, William Boone, Anthony Mathews, Thomas Sacheverell, Thomas Dale, John Dart, David Deas, Jordan Roche, Henry Gray.

  1750: John Rutledge, Thomas Drayton, George Austin, James Graeme, James Irving, Richard Singleton, Benjamin Smith, Thomas Glen.

Correspondence[2]
  1749: John Dart, David Deas, Jordan Roche, James Irving, George Austin, James Graeme, Andrew Rutledge, Isaac Mazyck.

Petitions and Accounts[2]
  1749: Richard Singleton, David Crawford.

1750: Isaac Mazyck, John Ouldfield, George Bellinger, Thomas Glen, Richard Singleton, John Mayrant, John Cordes, David Crawford, David Deas, Richard Beresford.

Commissary's Accounts²

1749: John Rutledge, George Cattell, Henry Gray, Thomas Sacheverell, James Irving.

Funds in the Treasury²

1749: Tacitus Gaillard, John Mayrant.

Negro and Slave Matters (various committees)

1749: Andrew Rutledge, John Rutledge, George Austin, William Brisbane, Thomas Glen, Peter Taylor, Thomas Dale, John Dart, William Boone, Anthony Mathews, James Irving, Zacharias Villepontoux.

On Religion²

1749: David Hext, Richard Singleton, Zacharias Villepontoux, Benjamin Smith, Isaac Mazyck.

1750: George Bellinger, George Cattell, Thomas Drayton, Benjamin Smith.

Burning Old Bills of Credit²

1749: Richard Beresford, Thomas Lloyd, William Brisbane, John Ouldfield.

Miscellaneous Ad Hoc Committees

1749: Thomas Dale, John Dart, David Deas, David Hext, Jordan Roche, Henry Gray, Stephen Miller, Jr., John Mayrant, James Irving, John Lloyd, William Allen, Peter Taylor, George Austin, Thomas Drayton, John Rutledge, Isaac Mazyck, William Boone, Anthony Mathews, Thomas Sacheverell. *1750:* Thomas Dale, David Deas, David Hext, Samuel Prioleau, Jordan Roche, Richard Beresford, Thomas Glen, James Irving, John Lloyd, Richard Singleton, Thomas Drayton, George Bellinger, Peter Taylor, William Brisbane, George Austin, George Cattell, John Rutledge, Isaac Mazyck, John Ouldfield, James Maxwell, William Boone, Anthony Mathews.

TABLE 7

Legislative Committee Assignments, by Parish, of the South Carolina Commons House of Assembly, January–August 1765

Lieutenant Governor: William Bull II

	TOTAL MEMBERSHIPS (*in brackets*)
Christ Church Parish	
Rutledge, John, Jr.	[10]

To draft bills (2)†; reply/consider governor/Council messages (3); miscellaneous ad hoc (5).

Williams, Robert [6]
  Reply/consider governor/Council messages; internal improvements (3); miscellaneous ad hoc (2).

Prince Frederick Parish

Murray, John [2]
  To draft bills; reply/consider governor/Council messages.

Prince George Winyaw Parish

Daniel, ——— [2]
  Powder receiver's accounts; internal improvements.

Prince William's Parish

Beale, John [5]
  Reply/consider governor/Council messages; treasurer's accounts; internal improvements (2); commissary's accounts.

St. Andrew's Parish

Drayton, William [7]
  To draft bills; powder receiver's accounts; internal improvements; miscellaneous ad hoc (4).
Ferguson, Thomas [9]
  Internal improvements (2); Negro and slave matters; miscellaneous ad hoc (6).
Smith, Thomas [11]
  To draft bills (2); reply/consider governor/Council messages (3); treasurer's accounts; internal improvements; burning old bills of credit; miscellaneous ad hoc (3).

St. Bartholomew's Parish

Logan, George [8]
  To draft bills (2); internal improvements (3); Negro and slave matters; miscellaneous ad hoc (2).
Lowndes, Rawlins [0]
  Speaker.
Parsons, James [18]
  To draft bills (5); internal improvements (3); Negro and slave matters; reply/consider governor/Council messages (4); miscellaneous ad hoc (5).
Skirving, James [12]
  To draft bills (2); reply/consider governor/Council messages; internal improvements (3); Negro and slave matters; miscellaneous ad hoc (5).

St. George Parish, Dorchester

Baker, Richard Bohun [1]
    To draft bills.

St. Helena's Parish

Gadsden, Thomas [10]
    To draft bills (2); reply/consider governor/Council messages; internal im-
provements (2); burning old bills of credit; miscellaneous ad hoc (4).
Moultrie, William [3]
    To draft bills (2); internal improvements.
Roper, William [5]
    To draft bills; internal improvements; on Charles Town; burning old bills
of credit; miscellaneous ad hoc.

St. James' Parish, Goose Creek

Fraser, Alexander [3]
    To draft bills (2); miscellaneous ad hoc.
McKensie, John [3]
    To draft bills; burning old bills of credit; miscellaneous ad hoc.
Motte, Jacob [7]
    To draft bills; internal improvements (2); on Charles Town; miscellaneous
ad hoc (3).
Parker, John [1]
    Burning old bills of credit.
Singleton, Richard [0]

St. James' Parish, Santee

Gaillard, Tacitus [6]
    To draft bills; miscellaneous ad hoc (5).
Lynch, Thomas [14]
    To draft bills (2); reply/consider governor/Council messages; internal
improvements; Negro and slave matters; miscellaneous ad hoc (9).
Oliphant, David [6]
    To draft bills; reply/consider governor/Council messages; armory/fortifica-
tions; tax bill; miscellaneous ad hoc (2).

St. John's Parish, Berkeley

Colleton, Sir John [2]
    Negro and slave matters; miscellaneous ad hoc.
Mazyck, Isaac [19]
    To draft bills; reply/consider governor/Council messages (6); treasurer's
accounts; on Charles Town (2); Negro and slave matters; burning old bills
of credit; miscellaneous ad hoc (7).

Wright, Thomas   [6]
> To draft bills; on Charles Town; miscellaneous ad hoc (4).

St. John's Parish, Colleton

Maxwell, William   [8]
> To draft bills (2); reply/consider governor/Council messages; on the estimate; internal improvements; commissary's accounts; miscellaneous ad hoc (2).

Simmons, Ebenezer   [3]
> To draft bills; miscellaneous ad hoc (2).

Wragg, William   [16]
> To draft bills (4); reply/consider governor/Council messages (2); on Charles Town; Negro and slave matters; miscellaneous ad hoc (8).

St. Mark's Parish

Richardson, Richard   [1]
> Miscellaneous ad hoc.

St. Michael's Parish, Charles Town

Brailsford, Samuel   [4]
> Reply/consider governor/Council messages; on the estimate; commissary's accounts; miscellaneous ad hoc.

Laurens, Henry   [13]
> Reply/consider governor/Council messages (3); to draft bills; treasurer's accounts; powder receiver's accounts; internal improvements; on Charles Town (2); burn old bills of credit; miscellaneous ad hoc (3).

Pinckney, Charles   [19]
> To draft bills (6); reply/consider governor/Council messages (4); powder receiver's accounts; on Charles Town (2); Negro and slave matters; miscellaneous ad hoc (5).

St. Paul's Parish

Bee, Thomas   [9]
> To draft bills; on the estimate; internal improvements; public accounts; miscellaneous ad hoc (5).

Gadsden, Christopher   [10]
> Reply/consider governor/Council messages (4); commissary's accounts; miscellaneous ad hoc (5).

Williamson, William   [6]
> Correspondence; reply/consider governor/Council messages; on the estimate; on Charles Town; miscellaneous ad hoc (2).

St. Peter's Parish

Blake, William   [4]
    To draft bills; internal improvements (2); Negro and slave matters.

St. Philip's Parish, Charles Town

Price, Hopkins   [3]
    Reply/consider governor/Council messages; powder receiver's accounts; on
    Charles Town.
Scott, William   [7]
    On the estimate; armory/fortifications; on Charles Town (2); Negro and
    slave matters; commissary's accounts; miscellaneous ad hoc.
Smith, Benjamin   [9]
    To draft bills; reply/consider governor/Council messages (3); tax bill;
    on Charles Town (2); miscellaneous ad hoc (2).

St. Stephen's Parish

Pomo'r, John   [2]
    Armory/fortifications; miscellaneous ad hoc.

St. Thomas and St. Dennis Parish

D'Oyley, Daniel   [9]
    To draft bills; reply/consider governor/Council messages (2); internal im-
    provements; miscellaneous ad hoc (5).
Manigault, Peter   [12]
    Speaker; correspondence; reply/consider governor/Council messages (2);
    internal improvements; tax bill; on Charles Town; Public accounts; mis-
    cellaneous ad hoc (5).

TABLE 8

Legislative Committee Memberships of the South Carolina Commons House of
Assembly, January–August 1765

Lieutenant Governor: William Bull II

Armory and Fortifications[2] (various committees)
    William Scott, John Pomo'r, David Oliphant.
Internal Improvements (various committees)
    Daniel D'Oyley, Peter Manigault, Robert Williams, ——— Daniel, John
    Beale, William Drayton, Thomas Ferguson, Thomas Smith, George Logan,
    James Parsons, James Skirving, Thomas Gadsden, William **Moultrie,**

William Roper, Jacob Motte, Thomas Lynch, William Maxwell, Henry Laurens, Thomas Bee, William Blake.

Tax Bill[2]

Peter Manigault, Benjamin Smith, David Oliphant.

On Charles Town (various committees)

Hopkins Price, William Scott, Benjamin Smith, Peter Manigault, William Roper, Jacob Motte, Isaac Mazyck, Thomas Wright, William Wragg, Henry Laurens, Charles Pinckney, William Williamson.

Public Accounts[2]

Peter Manigault, Thomas Bee.

Negro and Slave Matters (various committees)

William Scott, Thomas Ferguson, George Logan, James Parsons, James Skirving, Thomas Lynch, Sir John Colleton, Isaac Mazyck, William Wragg, Charles Pinckney, William Blake.

Commissary's Accounts[2]

William Scott, John Beale, William Maxwell, Samuel Brailsford, Christopher Gadsden.

Burning Old Bills of Credit[2]

Thomas Smith, Thomas Gadsden, William Roper, John McKensie, John Parker, Isaac Mazyck, Henry Laurens.

Powder Receiver's Accounts[2]

William Drayton, ——— Daniel, Hopkins Price, Henry Laurens, Charles Pinckney.

Correspondence[2]

Peter Manigault, William Williamson.

Reply to or Consider Messages from the Governor or Council (various committees)

John Rutledge, Jr., Robert Williams, John Murray, John Beale, Thomas Smith, James Parsons, James Skirving, Thomas Gadsden, Thomas Lynch, David Oliphant, Isaac Mazyck, William Maxwell, William Wragg, Peter Manigault, Hopkins Price, Benjamin Smith, Daniel D'Oyley, Samuel Brailsford, Henry Laurens, Charles Pinckney, Christopher Gadsden, William Williamson.

To Draft Bills (various committees)

John Rutledge, Jr., John Murray, William Drayton, Thomas Smith, George Logan, James Parsons, James Skirving, Richard Bohun Baker, Thomas Gadsden, William Moultrie, William Roper, Alexander Fraser, John McKensie, Jacob Motte, Tacitus Gaillard, Thomas Lynch, David Oliphant, Isaac Mazyck, Thomas Wright, William Maxwell, Ebenezer Simmons, William Wragg, Daniel D'Oyley, Benjamin Smith, Henry Laurens, Charles Pinckney, Thomas Bee, William Blake.

Treasurer's Accounts[2]

John Beale, Thomas Smith, Isaac Mazyck, Henry Laurens.

On the Estimate (of governmental expenses)[2]
William Maxwell, William Scott, Samuel Brailsford, Thomas Bee, William Williamson.

Miscellaneous Ad Hoc Committees
Richard Richardson, Samuel Brailsford, Henry Laurens, Charles Pinckney, Thomas Bee, Christopher Gadsden, William Williamson, Ebenezer Simmons, William Wragg, Isaac Mazyck, Thomas Wright, William Maxwell, William Scott, Benjamin Smith, John Pomo'r, Daniel D'Oyley, Peter Manigault, John Rutledge, Jr., Robert Williams, William Drayton, Thomas Ferguson, Thomas Smith, George Logan, James Parsons, James Skirving, Thomas Gadsden, William Roper, Alexander Fraser, John McKensie, Jacob Motte, Tacitus Gaillard, Thomas Lynch, David Oliphant, Sir John Colleton.

TABLE 9

Legislative Committee Assignments, by Parish, of the South Carolina Commons House of Assembly, 1772–1775

Governors: Lord Charles Greville Montagu, William Bull II, Lord William Campbell

TOTAL
MEMBERSHIPS
(*in brackets*)

Christ Church Parish

Rutledge, John, 1772–1775*   [30]
    1772: Correspondence; grievances; laws expired or near expiring; miscellaneous ad hoc. *1773:* Correspondence; reply/consider governor/Council messages (2)†; treasurer's accounts; privileges and elections; state of the province; grievances; laws expired or near expiring; miscellaneous ad hoc. *1774:* Correspondence; to draft bills (2); reply/consider governor/Council messages (2); petitions and accounts; grievances; on religion; miscellaneous ad hoc (4). *1775:* Correspondence; to draft bills; grievances; on trade; laws expired or near expiring.
Vanderhorst, Arnoldus, 1772–1775   [2]
    1772: Petitions and accounts; laws expired or near expiring.

Prince Frederick's Parish

Farar, Benjamin, 1773–1775   [2]
    1775: Internal improvements (2).
Gaillard, Theodore, Jr., 1772–1775   [8]
    1772: Petitions and accounts. *1773:* Armory/fortifications; laws expired or

near expiring; commissary's accounts. *1775:* Petitions and accounts; internal improvements; on trade; on Charles Town.

Prince George Winyaw Parish

Horry, Elias, Jr., 1772–1775 [4]
 1772: Grievances. *1773:* Commissary's accounts. *1775:* Petitions and accounts; on Charles Town.

Lynch, Thomas, 1772–1775 [25]
 1772: Correspondence; privileges and elections; internal improvements. *1773:* Correspondence; reply/consider governor/Council messages (2); grievances; privileges and elections; state of the province (2); laws expired or near expiring. *1774:* Correspondence; reply/consider governor/Council messages (2); grievances; privileges and elections; provincial poor and immigration; on religion; miscellaneous ad hoc (2). *1775:* Correspondence; reply/consider governor/Council messages; grievances; privileges and elections; internal improvements.

Prince William's Parish

Motte, Isaac, 1772–1775 [9]
 1773: Treasurer's accounts; state of the province. *1774:* Treasurer's accounts. *1775:* On religion; treasurer's accounts; petitions and accounts; militia and town watch; miscellaneous ad hoc (2).

Ward, John, 1772–1775 [9]
 1772: Correspondence; treasurer's accounts; militia and town watch. *1773:* Militia and town watch (2). *1775:* Armory/fortifications; internal improvements; on religion; militia and town watch.

St. Andrew's Parish

Bee, Thomas, 1772–1775 [36]
 1772: Correspondence; grievances; privileges and elections; internal improvements. *1773:* Correspondence; powder receiver's accounts; grievances; privileges and elections; courts of justice; internal improvements; miscellaneous ad hoc. *1774:* Correspondence; reply/consider governor/Council messages (2); powder receiver's accounts; grievances; privileges and elections; courts of justice; paper currency and legal tender. *1775:* Correspondence; to draft bills; reply/consider governor/Council messages (4); powder receiver's accounts; armory; grievances; privileges and elections; on religion; laws expired or near expiring; tax bill; on Charles Town (2); miscellaneous ad hoc (2).

Cattell, William, 1772–1775 [14]
 1772: Armory/fortifications; provincial poor and immigration. *1773:* Correspondence; armory/fortifications. *1774:* Correspondence; reply/consider governor/Council messages (2); armory/fortifications; paper currency and

legal tender. *1775:* Correspondence; armory/fortifications; on Charles Town
(2); miscellaneous ad hoc.

Scott, William, 1772–1775   [6]
   1773: Treasurer's accounts. *1774:* Treasurer's accounts; powder receiver's
   accounts. *1775:* Paper currency and legal tender; on Charles Town; militia
   and town watch.

St. Bartholomew's Parish

Lowndes, Rawlins, 1772–1775   [5]
   Speaker, 1772–1775. *1772:* Correspondence; grievances; privileges and
   elections. *1774:* Petitions and accounts. *1775:* Petitions and accounts.

Osborne, Thomas, 1772   [0]

Parsons, James, 1772–1775   [37]
   1772: Correspondence; grievances; privileges and elections; militia and
   town watch. *1773:* committee of the whole house (2); correspondence; to
   draft bills; reply/consider governor/Council messages (3); grievances; provincial poor and immigration; state of the province (2); miscellaneous ad
   hoc. *1774:* Correspondence; reply/consider governor/Council messages
   (3); grievances; courts of justice; provincial poor and immigration; miscellaneous ad hoc. *1775:* Correspondence; to draft bills (4); reply/consider
   governor/Council messages (2); grievances; internal improvements; laws
   expired or near expiring; on Charles Town; militia and town watch; miscellaneous ad hoc.

Skirving, William, 1773–1775   [9]
   1773: Internal improvements; militia and town watch; miscellaneous ad
   hoc. *1774:* On religion; miscellaneous ad hoc. *1775:* To draft bills (2);
   militia and town watch; miscellaneous ad hoc.

St. David's Parish

Powell, George Gabriel, 1773–1775   [13]
   1773: To draft bills; treasurer's accounts; miscellaneous ad hoc (2). *1774:*
   Reply/consider governor/Council messages (3); on religion; militia and
   town watch. *1775:* Reply/consider governor/Council messages (3); internal improvements.

Stuart, Charles Augustus, 1772   [2]
   Militia and town watch; miscellaneous ad hoc.

St. George Parish, Dorchester

Oliphant, David, 1772–1775   [8]
   1772: Correspondence; petitions and accounts. *1773:* Correspondence.
   1774: Correspondence; reply/consider governor/Council messages. *1775:*
   Correspondence; armory/fortifications; miscellaneous ad hoc.

Waring, Benjamin, 1772–1775   [9]
   1772: Treasurer's accounts; petitions and accounts; militia and town watch.

1773: Militia and town watch; commissary's accounts. *1774:* To draft bills; militia and town watch; commissary's accounts. *1775:* Commissary's accounts.

St. Helena's Parish

Barnwell, John, Jr., 1772   [2]
    Petitions and accounts; militia and town watch.
Heyward, Thomas Jr., 1772–1775   [25]
    1772: Correspondence; grievances. *1773:* Correspondence; reply/consider governor/Council messages; treasurer's accounts; grievances; privileges and elections. *1774:* Correspondence; grievances; privileges and elections; paper currency and legal tender; tax bill. *1775:* Correspondence; reply/consider governor/Council messages (3); petitions and accounts; armory/fortifications; grievances; privileges and elections; on religion (2); laws expired or near expiring; miscellaneous ad hoc (2).
Motte, Jacob, 1773–1775   [6]
    1773: Reply/consider governor/Council messages; treasurer's accounts; state of the province. *1774:* Treasurer's accounts. *1775:* Treasurer's accounts; on religion.
Sanders, William, 1773–1775   [1]
    1775: On religion.

St. James' Parish, Goose Creek

Izard, John, 1773–1775   [3]
    1774: Paper currency and legal tender; tax bill. *1775:* Armory/fortifications.
Parker, John, 1772–1775   [12]
    1772: Correspondence; treasurer's accounts. *1773:* Correspondence; powder receiver's accounts. *1774:* Correspondence; treasurer's accounts; powder receiver's accounts; paper currency and legal tender; on religion. *1775:* Correspondence; paper currency and legal tender; powder receiver's accounts.
Smith, Benjamin, 1772   [2]
    Treasurer's accounts; militia and town watch.
Smith, Thomas, of Broad Street, 1772   [0]

St. James' Parish, Santee

Douxsaint, Paul, 1772–1775   [8]
    1772: Treasurer's accounts; internal improvements. *1773:* Treasurer's accounts; laws expired or near expiring. *1774:* Treasurer's accounts; paper currency and legal tender; tax bill; miscellaneous ad hoc.
Horry, Thomas, 1772–1775   [9]
    1772: Correspondence; armory/fortifications; militia and town watch. *1773:* Militia and town watch. *1774:* To draft bills; militia and town watch. *1775:* Petitions and accounts; armory/fortifications; internal improvements.

St. John's Parish, Berkeley

Cordes, James, Jr., 1772–1775   [1]
   1775: On Charles Town.
Huger, John, 1773–1775   [0]
Moultrie, William, 1772–1773   [1]
   1772: Armory/fortifications.
Ravenal, James, 1773–1775   [1]
   1775: On Charles Town.

St. John's Parish, Colleton

Evance, Thomas, 1772–1775   [9]
   1772: Correspondence; petitions and accounts; commissary's accounts.
1773: Correspondence. *1774:* Correspondence. *1775:* Correspondence; powder receiver's accounts; petitions and accounts; miscellaneous ad hoc.
Gibbes, William, 1772–1775   [11]
   1772: Correspondence. *1773:* Treasurer's accounts; miscellaneous ad hoc.
1774: Treasurer's accounts. *1775:* To draft bills; treasurer's accounts; petitions and accounts; tax bill; on Charles Town (2); miscellaneous ad hoc.
Pinckney, Charles Cotesworth, 1772–1775   [25]
   1772: Correspondence; grievances; militia and town watch. *1773:* Correspondence; to draft bills; grievances; courts of justice; militia and town watch. *1774:* Correspondence; reply/consider governor/Council messages; petitions and accounts; grievances; courts of justice (2). *1775:* Correspondence; to draft bills; reply/consider governor/Council messages; petitions and accounts; grievances; tax bill; laws expired or near expiring; on Charles Town; militia and town watch; miscellaneous ad hoc (2).

St. Mark's Parish

Kershaw, Joseph, 1772–1775   [4]
   1773: Petitions and accounts. *1774:* Petitions and accounts. *1775:* Petitions and accounts; internal improvements.

St. Matthew's Parish

Gaillard, Tacitus, 1772–1775   [4]
   1772: Petitions and accounts. *1773:* Petitions and accounts; state of the province. *1775:* Internal improvements.
Huger, Isaac, 1772–1775   [4]
   1772: Miscellaneous ad hoc. *1773:* Petitions and accounts. *1774:* Petitions and accounts. *1775:* Armory/fortifications.

St. Michael's Parish, Charles Town

Brewton, Miles, 1772–1775   [29]
   1772: Correspondence; treasurer's accounts; grievances. *1773:* Correspon-

dence; treasurer's accounts; grievances; miscellaneous ad hoc (2). *1774:* Correspondence; joint conference committee; to draft bills (3); reply/consider governor/Council messages; petitions and accounts; grievances; paper currency and legal tender; on religion; on Charles Town; militia and town watch; miscellaneous ad hoc. *1775:* Correspondence; reply/consider governor/Council messages (3); grievances; on religion; on trade; tax bill.

Deas, David, Jr., 1774–1775   [6]
    1774: To draft bills; treasurer's accounts; paper currency and legal tender; on Charles Town. *1775:* Reply/consider governor/Council messages; tax bill.

Edwards, John, 1772–1775   [14]
    1772: Correspondence; petitions and accounts. *1773:* Correspondence; commissary's accounts. *1774:* Correspondence; to draft bills; reply/consider governor/Council messages; on Charles Town (2); miscellaneous ad hoc. *1775:* Correspondence; petitions and accounts; on religion; on trade.

Smith, Thomas Loughton, 1773–1775   [4]
    1773: Correspondence; treasurer's accounts. *1774:* Correspondence. *1775:* Correspondence.

St. Paul's Parish

Elliott, Benjamin, 1772–1775   [16]
    1772: Correspondence. *1773:* Correspondence; treasurer's accounts; powder receiver's accounts; privileges and elections; miscellaneous ad hoc. *1774:* Correspondence; powder receiver's accounts; privileges and elections. *1775:* Correspondence; to draft bills; powder receiver's accounts; privileges and elections; on Charles Town; miscellaneous ad hoc (2).

Ferguson, Thomas, 1772–1775   [19]
    1772: Grievances; internal improvements. *1773:* Correspondence; reply/consider governor/Council messages; treasurer's accounts; grievances; provincial poor and immigration; internal improvements. *1774:* Correspondence; reply/consider governor/Council messages; grievances. *1775:* Correspondence; to draft bills; reply/consider governor/Council messages; grievances; internal improvements; on Charles Town (2); miscellaneous ad hoc.

Haig, George, 1773–1775   [5]
    1773: Treasurer's accounts. *1774:* Treasurer's accounts. *1775:* Treasurer's accounts; petitions and accounts; miscellaneous ad hoc.

St. Peter's Parish

DuPont, Gideon, 1773–1775   [8]
    1773: Treasurer's accounts. *1774:* Treasurer's accounts; paper currency and legal tender. *1775:* Treasurer's accounts; petitions and accounts; paper currency and legal tender; on religion; on trade.

Gadsden, Christopher, 1772–1775   [25]

1772: Correspondence; grievances; privileges and elections; miscellaneous ad hoc. *1773:* Correspondence; reply/consider governor/Council messages (2); treasurer's accounts; state of the province (2); militia and town watch. *1774:* Correspondence; to draft bills (2); reply/consider governor/Council messages (2); courts of justice; provincial poor and immigration; paper currency and legal tender; tax bill; on Charles Town; militia and town watch; miscellaneous ad hoc (2). *1775:* Correspondence.

St. Philip's Parish, Charles Town

Laurens, Henry, 1773–1775 [0]
Pinckney, Charles, 1772–1775 [31]
   1772: Correspondence; militia and town watch. *1773:* Correspondence; reply/consider governor/Council messages (2); on the state of the province (2); treasurer's accounts; grievances; internal improvements; miscellaneous ad hoc. *1774:* Correspondence; to draft bills (3); reply/consider governor/Council messages; grievances; provincial poor and immigration; paper currency and legal tender; tax bill; on Charles Town; militia and town watch; miscellaneous ad hoc. *1775:* Correspondence; reply/consider governor/Council messages (3); grievances; tax bill (2); laws expired or near expiring.
Smith, Roger, 1772–1775 [14]
   1772: Correspondence; petitions and accounts; militia and town watch. *1773:* Correspondence; reply/consider governor/Council messages; petitions and accounts; militia and town watch. *1774:* On Charles Town; correspondence; to draft bills (2); militia and town watch. *1775:* Correspondence; petitions and accounts.

St. Stephen's Parish

Gaillard, John, 1772–1775 [5]
   1772: Powder receiver's accounts; militia and town watch. *1773:* Militia and town watch. *1774:* Powder receiver's accounts; militia and town watch.

St. Thomas and St. Dennis Parish

Atkin, James, 1772–1775 [8]
   1772: Laws expired or near expiring; militia and town watch. *1773:* militia and town watch; commissary's accounts. *1774:* To draft bills; militia and town watch; commissary's accounts. *1775:* Commissary's accounts.
Harleston, Edward,[3] 1772 [2]
   Powder receiver's accounts; internal improvements.
Harleston, Isaac, 1773–1775 [2]
   1773: Armory/fortifications. *1774:* Armory/fortifications.
Manigault, Peter, 1772–1773 [0]
   Speaker.

Wigfall, John. 1772–1775   [1]
   1772: Militia and town watch.

TABLE 10

Legislative Committee Memberships of the
South Carolina Commons House of Assembly, 1772-1775
Governors: Lord Charles Greville Montagu, William Bull II,
Lord William Campbell

Correspondence[2]
   1772: John Rutledge, Thomas Lynch, John Ward, Thomas Bee, Rawlins
Lowndes, James Parsons, David Oliphant, Thomas Heyward, Jr.,
Thomas Horry, Thomas Evance, William Gibbes, Charles Cotesworth
Pinckney, Miles Brewton, John Edwards, Benjamin Elliott, Christopher
Gadsden, Charles Pinckney, Roger Smith, John Parker.
   1773: John Rutledge, Thomas Lynch, Thomas Bee, William Cattell, James
Parsons, David Oliphant, Thomas Heyward, Jr., Thomas Evance,
Charles Cotesworth Pinckney, Miles Brewton, John Edwards, Thomas
Loughton Smith, Benjamin Elliott, Thomas Ferguson, Christopher
Gadsden, Charles Pinckney, Roger Smith, John Parker.
   1774: John Rutledge, Thomas Lynch, Thomas Bee, William Cattell, James
Parsons, David Oliphant, Thomas Heyward, Jr., Thomas Evance,
Charles Cotesworth Pinckney, Miles Brewton, John Edwards, Thomas
Loughton Smith, Benjamin Elliott, Thomas Ferguson, Christopher
Gadsden, Charles Pinckney, John Parker, Roger Smith.
   1775: John Rutledge, Thomas Lynch, Thomas Bee, William Cattell, James
Parsons, David Oliphant, Thomas Heyward, Jr., Thomas Evance,
Charles Cotesworth Pinckney, Miles Brewton, John Edwards, Thomas
Loughton Smith, Benjamin Elliott, Thomas Ferguson, Christopher
Gadsden, Charles Pinckney, Roger Smith, John Parker.
To Draft Bills (*various committees*)
   1773: James Parsons, George Gabriel Powell, Charles Cotesworth Pinckney.
   1774: James Atkin, John Rutledge, James Parsons, Benjamin Waring,
Thomas Horry, Miles Brewton, David Deas, Jr., John Edwards, Chris-
topher Gadsden, Charles Pinckney, Roger Smith.
   1775: John Rutledge, Thomas Bee, William Skirving, William Gibbes,
Charles Cotesworth Pinckney, Benjamin Elliott, Thomas Ferguson,
James Parsons.
Reply to or Consider Messages from the Governor or Council
   1773: Christopher Gadsden, Charles Pinckney, Roger Smith, Thomas Ferguson, Thomas Heyward, Jr., Jacob Motte, James Parsons, John Rutledge,
Thomas Lynch.
   1774: Christopher Gadsden, Charles Pinckney, John Edwards, Thomas Fergu-

son, Charles Cotesworth Pinckney, Miles Brewton, James Parsons, George Gabriel Powell, David Oliphant, Thomas Bee, William Cattell, John Rutledge, Thomas Lynch.

1775: Charles Pinckney, David Deas, Jr., Thomas Ferguson, Charles Cotesworth Pinckney, Miles Brewton, Thomas Heyward, Jr., James Parsons, George Gabriel Powell, Thomas Bee, Thomas Lynch.

Powder Receiver's Accounts[2]

1772: Edward Harleston, John Gaillard.

1773: Thomas Bee, John Parker, Benjamin Elliott.

1774: Thomas Bee, William Scott, John Parker, Benjamin Elliott, John Gaillard.

1775: Thomas Bee, John Parker, Thomas Evance, Benjamin Elliott.

Petitions and Accounts[2]

1772: Arnoldus Vanderhorst, Theodore Gaillard, Jr., David Oliphant, John Barnwell, Jr., Thomas Evance, Tacitus Gaillard, John Edwards, Roger Smith, Benjamin Waring.

1773: Joseph Kershaw, Tacitus Gaillard, Isaac Huger, Roger Smith.

1774: John Rutledge, Rawlins Lowndes, Charles Cotesworth Pinckney, Joseph Kershaw, Isaac Huger, Miles Brewton.

1775: Theodore Gaillard, Jr., Elias Horry, Jr., Isaac Motte, Rawlins Lowndes, Thomas Heyward, Jr., Thomas Horry, Thomas Evance, William Gibbes, Charles Cotesworth Pinckney, Joseph Kershaw, John Edwards, George Haig, Gideon DuPont, Roger Smith.

On the State of the Province

1773: Christopher Gadsden, Charles Pinckney, Jacob Motte, James Parsons, Isaac Motte, John Rutledge, Tacitus Gaillard, Thomas Lynch.

On Trade[2]

1775: John Rutledge, Theodore Gaillard, Jr., John Edwards, Gideon DuPont, Miles Brewton.

Treasurer's Accounts

1772: Miles Brewton, Paul Douxsaint, Benjamin Waring, John Ward, John Parker, Benjamin Smith.

1773: Gideon DuPont, Christopher Gadsden, Charles Pinckney, Thomas Loughton Smith, Benjamin Elliott, Thomas Ferguson, George Haig, William Gibbes, Miles Brewton, Paul Douxsaint, Thomas Heyward, Jr., Jacob Motte, George Gabriel Powell, Isaac Motte, William Scott, John Rutledge.

1774: Gideon DuPont, David Deas, Jr., George Haig, William Gibbes, Paul Douxsaint, Jacob Motte, John Parker, Isaac Motte, William Scott.

1775: Gideon DuPont, George Haig, William Gibbes, Jacob Motte, John Parker, Isaac Motte.

Armory[2] *and/or Fortifications* (sometimes separate committees, sometimes different nomenclature)

1772: Thomas Horry, William Moultrie, William Cattell.

1773: William Cattell, Theodore Gaillard, Jr., Isaac Harleston.

1774: William Cattell, Isaac Harleston.

1775: Thomas Horry, Thomas Heyward, Jr., John Izard, David Oliphant, John Ward, Thomas Bee, William Cattell, Isaac Huger.

Courts of Justice

1773: Thomas Bee, Charles Cotesworth Pinckney.

1774: Christopher Gadsden, Thomas Bee, James Parsons, Charles Cotesworth Pinckney.

Grievances[2]

1772: John Rutledge, Elias Horry, Jr., Thomas Bee, Rawlins Lowndes, James Parsons, Thomas Heyward, Jr., Miles Brewton, Thomas Ferguson, Christopher Gadsden, Charles Cotesworth Pinckney.

1773: John Rutledge, Thomas Lynch, Thomas Bee, James Parsons, Thomas Heyward, Jr., Miles Brewton, Thomas Ferguson, Charles Pinckney, Charles Cotesworth Pinckney.

1774: John Rutledge, Thomas Lynch, Thomas Bee, James Parsons, Thomas Heyward, Jr., Miles Brewton, Thomas Ferguson, Charles Pinckney, Charles Cotesworth Pinckney.

1775: John Rutledge, Thomas Lynch, Thomas Bee, James Parsons, Thomas Heyward, Jr., Miles Brewton, Thomas Ferguson, Charles Pinckney, Charles Cotesworth Pinckney.

Privileges and Elections[2]

1772: Thomas Lynch, Rawlins Lowndes, Thomas Bee, James Parsons, Christopher Gadsden.

1173: John Rutledge, Thomas Lynch, Thomas Bee, Thomas Heyward, Jr., Benjamin Elliott.

1774: Thomas Lynch, Thomas Bee, Thomas Heyward, Jr., Benjamin Elliott.

1775: Thomas Lynch, Thomas Bee, Thomas Heyward, Jr., Benjamin Elliott.

Provincial Poor and/or Immigration

1772: William Cattell.

1773: Thomas Ferguson, James Parsons.

1774: Charles Pinckney, Christopher Gadsden, Thomas Lynch, James Parsons.

Internal Improvements (various committees)

1772: Edward Harleston, Thomas Ferguson, Paul Douxsaint, Thomas Bee, Thomas Lynch.

1773: Charles Pinckney, Thomas Ferguson, William Skirving, Thomas Bee.

1775: Joseph Kershaw, Tacitus Gaillard, Thomas Ferguson, Thomas Horry, James Parsons, John Ward, Theodore Gaillard, Jr., Thomas Lynch, Benjamin Farar, George Gabriel Powell.

Paper Currency or Legal Tender (various committees)

1774: Thomas Bee, William Cattell, Thomas Heyward, Jr., John Izard, John Parker, Paul Douxsaint, David Deas, Jr., Gideon DuPont, Christopher Gadsden, Charles Pinckney, Miles Brewton.

1775: William Scott, Gideon DuPont, John Parker.

On Religion[2]

1774: John Rutledge, Thomas Lynch, William Skirving, George Gabriel Powell, John Parker, Miles Brewton.

1775: Isaac Motte, John Ward, Thomas Bee, Thomas Heyward, Jr., Jacob Motte, William Sanders, John Edwards, Gideon DuPont, Miles Brewton.

Tax Bill²

1774: Christopher Gadsden, Charles Pinckney, Paul Douxsaint, Thomas Heyward, Jr., John Izard.

1775: William Gibbes, Charles Cotesworth Pinckney, Miles Brewton, Charles Pinckney, David Deas, Jr., Thomas Bee.

Laws Expired or Near Expiring²

1772: James Atkin, John Rutledge, Arnoldus Vanderhorst.

1773: Paul Douxsaint, John Rutledge, Theodore Gaillard, Jr., Thomas Lynch.

1775: Charles Cotesworth Pinckney, Charles Pinckney, Thomas Heyward, Jr., James Parsons, John Rutledge, Thomas Bee.

On Charles Town (various committees)

1774: David Deas, Jr., John Edwards, Christopher Gadsden, Charles Pinckney, Roger Smith, Miles Brewton.

1775: Theodore Gaillard, Jr., Elias Horry, Jr., Thomas Bee, William Cattell, William Scott, James Parsons, James Cordes, Jr., James Ravenal, Benjamin Elliott, Thomas Ferguson, William Gibbes, Charles Cotesworth Pinckney.

Commissary's Accounts²

1772: Thomas Evance.

1773: James Atkin, John Edwards, Benjamin Waring, Theodore Gaillard, Jr., Elias Horry, Jr.

1774: James Atkin, Benjamin Waring.

1775: James Atkin, Benjamin Waring.

Militia and Town Watch (various committees)

1772: John Ward, James Parsons, Charles Augustus Stuart, Benjamin Waring, John Barnwell, Jr., Benjamin Smith, Thomas Horry, Charles Pinckney, Roger Smith, John Gaillard, James Atkin, John Wigfall, Charles Cotesworth Pinckney.

1773: John Ward, William Skirving, Benjamin Waring, Thomas Horry, Christopher Gadsden, Roger Smith, John Gaillard, James Atkin, Charles Cotesworth Pinckney.

1774: George Gabriel Powell, Benjamin Waring, Thomas Horry, Christopher Gadsden, Charles Pinckney, Roger Smith, John Gaillard, James Atkin, Miles Brewton.

1775: Isaac Motte, John Ward, William Scott, James Parsons, William Skirving, Charles Cotesworth Pinckney.

Miscellaneous Ad Hoc Committees (various subjects)

1772: Isaac Huger, Christopher Gadsden, Charles Augustus Stuart, John Rutledge.

1773: William Gibbes, Miles Brewton, Charles Pinckney, Benjamin Elliott, James Parsons, William Skirving, George Gabriel Powell, Thomas Bee, John Rutledge.

1774: Miles Brewton, Christopher Gadsden, Charles Pinckney, John Edwards,

Paul Douxsaint, James Parsons, William Skirving, John Rutledge, Thomas Lynch.
1775: William Gibbes, Charles Cotesworth Pinckney, Benjamin Elliott, Thomas Ferguson, George Haig, Thomas Evance, Thomas Heyward, Jr., James Parsons, William Skirving, David Oliphant, Isaac Motte, Thomas Bee, William Cattell.

Geographic Distribution of, Assignments to, and Membership of Selected Important Legislative Committees of the South Carolina Commons House of Assembly, 1736–1739

Lieutenant Governors: Thomas Broughton, William Bull I

Source: *The Colonial Records of South Carolina: The Journals of the Commons House of Assembly, 1736–1750,* edited by James Harrold Easterby and others.

TABLE II

Geographic Distribution of Assignments to Selected Important Legislative Committees of the South Carolina Commons House of Assembly, 1736–1739

PARISH	GEOGRAPHIC AREA	NUMBER OF REPRESENTATIVES	NUMBER OF COMMITTEE MEMBERSHIPS
Christ Church	Central Coastal	2	12
Prince Frederick's	Northwestern	2	10
Prince George Winyaw	Northeastern	2	4
St. Andrew's	Central	3	13
St. Bartholomew's	Southwestern and Coastal	4	11
St. George, Dorchester	West Central	2	2
St. Helena's	Southern Coastal	4	11
St. James', Goose Creek	Central	4	8
St. James', Santee	Coastal	2	6

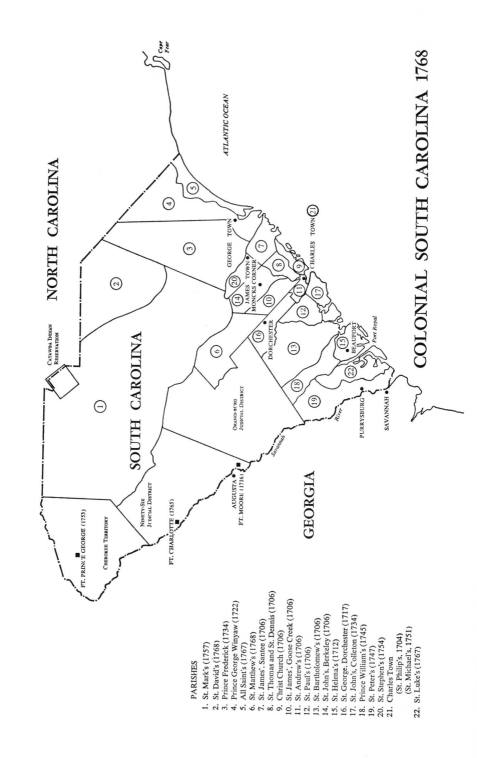

COLONIAL SOUTH CAROLINA 1768

NORTH CAROLINA

SOUTH CAROLINA

GEORGIA

ATLANTIC OCEAN

Cape Fear

Catawba Indian Reservation

Cherokee Territory

Ninety-Six Judicial District

Orangeburg Judicial District

Ft. Prince George (1753)

Ft. Charlotte (1765)

Ft. Moore (1716)

Augusta

Savannah River

Purrysburg

Savannah

Beaufort

Port Royal

Dorchester

George Town

James Town

Moncks Corner

Charles Town

PARISHES

1. St. Mark's (1757)
2. St. David's (1768)
3. Prince Frederick (1734)
4. Prince George Winyaw (1722)
5. All Saint's (1767)
6. St. Matthew's (1768)
7. St. James', Santee (1706)
8. St. Thomas and St. Dennis (1706)
9. Christ Church (1706)
10. St. James', Goose Creek (1706)
11. St. Andrew's (1706)
12. St. Paul's (1706)
13. St. Bartholomew's (1706)
14. St. John's, Berkeley (1706)
15. St. Helena's (1712)
16. St. George, Dorchester (1717)
17. St. John's, Colleton (1734)
18. Prince William's (1745)
19. St. Peter's (1747)
20. St. Stephen's (1754)
21. Charles Town
    (St. Philip's, 1704)
    (St. Michael's, 1751)
22. St. Luke's (1767)

GEOGRAPHIC AREA	NUMBER OF REPRESENTATIVES	NUMBER OF COMMITTEE MEMBERSHIPS
St. John's, Berkeley	Central	3	13
St. John's, Colleton	Southern Coastal	3	7
St. Paul's	Central	3	8
St. Philip's, Charles Town	Center Coastal	5	21
St. Thomas and St. Dennis	Central	3	11

TABLE 12

Assignments, by Parish, to Selected Important Legislative Committees
of the South Carolina Commons House of Assembly, 1736–1739

TOTALS
(*in brackets*)

Christ Church Parish

Bond, Jacob, 1736–1739* [9]
 Correspondence; on the estimate; fortifications; grievances; petitions and
 accounts; privileges and elections; public treasurer's accounts; joint conference; special messages.
Rutledge, Andrew, 1736–1739 [3]
 Correspondence; grievances; Indian affairs.

Prince Frederick Parish

Henning, Thomas, 1736–1739 [5]
 Armory; powder receiver's accounts; fortifications; public treasurer's accounts; burn old bills of credit.
Lewis, Maurice, 1736–1739 [5]
 Fortifications; grievances; privileges and elections; joint conference committees (2).

Prince George Winyaw Parish

Poole, William, 1736–1739 [2]
 On the estimate; public debt.
Whiteside, William, 1736–1739 [2]
 Petitions and accounts; special messages.

St. Andrew's Parish

Bull, William, II, 1736–1739   [4]
    Armory; correspondence; commissary's accounts; privileges and elections.
Drayton, Thomas, 1736–1739   [3]
    Commissary's accounts; privileges and elections; burn old bills of credit.
Roche, Jordan, 1736–1739   [6]
    On the estimate; petitions and accounts; Indian affairs; public treasurer's accounts; courts of justice; public debt.

St. Bartholomew's Parish

Champneys, John, 1736–1739   [5]
    On the estimate; petitions and accounts; tax bills; public treasurer's accounts; public debt.
Cochran, James, 1737–1739   [0]
Mathews, Anthony, 1736–1739   [4]
    Correspondence; commissary's accounts; grievances; public treasurer's accounts.
Peters, William, 1736–1739   [2]
    Petitions and accounts; privileges and elections.

St. George Parish, Dorchester

Izard, Walter, Jr., 1737–1739   [1]
    Public treasurer's accounts.
Postell, John, 1736–1739   [1]
    Armory.

St. Helena's Parish

Barnwell, Nathaniel, 1736–1739   [5]
    On the estimate; fortifications; petitions and accounts; special messages; public debt.
Bull, Stephen, 1737–1739   [2]
    Public treasurer's accounts; burn old bills of credit.
De la Bere, John,[1] 1737–1739   [0]
Parris, John,[1] 1736–1739   [1]
    Petitions and accounts.
Prioleau, Samuel, 1739   [3]
    Treasurer's accounts; burn old bills of credit; joint conference committees.
Thorpe, Robert,[1] 1737   [0]

St. James' Parish, Goose Creek

Maxwell, James, 1737–1739   [1]
    Powder receiver's accounts.

Morris, Samuel, 1737–1739   [2]
  Commissary's accounts; tax bill.
Singleton, Richard, 1737–1739   [0]
Taylor, Peter, 1736–1739   [5]
  Correspondence; commissary's accounts; grievances; petitions and accounts;
  treasurer's accounts.

St. James' Parish, Santee

De St. Julien, Peter, 1736–1739   [4]
  Powder receiver's accounts; fortifications; Indian affairs; joint conference
  committees.
Serré, Noah, 1736–1739   [2]
  Correspondence; burn old bills of credit.

St. John's Parish, Berkeley

Broughton, Andrew, 1736–1739   [3]
  On the estimate; petitions and accounts; privileges and elections.
Cordes, Thomas, 1736–1739   [6]
  Armory; grievances; privileges and elections; Indian affairs; treasurer's ac-
  counts; joint conference committees.
Le Bas, James,[1] 1736–1738   [3]
  Grievances; petitions and accounts; treasurer's accounts.
Monck, Thomas, 1738-1739   [1]
  Public treasurer's accounts.

St. John's Parish, Colleton

Drake, William, 1737–1739   [0]
Hext, Alexander, 1736–1739   [6]
  Armory; on the estimate; fortifications; privileges and elections; Indian af-
  fairs; joint conference committees.
Hext, David, 1736–1739   [1]
  Burn old bills of credit.

St. Paul's Parish

Bedon, Richard,[1] 1736–1739   [3]
  Armory; fortifications; treasurer's accounts.
Elliott, Joseph, 1739   [0]
Hyrne, Henry, 1736–1739   [5]
  Correspondence; on the estimate; petitions and accounts; tax bill; burn
  old bills of credit.
Miles, Jeremiah,[1] 1736–1737   [0]
Younge, Robert, 1737–1739   [0]

St. Philip's Parish, Charles Town

Brewton, Robert, 1736–1739   [3]
     Correspondence; commissary's accounts; treasurer's accounts.
Dart, John, 1736–1739   [6]
     Correspondence; powder receiver's accounts; petitions and accounts; Indian affairs; treasurer's accounts; joint conference committees.
Mazyck, Isaac, 1736–1739   [5]
     Armory; correspondence; powder receiver's accounts; treasurer's accounts; courts of justice.
Pinckney, Charles, 1736–1739   [0]
     Speaker.
Whitaker, Benjamin, 1736–1739   [7]
     Correspondence; on the estimate; grievances; Indian affairs; courts of justice; joint conference committees; special messages.

St. Thomas and St. Dennis Parish

Bonny, Thomas, 1736–1739   [2]
     Powder receiver's accounts; fortifications.
Paget, John, 1737–1738   [0]
Trewin, William, 1736–1739   [3]
     Grievances; Indian affairs; joint conference committees.
Vicaridge, John,[1] 1736–1737   [6]
     Powder receiver's accounts; fortifications; petitions and accounts; Indian affairs; treasurer's accounts; joint conference committees.

TABLE 13

Memberships of Selected Important Legislative Committees of the
South Carolina Commons House of Assembly, 1736–1739

Privileges and Elections[2]
     William Peters, Jacob Bond, Maurice Lewis, Andrew Broughton, Alexander Hext, Thomas Cordes, William Bull II, Thomas Drayton.
Indian Affairs
     Jordan Roche, Benjamin Whitaker, Thomas Cordes, William Trewin, John Vicaridge, Alexander Hext, Peter de St. Julien, John Dart, Andrew Rutledge.
Tax Bills[2]
     Henry Hyrne, John Champneys, Samuel Morris.
Armory[2]
     Thomas Henning, William Bull II, Alexander Hext, Richard Bedon, John Postell, Thomas Cordes, Isaac Mazyck.
Correspondence[2]
     Jacob Bond, Robert Brewton, Andrew Rutledge, William Bull II, Peter

Taylor, Noah Serré, Henry Hyrne, John Dart, Isaac Mazyck, Benjamin Whitaker, Anthony Mathews.

Public Debt[2]

William Poole, Jordan Roche.

Special Messages (one committee of many)

William Whitesides, Jacob Bond, Nathaniel Barnwell, Benjamin Whitaker.

Burn Old Bills of Credit[2]

Thomas Henning, Stephen Bull, Henry Hyrne, Noah Serré, Thomas Drayton, David Hext, Samuel Prioleau.

The Estimate[2] (for tax purposes)

Jacob Bond, Andrew Broughton, Henry Hyrne, Benjamin Whitaker, Alexander Hext, John Champneys, Jordan Roche, Nathaniel Barnwell, William Poole.

Fortifications

John Vicaridge, Jacob Bond, Thomas Henning, Maurice Lewis, Peter de St. Julien, Thomas Bonny, Alexander Hext, Richard Bedon, Nathaniel Barnwell.

Grievances[2]

James Le Bas, Peter Taylor, William Trewin, Jacob Bond, Maurice Lewis, Thomas Cordes, Anthony Mathews, Benjamin Whitaker, Andrew Rutledge.

Courts of Justice

Jordan Roche, Isaac Mazyck, Benjamin Whitaker.

Commissary's Accounts[2]

Robert Brewton, Peter Taylor, Samuel Morris, Anthony Mathews, Thomas Drayton, William Bull II.

Powder Receiver's Accounts[2]

Thomas Bonny, John Dart, Peter de St. Julien, John Vicaridge, Thomas Henning, Isaac Mazyck, James Maxwell.

Petitions and Accounts[2]

Henry Hyrne, Andrew Broughton, James Le Bas, Peter Taylor, John Parris, John Vicaridge, William Whiteside, Jordan Roche, John Champneys, Nathaniel Barnwell, John Dart, William Peters.

Public Treasurer's Accounts[2] (two committees, due to the death of the public treasurer)

Walter Izard, Jr., Jordan Roche, Jacob Bond, Peter Taylor, James Le Bas, Thomas Monck, Robert Brewton, Richard Bedon, John Dart, Isaac Mazyck, Anthony Mathews, John Vicaridge, John Champneys, Thomas Henning, Thomas Cordes, Stephen Bull, Samuel Prioleau.

Joint Conference Committees (a small sample of several)

Peter de St. Julien, William Trewin, John Vicaridge, Jacob Bond, Maurice Lewis, Thomas Cordes, Benjamin Whitaker, Alexander Hext, John Dart, Samuel Prioleau.

Bibliography

I. GUIDES AND INDEXES

Andrews, Charles M. *Guide to the Materials for American History to 1783 in the Public Record Office of Great Britain.* 2 vols. Carnegie Institution Publication No. 90A. Washington, D.C.: Carnegie Institution, 1912–1914.

———, and Davenport, Francis G. *Guide to the Manuscript Materials for the History of the United States to 1783, in the British Museum, in Minor London Archives, and the Libraries of Oxford and Cambridge.* Carnegie Institution Publication No. 90. Washington, D.C.: Carnegie Institution, 1908.

Born, Lester K. *British Manuscript Project: A Checklist of the Microfilms Prepared in England and Wales for the American Council of Learned Societies, 1941–1945.* Washington, D.C.: Library of Congress, 1955.

Cohen, Hennig. *Articles in Periodicals and Serials on South Carolina Literature and Related Subjects, 1900–1955.* Columbia: South Carolina Archives, 1956.

Easterby, James Harrold. *Guide to the Study and Reading of South Carolina History: A General Classified Bibliography.* 2 vols. to date. Columbia: South Carolina Historical Commission, 1949—.

———. *List of Publications of the South Carolina Archives Department.* Columbia: South Carolina Archives, 1957—.

Greene, Jack Philip. "The Publication of the Official Records of the Southern Colonies." *William and Mary Quarterly,* 3d ser., 14 (1957): 268–80.

Griffin, Grace Gardner. *A Guide to Manuscripts Relating to American History in British Depositories Reproduced for the Division of Manuscripts.* Washington, D.C.: Library of Congress, 1946.

Hamer, Philip M., ed. *A Guide to Archives and Manuscripts in the United States.* New Haven: Yale University Press, 1961.

Handlin, Oscar, et al. *Harvard Guide to American History.* Cambridge: Harvard University Press: Belknap Press, 1960.

Jenkins, William Sumner. *Guide to the Microfilm Collections of Early State Records*. Washington, D.C.: Library of Congress, 1950.

Lee, Charles E., and Green, Ruth. "A Guide to the Commons House Journals of the South Carolina Assembly, 1692–1721." *South Carolina Historical Magazine* 68 (1967), no. 2: 85–96; no. 3: 165–83.

————. "A Guide to South Carolina Council Journals, 1671–1775." *South Carolina Historical Magazine* 68 (1967), no. 1: 1–13.

————. "A Guide to the Upper House Journals of the South Carolina General Assembly, 1721–1775." *South Carolina Historical Magazine* 67 (1966), no. 4: 187–202.

Prior, Mary B., et al. *Consolidated Index, I-XL, 1900–1939, to the South Carolina Historical Magazine with Subject Index, I-LXI, 1900–1960*. Charleston: South Carolina Historical Society, 1961.

Public Record Office. *Guide to the Contents of the Public Record Office*. 2 vols. London: Her Majesty's Stationery Office, 1963. (Replaces the older guide by M. S. Giuseppi.)

Pugh, R. B. *The Records of the Colonial and Dominion Office*. Public Record Office Handbook No. 3. London: Her Majesty's Stationery Office, 1963.

II. PRIMARY MATERIAL

Manuscript Sources

British Public Record Office. London, England.

Colonial Office Documents. Herein are class 5 records dealing with correspondence of South Carolina Governors, tax records, Assembly journals, and other miscellaneous entries, including laws, correspondence, and colonial newspapers. (Microfilm copies.) Cited in the notes as PRO CO.

Charleston Library Society. Charleston, South Carolina.

Early South Carolina Newspapers Collection. Includes microfilm reproductions of colonial and early national holdings from 1732 to the 1830s. The *South Carolina Gazette* (cited in the notes as *SCG*) and the *South Carolina Gazette and Country Journal* are excellent sources of information.

Library of Congress. Washington, D.C.

Fulham Palace Records. Transcripts of parish vestries and religious correspondence from the colonies to Anglican authorities in Great Britain.

Pinckney Papers. Correspondence and documents of this leading South Carolina family, particularly helpful in the later colonial days.

Miscellaneous Collections. South Carolina manuscripts relating to government, Indian affairs, and correspondence of leading figures are of value.

Records of the States of the United States. Edited by William S. Jenkins. The South Carolina Records. The Journals of the Commons House of Assembly (42 manuscript volumes on 19 reels of microfilm). Cited in the notes as *JCHA* (Jenkins). Journals of the Council and the Upper House of Assembly (38 manuscript volumes on 16 reels of microfilm).

South Carolina Archives Department. Columbia, South Carolina.

Charles Garth Letterbook. Letters and documents from and to the General

Assembly joint committee on correspondence and its colonial agent in London, 1766–1775.

Peter Burke Diary. Edited by John Franklin Jameson. Typescript copy, n.d. (ca. 1750). Memoirs of a soldier of fortune and civil engineer; particularly enlightening for an account of the Commons House of Assembly and its committee on fortifications in the 1740s.

Journals of the Commons House of Assembly, 1692–1775 (42 manuscript volumes, also available on Library of Congress microfilm). Cited in the notes as JCHA (Arch.). The most valuable source of information about South Carolina's legislative committee system.

Journals of the Upper House of Assembly and His Majesty's Council (38 manuscript volumes, also available on Library of Congress microfilm). Material about the Council's committees and joint committees.

South Carolina Historical Society. Charleston, South Carolina.

Barnwell Correspondence. Memorials and correspondence of John Barnwell, South Carolina's agent and legislative leader during the Revolution of 1719 and the 1720s.

Henry Laurens' Letterbooks. Correspondence of one of the most influential political leaders of colonial and revolutionary days.

St. Cecilia Society Founders Manuscript. A list of the officers of the most influential society in the colony.

Other collections. Herein are a wealth of letters, records, and journals concerning colonial South Carolina.

South Caroliniana Library, University of South Carolina. Columbia, South Carolina.

Childberry School Manuscripts. Records of the school's trustees indicate the interrelationship between colonial executives and legislators in nongovernmental affairs.

Council of Safety Papers. Correspondence, currency, and records of the executive committee of the extralegal Provincial Congresses of 1775–1776.

Manigault Family Papers. The personal records of a leading Huguenot family of planter-merchants.

University of California, Santa Barbara, Library. Santa Barbara, California.

Louis K. Koontz Collection. Includes transcripts of British and French archival materials which are particularly helpful in understanding intercolonial relations.

University of North Carolina Library. Chapel Hill, North Carolina.

Southern Historical Collections. Bull Family Papers. Records of this prominent South Carolina family's financial holdings and business connections.

Printed Sources

Adair, James. *History of the American Indians.* London, 1775. Edited by Samuel Cole Williams. Nashville: Kingsport Press, 1953.

A reliable source on Southern Indians written by a South Carolina Indian trader who was involved in provincial Indian affairs.

Atkin, Edmund. *Indians of the Southern Frontier: The Edmund Atkin Report and Plan of 1775.* Edited by Wilbur R. Jacobs. Columbia: University of South Carolina Press, 1954.

Accurately describes Southern Indians and colonial Indian policy. The editor presents a lucid biographical sketch of Atkin, president of the South Carolina Council and first superintendent of Indian affairs for the Southern colonies.

Burke, Edmund. *Burke's Speeches: On American Taxation, On Conciliation with America, and letter to the Sheriffs of Bristol.* London: Macmillan and Co., 1956.

The speech on conciliation shows great insight into the nature of Southern colonial leaders' political values.

Carroll, Bartholomew Rivers, ed. *Historical Collections of South Carolina; Embracing many rare and valuable pamphlets and other accounts, relating to that State, from its first discovery to its Independence, in the year 1776.* 2 vols. New York: Harpers, 1836.

Contemporary accounts, useful for their background of political, religious, and economic events. Particularly helpful were the selections by Alexander Hewatt (1:xxi–533), Governor James Glen (2:193–272), and Francis Yonge (2:141–92).

Cooper, Thomas, and McCord, David J. *The Statutes at Large of South Carolina.* 10 vols. Columbia: A. S. Johnston, 1836–1841.

Includes the laws passed by the colonial legislature.

Drayton, John. *Memoirs of the American Revolution.* Charleston: 1820.

The reflections and papers of South Carolina assemblyman, councilor, and revolutionary leader William Henry Drayton, as written by his son.

Gadsden, Christopher. *The Writings of Christopher Gadsden, 1746–1805.* Edited by Richard Walsh. Columbia: University of South Carolina Press, 1967.

A compilation of the written work of the famous Southern revolutionary.

Garth, Charles. "Charles Garth Correspondence." Edited by John Barnwell. *South Carolina Historical and Genealogical Magazine* 28–31, 33 (1927–1931, 1933), passim.

Letters between the legislative committee on correspondence and the South Carolina agent in London.

Herbert, Colonel John. *Journal of Colonel John Herbert, Commissioner of Indian Affairs for the Province of South Carolina, October 17, 1727 to March 19, 1727/1728.* Edited by Alexander Samuel Salley. Columbia: South Carolina Historical Commission, 1936.

Reports of a Commons member and Indian commissioner describing his Indian diplomacy in the field.

Jensen, Merrill, ed. *English Historical Documents: American Colonial Documents to 1776.* Vol. 9. London: Eyre and Spottiswoode, 1955.

Includes contemporary comments on the colony's government, sectionalism, and economy.

Laurens, Henry. "Correspondence of Henry Laurens." Edited by John W. Barnwell. *South Carolina Historical and Genealogical Magazine* 28–31 (1927–1930), passim.

Most of the letters are concerned with business, social, and general political matters prior to 1755.

———. "Letters [of and to] Henry Laurens." *South Carolina Historical and Genealogical Magazine* 1–4 (1900–1905), 13–24 (1912–1923), passim.

Family correspondence, letters written in his official capacities, and correspondence with leading figures of the colonial and revolutionary periods.

Leigh, Sir Egerton, Bart. *Considerations in certain transactions of the Province of South Carolina, Containing a view of the Colony's legislature with observations to their resemblence to the British model.* London: T. Codell, 1774.

Written by a staunch royalist and chief placeman of the colony. It is critical of the Commons and the entire movement toward greater self-government.

Quincy, Josiah, Jr. "The Journal of Josiah Quincy, Jr., 1773." Edited by Mark A. de Wolfe Howe. *Massachusetts Historical Society Proceedings* 49 (1915–1916): 424–81.

An accurate contemporary appraisal of South Carolina society and politics by a perceptive Massachusetts traveller.

Ramsay, David, M.D. *Ramsay's History of South Carolina: from its first settlement in 1670 to the year 1808.* 2 vols. Spartanburg, S.C.: Reprint Co., 1959–1960.

The first major history of South Carolina written after the Revolutionary War. For the purpose of this study the book's greatest strength is in the revolutionary period.

———. *The History of the American Revolution.* 2 vols. Philadelphia: R. Aitpen and Son, 1789.

Considered to be the first significant contemporary history of the American Revolution.

Saint Helena's Parish, South Carolina. *Minutes of the Vestry of St. Helena's Parish, South Carolina, 1726–1821.* Columbia: South Carolina Archives, 1919.

Describes the typical activities of a country parish vestry committee, the chief element of local government in colonial South Carolina.

Smith, Sir Thomas. *De republica Anglorum, A Discourse on the Commonwealth of England.* Cambridge, England: Cambridge University Press, 1906.

Contains an insightful view of sixteenth-century British parliamentary government including the early use of legislative committees.

South Carolina, Board of Commissioners for Indian Affairs. *The Colonial Records of South Carolina: Journals of the Board of Commissioners for Indian Affairs, September 20, 1710–August 29, 1718.* Edited by William L. McDowell. Columbia: South Carolina Archives, 1955.

Records of the meetings of this board. It is an example of the widespread use of quasi-executive committees in the colony's administration.

———. *The Colonial Records of South Carolina. Documents relating to Indian Affairs, May 21, 1750–August 7, 1754: The South Carolina Indian Books.* Edited by William L. McDowell. Ser. 2. Columbia: South Carolina Archives, 1958.

Includes correspondence, diplomatic records, military, and trade matters for that period.

South Carolina, Commons House of Assembly. *The Colonial Records of South Carolina: The Journals of the Commons House of Assembly, 1736–1750.* Edited by James Harrold Easterby, Ruth Green, and Charles E. Lee. 9 vols. to date. Columbia: South Carolina Archives, 1951—. Cited in the notes as *JCHA* (Easterby).

A well-edited record of many phases of governmental activity. This is the best source of information regarding legislative committees.

————. *The Journals of the Commons House of Assembly of South Carolina, 1692–1735.* Edited by Alexander Samuel Salley. 21 vols. Columbia: South Carolina Historical Commission, 1907–1947. Cited in the notes as *JCHA* (Salley).

This series is incomplete in its coverage after the proprietary period.

————. *The Journal of the Commons House of Assembly of South Carolina, January 8, 1765–August 9, 1765.* Edited by Alexander Samuel Salley. Columbia: South Carolina Historical Commission, 1949.

Relates the activity of the Commons House during the Stamp Act crisis.

South Carolina, Council of Safety. "Papers of the [First and Second] Council[s] of Safety." Edited by Alexander Samuel Salley. *South Carolina Historical and Genealogical Magazine* 1 (1900): 41–75, 119–35, 184–205, 279–310; 2 (1901): 2–26, 97–107, 169–93, 257–69.

The voluminous correspondence and records of the Provincial Council of Safety, the real executive force in the colony from June 1775, to March 1776. This collection indicates the widespread use of extralegal committees throughout the province.

South Carolina, General Assembly. *The St. Augustine Expedition of 1740: A Report to the South Carolina General Assembly.* [Introduction by J. T. Lanning] Columbia: South Carolina Archives Department, 1954.

An account of an unsuccessful invasion of Florida, composed by a joint committee of the legislature.

South Carolina, His Majesty's Council. *Journal of His Majesty's Council for South Carolina, May 29, 1721–June 10, 1721.* Edited by Alexander Samuel Salley. Columbia: South Carolina Historical Commission, 1930.

Provides a view of the Council in its energetic youth.

South Carolina, Provincial Congress. *Extracts from the Journals of the Provincial Congresses of South Carolina, 1775–1776.* Edited by William Edwin Hemphill and Wylma Anne Wates. Columbia: South Carolina Archives, 1955.

Provide an understanding of the colony's extralegal legislature of 1775–1776. The vital role of the committee system and its transition from the Commons House of Assembly can be seen.

South Carolina and American General Gazette. Marriage Notices in the South Carolina and American Gazette from May 30, 1766, to February 28, 1781, and Its Successor the Royal Gazette, 1781–1782. Edited by Alexander Samuel Salley. Columbia: South Carolina Historical Commission, 1914.

Indicates the interrelationship of important families whose representatives dominated legislative committees.

The South Carolina Gazette, 1732–1775. Edited by Hennig Cohen. Columbia: University of South Carolina, 1953.

Contains representative articles from the colony's chief newspaper which accurately portray provincial life. The editor provides an excellent biographical sketch of Peter Timothy, a member of the Commons House, printer and publisher, and active leader of revolutionary extralegal organizations.

South Carolina Historical Society. *Collections.* 5 vols. Charleston: South Carolina Historical Society, 1857–1897.

One of the richest sources of published materials on Colonial South Carolina. The abstracts of official correspondence, materials in British depositories, and the Journals of the Council of Safety were useful.

Timothy, Peter. *Letters of Peter Timothy, Printer of Charleston, to Benjamin Franklin.* Edited by Douglas C. McMurtie. Chicago: Black Cat Press, 1935.

Webster, Pelatiah. *Journal of a Voyage to South Carolina by Pelatiah Webster in 1765.* Edited by T. P. Harrison. Charleston: South Carolina Historical Society, 1898.

Includes an excellent description of the South Carolina State House where legislative committees met.

Woodmason, Reverend Charles. *The South Carolina Backcountry on the Eve of the Revolution: The Journal and Other Writings of Charles Woodmason, Anglican Itinerant.* Edited by Richard J. Hooker. Chapel Hill: University of North Carolina Press, 1953.

A well-edited account of a fluent, opinionated British cleric in the South Carolina backcountry. Woodmason, a royalist, upcountry supporter, was often critical of the Commons House.

Maps

Mitchell, John. "Map of the British and French Dominions in North America." London, 1755. Photostat, University of California, Santa Barbara, Library.

Purcell, Joseph. "A Map of the Southern Indian District of North America compiled under the direction of John Stuart, esq.; His Majesty's Superintendent of Indian Affairs." London, 1773. Photostat, University of California, Santa Barbara, Library.

III. SECONDARY MATERIALS

Unpublished Master's Theses and Doctoral Dissertations

Attig, Clarence J. "William Henry Lyttleton: A Study of Colonial Administration." Ph.D. dissertation, University of Nebraska, 1958.

Carter, Mary F. "Governor James Glen: A Study in Colonial Administrative Policies." Ph.D. dissertation, University of California, Los Angeles, 1951.

Kaminer, Gugielma Melton. "A Dictionary of South Carolina Biography during the Royal Period, 1719–1776." Master's thesis, University of South Carolina, 1926.

Mancuse, William Augustus. "The Origin and Operation of the State Legislative Committee System." Master's thesis, University of Virginia, 1924.

Sirmans, M. Eugene, Jr. "Masters of Ashley Hall: A Biographical Study of the Bull Family of South Carolina, 1670–1737." Ph.D. dissertation, Princeton University, 1959.

Zahniser, Marvin Ralph. "The Public Career of Charles Cotesworth Pinckney." Ph.D. dissertation, University of California, Santa Barbara, 1963.

Published Works

Alden, John Richard. *John Stuart and the Southern Colonial Frontier: A Study of Indian Relations, War, Trade, and Land Problems in the Southern Wilderness, 1754–1775.* Ann Arbor: University of Michigan Press, 1944.

Andrews, Charles McLean. *The Colonial Period in American History.* 4 vols. New Haven: Yale University Press, 1934–1938.

Aptheker, Herbert. *The Colonial Era.* New York: International Publishers Co., 1959.

Ball, William Watts. *The State That Forgot: South Carolina's Surrender to Democracy.* Indianapolis: Bobbs-Merrill Co., 1932.

Barber, James David. *Power in Committees: An Experiment in the Governmental Process.* Chicago: Rand McNally and Co., 1966.

Barry, Richard. *Mr. Rutledge of South Carolina.* New York: Duell, Sloan, and Pearce, 1942.

Boorstin, Daniel. *The Americans: The Colonial Experience.* New York: Random House, 1958.

Bowes, Frederick P. *The Culture of Early Charleston.* Chapel Hill: University of North Carolina Press, 1943.

Bridenbaugh, Carl. *Cities in Revolt: Urban Life in America, 1743–1776.* New York: Alfred A. Knopf, 1955.

———. *Cities in the Wilderness: The First Century of Urban Life in America, 1625–1742.* New York: Alfred A. Knopf, 1960.

———. *Myths and Realities: Societies of the Colonial South.* Baton Rouge: Louisiana State University Press, 1952.

Brown, Richard Maxwell. *The South Carolina Regulators.* Cambridge: Harvard University Press, Belknap Press, 1963.

Brown, Robert Elden, and Brown, B. Katherine. *Virginia, 1705–1786: Democracy or Aristocracy?* East Lansing: Michigan State University Press, 1964.

Bryce, James Viscount. *The American Commonwealth.* New York: Macmillan Co., 1910.

Buckley, William F., Jr. *The Committee and Its Critics: A Calm Review of the House Committee on Un-American Activities.* New York: G. P. Putnam's Sons, 1962.

Calhoon, Robert M., and Weir, Robert M. "The Scandalous History of Sir Egerton Leigh." *William and Mary Quarterly,* 3d ser., 26, no. 1 (1969): 31–46.

Cartwright, Dorwin, and Zander, Alvin, eds. *Group Dynamics and Theory.* Evanston, Ill.: Row, Peterson, 1953.

Clapp, Charles L. *The Congressman: His Work as He Sees It.* Washington, D.C.: Brookings Institution, 1963.

Clarke, Desmond. *Arthur Dobbs, Esquire, 1689–1765, Surveyor General of Ireland, Prospector, and Governor of North Carolina.* Chapel Hill: University of North Carolina Press, 1957.

Clarke, Mary Patterson. *Parliamentary Privilege in the American Colonies.* New Haven: Yale University Press, 1943.

Collins, Barry E., and Guetzkow, Harold. *A Social Psychology of Group Processes for Decision Making.* New York: John Wiley and Sons, 1964.

Collins, E. D. "Committees of Correspondence of the American Revolution." *American Historical Association Annual Report, 1901* 1: 243–71.

Crane, Verner W. *The Southern Frontier, 1670–1732.* Durham, N.C.: Duke University Press, 1928.

Dabney, William M., and Dargan, Marvin. *William Henry Drayton and the American Revolution.* Albuquerque: University of New Mexico Press, 1962.

Dalcho, Frederick, M.D. *An Historical Account of the Protestant Episcopal Church in South Carolina, from the first settlement of the Province, to the War of the Revolution; with notices of the present state of the church in each parish; and some accounts of the early Civil History of Carolina never before published.* . . . Charleston: E. Thayer, 1820.

Dickerson, Oliver Morton. *American Colonial Government, 1696–1765: A Study of the British Board of Trade in Its Relations to the American Colonies, Political, Industrial, and Administrative.* New York: Russell and Russell Publishers, 1962.

Doyle, John Andrew. *The English Colonies in America.* Vol. 1, *Maryland, Virginia, and the Carolinas.* New York: Henry Holt, 1882.

Galloway, George. *History of the House of Representatives.* New York: Thomas Y. Crowell Co., 1961.

Gipson, Lawrence Henry. *The British Empire before the American Revolution.* 12 vols. to date. New York: Alfred A. Knopf, 1936—. (Volumes 2, 9, and 12 were particularly helpful.)

Golembriewski, Robert. *The Small Group.* Chicago: University of Chicago Press, 1962.

Greene, Everts Boutell. *The Provincial Governor in the English Colonies in North America.* New York: Longmans, 1898.

Greene, Jack Philip. "Bridge to Revolution: The Wilkes Fund Controversy in South Carolina, 1769–1775." *Journal of Southern History* 39 (1963): 19–52.

———. "The Gadsden Election Controversy and the Revolutionary Movement in South Carolina." *Mississippi Valley Historical Review* 46 (1959): 469–92.

———. *The Quest for Power: The Lower Houses of Assembly in the Southern Royal Colonies, 1689–1776.* Chapel Hill: University of North Carolina Press, 1963.

———. "The Role of the Lower Houses of Assembly in Eighteenth-Century Politics." *Journal of Southern History* 37 (1961): 451–74.

Harlow, Ralph Volney. *A History of Legislative Methods in the Period before 1825.* New Haven: Yale University Press, 1917.

Hennig, Hellen Kohn. *Great South Carolinians, From Colonial Days to the Confederate War.* Chapel Hill: University of North Carolina Press, 1940.

Homans, George. *The Human Group.* New York: Harcourt, Brace, 1950.

Hunt, Agnes. *The Provincial Committees of Safety and the American Revolution.* Cleveland: Western Reserve University Press, 1904.

Hunt, Edward Eyre. *Conventions, Committees and Conferences, and How to Run Them.* New York: Harpers, 1925.

Jacobs, Wilbur R. *Diplomacy and Indian Gifts.* Stanford: Stanford University Press, 1950.

Jameson, John Franklin. "The Origin of the Standing-Committee System in American Legislative Bodies." *Political Science Quarterly* 9 (1894): 246–67.

Jernegan, Marcus Wilson. *The American Colonies, 1492–1759: A Study of Their Political, Economic, and Social Development.* New York: Frederick Ungar Publishing Co., 1959.

Johnson, Joseph. *Traditions and Reminiscences of the American Revolution in the South. . . .* Charleston: Walker and James, 1851.

Kammerer, Gladys Marie. *The Staffing of the Committees of Congress.* Lexington: University of Kentucky Press, 1949.

Koontz, Louis Knott. *Robert Dinwiddie: His Career in American Colonial Government and Westward Expansion.* Glendale, Calif.: Arthur H. Clark Co., 1941.

Labaree, Leonard Woods. *Royal Government in America: A Study of the British Colonial System in America before 1783.* New York: Frederick Ungar Publishing Co., 1958.

Landrum, John Belton O'Neal. *Colonial and Revolutionary History of Upper South Carolina.* Greenville, S.C.: Reprint Co., 1959.

Leake, James Miller. *The Virginia Committee System and the American Revolution.* Baltimore: Johns Hopkins University Press, 1917.

Lonn, Ella. *The Colonial Agents of the Southern Colonies.* Chapel Hill: University of North Carolina Press, 1945.

Luce, Robert. *Legislative Assemblies: Their Framework, Make-up, Characteristics, Habits, and Manners.* Boston: Houghton Mifflin Co., 1924.

―――. *Legislative Principles: The History and Theory of Lawmaking by Representative Government.* Boston: Houghton Mifflin Co., 1930.

―――. *Legislative Procedures and the Course of Business in Framing of Statutes.* Boston: Houghton Mifflin Co., 1922.

McCrady, Edward. *The History of South Carolina under the Proprietary Government, 1670–1719.* New York: Macmillan Co., 1897.

―――. *The History of South Carolina under the Royal Government, 1719–1776.* New York: Macmillan Co., 1901.

―――. *The History of South Carolina in the Revolution.* New York: Macmillan Co., 1901.

McDonald, Forest. *E. Pluribus Unum: The Formation of the American Republic, 1776–1796.* Boston: Houghton Mifflin Co., 1965.

Main, Jackson Turner. *The Social Structure of Revolutionary America.* Princeton: Princeton University Press, 1965.

Mann, Richard D. "A Review of the Relationships between Personality and Performance in Small Groups." *Psychological Bulletin* 56 (1959): 241–70.

Meriwether, Robert Lee. *The Expansion of South Carolina, 1729–1765.* Kingsport, Tenn.: Southern Publishers, 1940.

Merrens, Harry Roy. *Colonial North Carolina in the Eighteenth Century: A Study in Historical Geography.* Chapel Hill: University of North Carolina Press, 1964.

Milling, Chapman James. *Red Carolinians.* Chapel Hill: University of North Carolina Press, 1940.

Mills, Robert. *Statistics of South Carolina, Including a View of Its Natural, Civil and Military History, General and Particular.* Charleston: Hurlburt and Lloyd, 1826.

Morgan, Edmund S. "The Puritan Ethic and the American Revolution." *William and Mary Quarterly,* 3d ser., 24, no. 1 (1967): 3–43.

Namier, Sir Louis Bernstein. "Charles Garth and His Connexions." *English Historical Review* 54 (1939): 443–70, 632–52.

Nettels, Curtis Putnam. *The Money Supply of the American Colonies before 1720.* Madison: University of Wisconsin Press, 1934.

———. *The Roots of American Civilization: A History of Colonial Life.* New York: Appleton-Century-Crofts, 1938.

O'Donnel, James H. "A Loyalist View of the Drayton-Tennent-Hart Mission to the Upcountry." *South Carolina Historical Magazine* 67 (1966): 15–29.

Osgood, Herbert Levi. *The American Colonies in the Eighteenth Century.* 4 vols. Glouchester, Mass.: Peter Smith, 1962.

Peckham, Howard H. *The Colonial Wars, 1689–1762.* Chicago: University of Chicago Press, 1964.

Ravenal, Harriet Horry. *Eliza Pinckney.* New York: Charles Scribner's Sons, 1896.

Rhett, Robert Goodwyn. *Charleston: An Epic of Carolina.* Richmond, Va.: Garrett and Massie, Inc., 1940.

Rhode, William E. *Committee Clearance of Administrative Decisions.* East Lansing: Michigan State University Press, 1959.

Rogers, George C., Jr. *Evolution of a Federalist: William Loughton Smith of Charleston (1758–1812).* Columbia: University of South Carolina Press, 1962.

Rossiter, Clinton. *1789: The Grand Convention.* New York: Macmillan Co., 1966.

Ryan, Francis Winkler, Jr. "The Role of South Carolina in the First Continental Congress." *South Carolina Historical Magazine* 60 (1959): 147–53.

———. "Travelers in South Carolina in the Eighteenth Century." *Year Book, City of Charleston,* 1948, pp. 184–256.

Salley, Alexander Samuel. "The Boundary Line between North Carolina and South Carolina." *Bulletin of the South Carolina Historical Commission,* No. 10 (1930): 1–23.

———. "The Fundamental Constitutions of Carolina." *Proceedings of the South Carolina Historical Society,* 1934, pp. 25–31.

————. *The State Houses of South Carolina, 1751–1936.* Columbia: South Carolina Archives, 1936.

Schaper, William A. "Sectionalism and Representation in South Carolina: A Sociological Study." *American Historical Association Annual Report, 1900* 1: 237–464.

Schlesinger, Arthur M. *Prelude to Independence: The Newspaper War on Britain, 1764–1776.* New York: Alfred A. Knopf, 1958.

Sellers, Lelia. *Charleston Business on the Eve of the American Revolution.* Chapel Hill: University of North Carolina Press, 1934.

Sherman, Richard P. *Robert Johnson: Proprietary and Royal Governor of South Carolina.* Columbia: University of South Carolina Press, 1967.

Simms, William Gilmore. *The History of South Carolina from its first European discovery to its erection into a Republic; With a supplementary book bringing the narrative down to the present time.* New York: Redfield, 1860.

Sirmans, M. Eugene, Jr. *Colonial South Carolina: A Political History, 1663–1763.* Chapel Hill: University of North Carolina Press, 1966.

————. "The South Carolina Royal Council, 1720–1763." *William and Mary Quarterly,* 3d ser., 38 (1961): 373–92.

Skaggs, Marvin Lucas. *North Carolina's Boundary Disputes Involving Her Southern Line.* Chapel Hill: University of North Carolina Press, 1941.

Smith, William Roy. *South Carolina as a Royal Province, 1719–1776.* New York: Macmillan Co., 1903.

Thibaut, John W., and Kelley, Harold H. *The Social Psychology of Groups.* New York: John Wiley and Sons, 1961.

Trecker, Audrey, and Trecker, Harleigh B. *Committee Common Sense.* New York: Whiteside, 1954.

Turner, Frederick Jackson. *The Frontier in American History.* New York: Holt, Rhinehart and Winston, 1962.

Verba, Sidney. *Small Groups and Political Behavior.* Princeton: Princeton University Press, 1962.

Ver Steeg, Clarence. *The Formative Years: 1607–1763.* New York: Hill and Wang, 1964.

Wallace, David Duncan. *A Constitutional History of South Carolina, 1725–1775.* Abbeville, S.C.: H. Wilson, 1899.

————. *A History of South Carolina.* 4 vols. New York: American Historical Society, 1934.

————. *The Life of Henry Laurens and a Sketch of the Life of Lieutenant-Colonel John Laurens.* New York: G. P. Putnam's Sons, 1934.

————. *A Chapter of South Carolina History.* Publications of the Vanderbilt Southern History Society. Nashville, Tenn.: Cumberland Presbyterian Publishing House, 1900.

————. *South Carolina: A Short History, 1520–1948.* Columbia: University of South Carolina Press, 1961.

Walsh, Richard. *Charleston's Sons of Liberty: A Study of the Artisans, 1763–1789.* Columbia: University of South Carolina Press, 1959.

Webb, Stephen Saunders. "The Strange Career of Francis Nicholson." *William and Mary Quarterly,* 3d ser., 23, no. 4 (October 1966): 513–48.

Webber, Mabel L. "The Pinckney Family of South Carolina." *South Carolina Historical and Genealogical Magazine* 39 (1938): 15–35, 174–75.

Weir, Robert M. "The Harmony We Were Famous For: An Interpretation of Pre-Revolutionary South Carolina Politics." *William and Mary Quarterly,* 3d ser., 26, no. 4 (October 1969): 473–501.

Wertenbaker, Thomas Jefferson. *The Old South: The Founding of American Civilization.* New York: Charles Scribner's Sons, 1942.

Whitney, Edson Leone. *Government of the Colony of South Carolina.* Baltimore: Johns Hopkins University Press, 1895.

Wilson, Woodrow. *Congressional Government: A Study in American Politics.* Boston: Houghton Mifflin Co., 1885.

Winslow, Clinton Ivan. *State Legislative Committees: A Study in Procedure.* Baltimore: Johns Hopkins University Press, 1931.

Winsor, Justin M., ed. *Narrative and Critical History of America.* 8 vols. Boston: Houghton Mifflin Co., 1884–1889.

Zemsky, Robert M. "Power, Influence, and Status: Leadership Patterns in the Massachusetts Assembly, 1740–1755." *William and Mary Quarterly,* 3d ser., 26, no. 4 (October 1969): 502–20.

Index

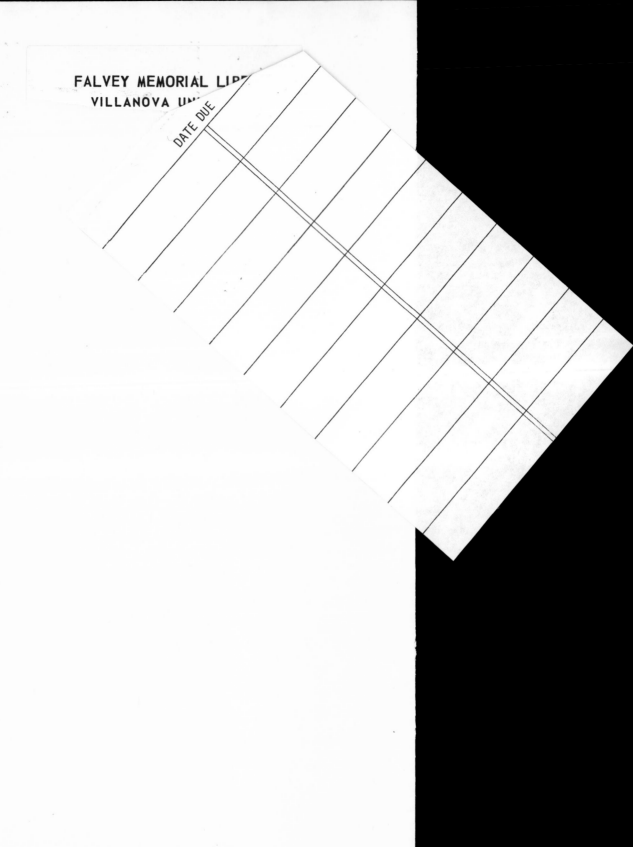